# SIMULATION AND SOCIETY:

## An Exploration of Scientific Gaming

JOHN R. RASER

*Claremont Graduate School*

*and*

*Western Behavioral Sciences Institute*

ALLYN AND BACON, INC.

BOSTON

Dedicated to Bud Crow, an inveterate gamesman, who will see his helping hand on every page.



Library of Congress Catalog Card Number: 69-14514

Printed in the United States of America

Third printing . . . May, 1971

# Contents

## PART II
## THE USES OF SIMULATION-GAMING

# Preface

This book is designed to introduce social scientists to a sphere of activity with which they may not be familiar, that of simulation and gaming. It is particularly designed for undergraduate and graduate students of sociology, history, political science, psychology, economics, and anthropology, disciplines in which the simulation technique is becoming a major research and teaching device. Those who are already familiar with simulation will find that in some places I have elaborated on what, to them, is the obvious. Those unacquainted with social science techniques will occasionally find unfamiliar terminology, although I have tried either to avoid it or where necessary to explain. The volume, then, is intended to be an introduction to, a methodological examination into, and a survey of the field of simulation and gaming in the social sciences.

Most of the work was done while I was Visiting Research Political Scientist at the Mental Health Research Institute, University of Michigan, on leave from the Western Behavioral Sciences Institute. I am indebted to J. David Singer, a warm critic, for his office and hospitality, and to John Rader Platt, Acting Director of the M.H.R.I. I thank Susan Jones and Toni Volcani for extensive assistance with editing my often incomprehensible writing and atrocious grammar. Ann Clawson performed the drudgery of typing the manuscript. I am especially indebted to Warren Phillips, Karl Deutsch, Wayman J. Crow, Harold Guetzkow, and Donald T. Campbell, who read preliminary drafts and offered valuable comments. They improved the manuscript greatly, and I am much in their debt. Any errors that remain are, of course, also partly their responsibility.

My deepest debts are to my friends, Wayman J. Crow, Toni Volcani, Richard Farson, and Harold Guetzkow, all of whom keep pointing to new doors ready to be opened. I stand on their shoulders, but I do not hold them responsible for my faulty vision.

J. R. R.
Ann Arbor
January, 1968

# Introduction

There are many ways of viewing man, each of which has different consequences for normative attitudes and values. The oldest and simplest view is that man is the product of the all-effecting hand of an ominiscient and omnipresent God. The anthropological concept of man, embodied in the term *homo sapiens*, is in conformity with the assertion of Thomas Aquinas that man is the "reasoning animal." The Freudian, or psychological, view of man, on the other hand, is rooted in the belief that human behavior is in large measure the product of subrational and often unconscious forces operating at the emotional level. Still another and currently fashionable formulation, the behavioristic view, declares that human behavior is the mechanistically determined product of a complex biogenetic, socio-economic matrix.

But Johan Huizinga has argued in a delightful book[1] that all of these formulations ignore one of the most obvious aspects of human nature: Human beings like to play. Man is, among other things, *homo ludens*—a playing animal. Much as Aquinas saw all human institutions and culture—the family, the state, religion, science, art and philosophy—as structured around the central edifice of reason; much as Freud saw them as derived from sublimated and re-channeled sexual drive, the "libido," so Huizinga proposes that most human institutions and human activities are in large part simply the product of the human desire to engage in ever more elaborate, subtle, and satisfying forms of play. This is not the kind of "play" to which Eric Berne[2] refers—the destructive manipulation of self and others arising from an inability or unwillingness to face life directly as responsible human beings. Huizinga is talking about "play" in the joyous sense of the puppy who chases the ball, the child who builds an ornate tower of blocks, the young man who grinds himself to exhaustion in a football game, the amateur musician who spends an hour at his piano, the writer who creates an intricate structure of words, or the couple who trace the mazes of one another's senses to delicious, dissolving peaks of erotic delight. This kind of play is magical activity that needs no justification or outside source of legitimacy. It is its own reward. And so, suggests Huizinga, is nearly everything we do. But because somewhere along the evolutionary line we forgot that we were playing, life often becomes a desperate search for "meaning" in activities, many which have no significance other than their own existence.

Huizinga's provocative view of man as *homo ludens* is probably no more adequate a description of human complexity or explanation of human institutions than are the concepts of "rational man," "irrational man," or "man as mechanism." But Huizinga's view does capture a central truth: men enjoy playing. If we were to look at man from Huizinga's perspective, we might find some important clues to human activities. In any case, this book is about a research technique that accidentally turns out to capitalize on man's desires for situational involvement for its own sake, for the construction of esthetically satisfying systems, for the joy of unearthing compelling symbolisms; and on man's delight in the creation of elaborate analogies.

This book is about "games" and "simulations," by means of which serious scholars approach serious, even crucial, problems by creating artificial worlds in a manner not entirely dissimilar to that of children playing house or building a space-ship out of cardboard cartons and chairs. This book is about "models," which Huizinga might view as adult toys, that researchers and theorists construct and play with to advance the purposes of scholarship. This book is about the men who build and play these games, or who develop and operate these simulations; and about what these scholars are trying to do and why they are trying to do it. I will be discussing people who, in all seriousness, are attempting to cope with real human problems, problems as complex as bureaucratic decision-making and as deadly as thermonuclear warfare, by using some of the principles Huizinga has set forth. Research scholars are trying to solve such problems by creating games (or simulations), by playing them or arranging for others to play, and by analyzing the way they are played—be the players human subjects or computers.

Why a methodology book about simulation? Because the type of thinking employed in constructing and operating a simulation and in developing its cousins—systems analysis, operations research, and systems design—has become a powerful social force in the contemporary world. Robert Boguslaw[3] argues that those who use these methods, the "social engineers" of our times, are creating a world based on sets of values that may be quite at variance with many of our traditional aspirations. Unless we understand the "systems" approach, both its great usefulness and its potential dangers, we may have to adjust to a world in which the humanistic, individualistic values have been submerged.

Certainly, as this book will document, the resources of universities, government agencies, private industry, and research institutes are being allocated in increasing amounts to one or another variant of simulation work. Such scholarly journals as *Management Science, Behavioral Science, Journal of Conflict Resolution,* and *The American Behavioral Scientist,* are devoting more and more of their pages to discussions of simulations and gaming. In 1963, when an American researcher toured Europe and spoke about simulation and gaming at professional meetings, he had to explain what he meant. But in 1967, when NATO held a summer conference in Paris on "The Simulation of Human Behavior," which was attended by more than 80 European participants, an entire meeting was devoted to an extremely sophisticated discussion of the issues and problems.

Simulation is "In." Simulation is likely to become a standard research technique due to the following developments in the social sciences: dramatic advances in machine computational and analogizing capabilities; greater emphasis on rationalized decision-making procedures; increased recognition that understanding social phenomena requires examining complex systems of interaction rather than isolated entities; a growing tendency to approach problems from the perspective of several disciplines simultaneously; and the increased popularity of a philosophy of the social sciences that insists on multi-variate analysis, rigorous specification of assumptions and relationships, and theories that are temporally dynamic rather than static. Also, social scientists increasingly are recognizing that many of our common sense thoughts and practices are partially inconsistent with each other. They could lead to serious clashes, conflicts, and deadlocks if they were carried further toward their full implications. But modern technology, by increasing our powers and multiplying our contacts, does just that: It makes the hidden dangers and surprises in our practices acute. Simulation then becomes an early warning system, a cheap form of experiment to help us discover something about ourselves and our world.

Simulation is "In" also because it seems to offer intriguing possibilities as an effective teaching tool in an era when disillusionment with traditional teaching methods is widespread. Finally, and we suspect not least important, simulation is "In," because it is an activity offering an intellectual challenge second to none, and because it is gripping, exciting, and fun, an enthralling activity. We have come full circle to Johan Huizinga.

Before going further, I should like to distinguish between simulations, games, and "game theory," for this is not a book about game theory and the various social, political, and strategic extrapolations sometimes drawn from it. Richard Brody has clearly drawn the distinction between "game theory" and the operating models called political or social "games," or "simulations."

> The Theory of Games ("Game Theory") provides a means of describing the strategic behavior of one or more actors who have to make choices in conflict situations (games) in which the payoffs (potential outcomes) are a function of the choices made by all parties to the conflict. The Game Theory model is normative, in that it prescribes the choice or combination of choices which lead to the *best* payoff under the circumstances of a given conflict situation. The theory, moreover, postulates a "rational" actor who will always follow this best strategy. A political game (or simulation) is an operating model which

> represents an attempt on the part of the theorist, through the representation of an empirical system, to provide himself with information about real states of the system.[4]

In other words, *game theory* is a set of mathematical tools for dealing with explicit types of conflict situations. It is used to bring clarity to such social and political variables as information patterns, distribution of power and resources, goals, feasibility of various strategies, the different effects of moves made openly or secretly, and coalition formation. *Games* and *simulations*, on the other hand, are attempts by theorists to construct operating models of complex social and physical systems.

I have not yet distinguished between "games" and "simulations." Indeed, the distinction is usually not made by those working in the field; the terms are generally used interchangeably. Still, there seems to be a subtle difference even in the conventional terminology. The more explicit is the "operating model" to which Brody refers, that is, the greater the extent to which all the seemingly salient variables are formally preprogrammed and the more it is believed that the model is a complete and accurate analogue to some "referent" system, the more likely it is that the model will be called a *simulation*. On the other hand, the more informal and tentative the model and the more it relies on human participants as an intrinsic component in its operation, the more likely it will be called a *game*.

There is another way in which games and simulations may be distinguished. In its structure, its rules, the nature of its pieces, chess is a model or a *simulation* of medieval warfare. When two people use that structure and manipulate those pieces in accordance with the rules, they are in one sense simulating something, perhaps the role of strategists of medieval warfare; but in more conventional terms, they are *playing* chess—that is, the human element is introduced into the model. This may be, as it seems, a trivial dispute over terminology, but it may also suggest why many "gamers" or "simulators" use the two terms interchangeably. Nevertheless, as I have indicated, there are some bases for differentiating between games and simulations. As we explore the differences between theories, models, and simulations, in Chapter 1, and then examine some of the philosophical and methodological problems of simulating social systems, in Chapter 2, the reasons for clearly distinguishing between games and simulations—or for taking a "gaming" approach to simulating—will emerge.

Familiarity with simulation is a prerequisite for understanding contemporary social and behavioral science research and teaching techniques. In addition, there is an important reason for examining the *methodological* aspects of gaming and simulation. Simulation is, in essence, the process of analogizing. So is all science. One examines a universe or an entity that is supposed to be *representative* of another universe or entity and argues that the laws that can be demonstrated as applying to the one under study also can be generalized—over greater numbers, over time, or over some other gap—to the referent universe. Thus, the problems of theory building, sampling, hypothesis testing, inference, and validity, which are the stuff of gaming and simulation efforts, are also the stuff of all scientific endeavor. By exploring these problems in connection with simulation, we will be exploring them also in the general sense. And because simulation is a very specific and somewhat unusual genre of scientific analogizing, the discussion will highlight some kinds of problems and promises that would not be dealt with in a volume concerned with other tools of the behavioral sciences workbench.

This book is designed to acquaint the reader with gaming and simulation efforts as they have developed during this century, but primarily since 1956. There are other books that deal with particular simulations, their development and uses.[5] This book, however, has a different purpose: to examine the history of simulations, discuss their theoretical and philosophical underpinnings, analyze some of their strong and weak points, deal with questions of validity and usefulness within a variety of contexts, and try to project some future directions for the field. In other words, this book addresses the questions: What are simulators doing and why are they doing it?"

## FOOTNOTES

1. Johan Huizinga, *Homo Ludens* (Boston: Beacon Press, 1950).
2. Eric Berne, *Games People Play* (New York: Grove Press, 1964).
3. Robert Boguslaw, *The New Utopians: A Study of System Design and Social Change* (Englewood Cliffs, New Jersey: Prentice-Hall, 1965).
4. Harold Guetzkow, Chadwick Alger, Richard Brody, Robert Noel and Richard Snyder, *Simulation in International Relations: Developments for Research and Teaching* (Englewood Cliffs, New Jersey: Prentice-Hall, 1963), pp. 211–12.
5. cf. Guetzkow *et al., op. cit.*; or Guy H. Orcutt, Martin Greenberger, John Korbel, and Alice M. Rivlin, *Microanalysis of Socioeconomic Systems: A Simulation Study* (New York: Harper & Row, 1961); Andrew M. Scott, William A. Lucas, and Trudi Lucas, *Simulation and National Development* (New York: John Wiley & Sons, Inc., 1966); or Claude McMillan and R. F. Gonzales, *Systems Analysis: A Computer Approach to Decision Models* (Homewood, Illinois: Richard D. Irwin, Inc., 1965).

# PART I

# Anatomy of a Technique

This is a very obscure question and we shall need keen sight to see our way. Now, as we are not remarkably clever, I will make a suggestion as to how we should proceed. Imagine a rather short-sighted person told to read an inscription in small letters from some way off. He would think it a godsend if someone pointed out that the same inscription was written up elsewhere on a bigger scale, so that he could first read the larger characters and then make out whether the smaller ones were the same.

No doubt, said Adeimantus; but what analogy do you see in that to our inquiry?

I will tell you. We think of justice as a quality that may exist in a whole community as well as in an individual, and the community is the bigger of the two. Possibly, then, we may find justice there in larger proportions, easier to make out. So I suggest that we should begin by inquiring what justice means in a state. Then we can go on to look for its counterpart on a smaller scale in the individual.

Socrates—*Republic*, by Plato

# I

# WHAT AND WHY IS A SIMULATION?

"Metaphor is man's pogo stick for crossing the terrain of knowledge."
Anonymous

As the fifteen uniformed Navy officer-candidates enter the large auditorium, they break rank and dash into one of five sets of partitioned cubicles or "offices." The sets of offices are widely separated from each other. Over each set of three offices is a placard bearing the name of a "nation"—ALGO, ERGA, INGO, OMNE, UTRO—and above each placard is the "nation's" flag.

In each set of offices, the nation's three decision-makers settle down to work. The chief decision-maker of UTRO smiles in satisfaction as he scans the reports from the calculation room, noting that his national standard of living has increased since the last period, that his proposed alliance with INGO has been ratified, and that due to a research-and-development breakthrough, his large nuclear force is becoming invulnerable. The foreign minister of ALGO scowls as he sits in his office across the room, hurriedly reading the mimeographed newspaper "World Times," for he discovers that a secret message to his ally, ERGA, has been intercepted by enemy intelligence and has been printed for all the "world" to see. His plans have gone awry. The economic minister is busily drafting a proposal for a trade agreement with OMNE. In a few minutes, the decision-makers of each "nation" assemble in their chief decision-maker's office for a cabinet meeting.

Some weeks later in the "real world," a report goes to the United States Department of Defense stating that some of the social-psychological assumptions underlying the proposal to develop an Anti-Ballistic Missile Defense System have been thrown into serious question in a "simulation" . . .

A group of general officers from all the services bend over desks in a cramped underground room dominated by the hum of air conditioning equipment. They are in a crisis meeting. One officer says: "But Chairman Kosygin, if we try to exploit this American mistake, the French may be very upset since some of their interests are involved." To which the reply comes: "Nevertheless, Comrade Talenskii, my belief is that it's worth the risk for the sake of weakening the Chinese position in Southeast Asia. I talked to Mao at lunch and . . ."

Having played out a "scenario," the setting of which is the Kremlin, these American military officers go to their beds that night with a new grasp of the complex ramifications that may result from any decision they make. . . .

Special staff assistants to the Council of Economic Advisors pore over the printout from a large computer, charting the progress of the economy during the next six months. They look worried. They check the inputs again, satisfying themselves that all the parameters are accurate and the assumptions in the program realistic. They begin to draft a recommendation to the President on increasing the corporate tax rate. . . .

All of these people are engaged in role playing, crisis gaming, economic modeling, scenario construction, contingency planning—or, to use a more comprehensive and common term—*simulation.*

According to the dictionary, a *simile* is a figure of speech directly expressing a resemblance in one or more points of one thing to another, while to "simulate" is to "assume or have the appearance of" something. The word "simulation" has a wide variety of meanings. In popular usage, it is often a fancy term for an imitation, for something that is false or "phony," a copy of something but not the real thing, as were the "genuinely beautiful scintillating simulated diamonds" that a 50,000-watt Texas radio station recently advertised for $2.00. In the biological sciences, "simulation" is used in the same way to denote an organism's assumption of deceptive features such as color or structure to protect itself from its enemies. Thus, a chameleon mimics or "simulates" the color of its background, and some insects in the course of their evolution have assumed the shape and color of a twig or leaf of the plant they inhabit, and thus blend protectively into their environment. (In the Spanish language, the connotation of the word "simulación" is *only* that of deception or phoniness, a fact that has caused more than one intercultural difficulty for North American researchers who have used the technique in Latin America!)

However, "simulation" also may mean simply that one thing is much like another, that it reproduces the characteristics of something else in certain important respects, but is otherwise somewhat different. Thus, an ultra-violet light may be thought of as a simulation of sunlight, acrylic pile may be a simulation of lamb's wool, and oleomargarine may be a simulation of butter. In such cases, there is not necessarily any intent to deceive; there is simply an attempt to provide a functional substitute for something else. (Though the uproar about coloring margarine yellow, stirred up by the dairy industry, suggests that in this case some people were worried about deception.)

Metaphor is merely a simile with the "like" or "as" left out; indeed, some people have claimed that all language is metaphor.

"Strictly speaking," says Fowler, "metaphor occurs as often as we take a word out of its original sphere and apply it to new circumstances"; he then points out that there are eight different metaphors in that sentence!

In a similar way, almost anything can be considered a "simulation" of something else. The typewriter I am using, it could be claimed, is a simulated pen, for it serves the same function. The sweater I am wearing could be considered a simulated pelt, for it is analogous to and serves the same function as a coat of fur. Any substitute for or representation of something else may be considered a simulation. A picture may be thought of as a simulation of what it portrays. A book may provide a simulated experience. An air conditioner may be simulated cool weather. Most human artifacts are analogous to something in nature and hence are simulations.

Man has a penchant for copying, imitating. He imitates because he sees a way to make more cheaply, safely, or effectively something that occurs in nature. He also imitates because it is esthetically satisfying to carve, to paint, or to build; imitating is fun.

Man uses verbal or logical analogies because they are esthetically pleasing or because they communicate vividly: "The vessel ploughed through the water." And as we saw above, analogy, or metaphor, is so deeply embedded in language that we are unaware of all but the most obvious. Verbal and logical analogies might almost be called the foundations of thought. By the use of analogy, what is abstract may be made concrete, and what is complex may be made simple. Thus, in the words of Socrates, Plato told his audience that the just man can be understood more clearly by examining the man "writ large," the just state. John of Salisbury reversed Plato by describing the state as a man, with the king as the head, the soldiers as the arms, and God as the soul. And Jesus told his followers that the man of true faith is like a lily of the field that takes no thought of the morrow.

Such analogies and similes are bridges that enable us to move from the simple, the concrete, and the specific, to the complexities and abstractions with which we wish to grapple. Analogies are tools for turning the *symbolic* into the *iconic*, thus giving form and substance to what is illusive and invisible. Think of the power of the Cross as a Christian symbol, an enormously economical abstraction; and of the even greater emotional and intellectual power of a painting (an "ikon") of the Crucifixion.

When the social scientists speak of "simulation," however, they are restricting the term to a much narrower sense than that used in the paragraphs above. Before it is possible to understand just how and why social scientists use simulation, it is necessary to grasp the exact sense in which they use the word.

Attempting to find an exact definition for the term "simulation" is a little like playing Twenty Questions. It is possible to agree that a simulation has certain characteristics and lacks others; it is possible to lead the inquirer slowly towards a more complete comprehension by using examples rather than by giving an abstract description. But, as with the slave boy who found under Socrates' questioning that he knew the principles of geometry even though he hadn't known he knew them, a real understanding of simulation depends on evoking the internalized experiences and conceptualizing ability of the questioner. A simulation should be seen, or built, or operated, or played—*then* one understands what a simulation is. But since we cannot do this within the format of a book, we must begin with a set of abstract entities. Hopefully, you will find your understanding increasing as illustrations are added to explanation.

## THEORIES, MODELS, AND SIMULATIONS

A simulation is a special kind of *model*, and a model is a special way of expressing *theory*. So we must first understand what a theory is. A theory is a set of statements about some aspect of reality, such as a past reality, a present reality, or a predicted reality. A theory attempts to describe the *components* of that reality and to specify the nature of the relationships among those components.

Karl Deutsch explains that:

> . . . theories are not only sets of propositions about reality but they are also at the same time a special class of languages about this reality, with a very limited vocabulary and relatively few connecting rules, but with relatively stringent criteria for relevance and verifiability.[1]

A theory (or a "theorem") usually deals with aspects of reality that are not immediately evident to the senses. For example, a basic theorem of human behavior holds that "men will act on the basis of what they perceive." A less global set of statements about a more restricted aspect of reality is, "If a political system is to persist, it must provide for the input of at least a minimal level of support for the regime."

In the physical sciences, when a theory is tested and found to describe adequately the aspect of reality with which it deals, it is called a *law*. Newton's third law of motion is an example: "Every action has an equal and opposite reaction"; In the social sciences, however, we avoid so positive a statement and we talk about a *probability*. In a later chapter, I will discuss the problems of theory-building, part-theories, and hypotheses; here, my chief purpose is to show how a *model* is related to a *theory*.

A theory may be expressed verbally (as I did above) or mathematically; "$E = mc^2$" is one of the most beautiful and economical examples of a mathematical expression. A third way of expressing theory is by means of a model. One example of this sort of expression is the physical model of a methane molecule with which some of you may be familiar—a Tinker Toy construction of five round balls connected by nine rods, pictorially represented thus:

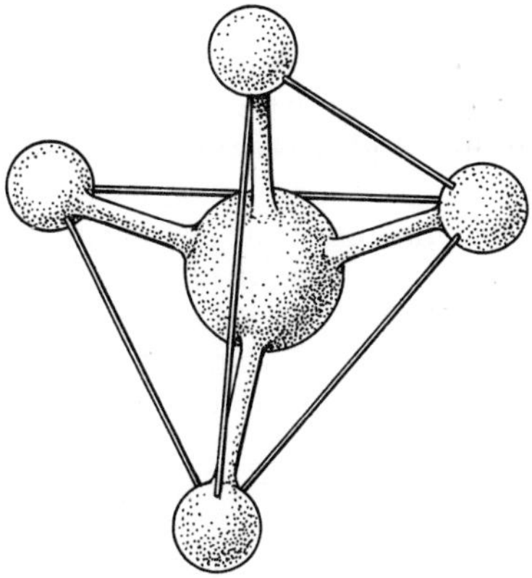

The methane molecule constitutes a "system." A system is a portion of reality in which we are interested, composed of related units (the one carbon and four hydrogen atoms) and the relationships among them (expressed in the model by the rods which unite them). Of course, each unit is composed of sub-systems, and the total system may be part of a larger system; but for the purposes of the model, these other systems can be ignored.

In constructing the model, as in constructing the theory that it expresses, it is necessary first to identify the components of the system and then to specify the relationships among them, as we did above. With most theories, a process of abstraction is necessary. That is, one postulates that certain aspects of the system are relevant to the problem at hand and that certain aspects are not. Only those aspects that are judged important are included in the model. Through this process of identification and specification, redundant and distracting details are eliminated. In the simple model of the methane molecule, details of the structure of the atoms and the nature of the bonds between them are ignored. Thus, the model is "cleaner," less complex, and more understandable. The model is "good" to the extent that one has selected wisely what to include and what to ignore and to the extent that the relationships among the components of the model are correctly specified.

An example can illustrate the power of such a visual formulation.

When Jacobus Hendricus van't Hoff first constructed this model in 1874, he effected a breakthrough in conceptualization on which the structure theory of chemistry has been based ever since. He pointed out that some properties of substances could be explained simply by the assumption that the four bonds formed by a carbon atom are directed towards the corners of a tetrahedron, with the carbon atom at its center, as shown in the drawing.

Even a "wrong" model may have great power, as we shall discuss in detail in later chapters. For example, at the time of Plato, the Greeks visualized the universe as consisting of four elements: fire, air, earth, and water. Plato and his students combined this model with an atomic theory that postulated five kinds of atoms, each represented by one of the five natural polyhedrons; the tetrahedron, the cube, the octahedron, the dodecahedron (twelve-faced solid), and the icosahedron (twenty-faced solid). Fire consisted of tetrahedron atoms, earth of cube atoms, air of octahedrons, and water of icosahedron atoms. When fire acted on water, it turned it into hot air, or steam, by breaking up the icosahedron into three atoms—two octahedrons and a tetrahedron! What of the dodecahedron? It was the "celestial atom," which accounted for the twelve signs of the Zodiac, that underlay the twelve months of the year. We can say with certainty that these models are "wrong." Yet, what power they had to stimulate dreams and scientific thought! Surely the concept of molecular changes in chemistry, the vision of elements composed of different kinds of atoms, the insight that crystalline structure reveals molecular and atomic structure were all stimulated and advanced by these "wrong" models.

Illustrations aside, there are important distinctions between *theories* and *models*. As Abraham Kaplan points out:

> In a strict sense, not all theories are in fact models; in general we learn something about the subject-matter *from* the theory, but not by investigating properties of the theory. The theory *states* that the subject-matter has a certain structure, but the theory does not necessarily *exhibit* that structure in itself.[2]

Kaplan's point is clear when we consider the difference between the statement of theory, "A molecule of methane is composed of one carbon-atom and four hydrogen atoms," and the Tinker Toy model of balls and rods. The model is *in itself* a system whose elements and structure are either physical or symbolic representations (or both) of what is being modeled (the *referent* system). Investigating the structure tells us something about the structure of the referent system. With our Tinker Toy methane model, we can physically explore the structure. We can learn something not only about the referent but also about the larger system of which it may be a part, for we can add a carbon atom and three straight and two curved rods showing the carbon-carbon double bond to model ethylene—and continue these manipulations indefinitely. The model may be said to be "valid" to the extent that investigations in the model provide the same outcomes as would investigations in the referent system. A model is thus a specific form of a theory; it allows us, in a sense, to "play" with the theory in a rather concrete, physical way.

What is a simulation? How does it differ from a model? To answer these questions, it is first necessary to discuss *structure* and *process* in systems. James G. Miller, in his articles "Living Systems: Basic Concepts," has offered formal definitions.

> The *structure* of a system is the arrangement of its subsystems and components in three-dimensional space at a given moment of time. . . . This may remain relatively fixed over a long period or it may change from moment to moment, depending upon the characteristics of the process in the system. This process halted at any given moment—as when motion is frozen by a high-speed photograph—would reveal the three-dimensional spatial arrangement of the system's components as of that instant. When anatomists study structure they use dead, often fixed, material in which no further activity can be expected to occur. Similarly historians study the relationships among units of a society at a given period. These are studies of structure.
>
> All change over time of matter-energy or information in a system is *process*. If the equation describing a process is the same no matter whether the temporal variable is positive or negative, it is a *reversible* process; otherwise it is *irreversible*. Process includes the on-going *function* of a system, reversible actions succeeding each other from moment to moment. . . . Process also includes history, less readily reversed changes like mutations, birth, growth, development, aging and death; changes which commonly follow trauma or disease; and the changes resulting from learning which is not later forgotten. Historical processes alter both the structure and the function of the system.[3]

Following Miller's definition, we can see that if the entity being studied is conceived of as a system, then the component parts and the static relationships among them are the *structure* of the system, whereas the changes that occur in those components and in the relationships among them over time are the *processes* characteristic of the system. It is just this distinction that is crucial to understanding how a simulation differs from a model, as is apparent in this lucid definition by Wayman Crow.

> As a model is a specific form of theory, so a simulation is a specific variety of model, distinguished by the fact that a simulation is a dynamic or operating model; therefore changes over time in the model correspond to changes over time in the system being modeled. In a model, the structural relationships are isomorphic with that being modeled; in a simulation, in addition, the *functional* relationships among the structural elements are isomorphic with that being represented. A simulation of another system therefore involves abstracting not only the static, structural relationships, but the dynamic, process relationships as well. With the incorporation of functional relations into a

model it becomes an operational and dynamic representation of *process*—a simulation. It is the exhibition of process that distinguishes simulations from such static models as blueprints, dolls, etc.

In sum, then, simulations belong to that class of theory called models, since, the structure of the theory exhibits the structure of the subject-matter, and are distinguished from other models in that they exhibit, in addition, the functional relations among the structural elements; by virtue of their dynamic, operating properties, simulations tell us something about the processes occurring in the system being modeled, since changes over time in the simulation correspond to changes in the system under investigation.[4]

This distinction between models and simulations—that a simulation is an *operating* model that displays processes over time and that thus may develop dynamically—is accepted by most scholars conversant with the field. Richard Dawson suggests that "Simulation . . . refers to the construction and manipulation of an operating model . . . ,"[5] whereas Sidney Verba elaborates on the description given above.

> A simulation is a model of a system. Other models . . . may attempt to represent a system through verbal means, mathematical means, or pictorial means. Like simulations, they involve the abstraction of certain aspects of the system one is studying and an attempt to replicate these aspects by other means, such as words or mathematical symbols. But the simulation model differs in that it is an *operating* model. Once the variables that have been selected are given values within the simulation and the relations among the variables are specified, the model is allowed to operate. It may operate through the interaction of people who play roles within the model; or it may operate on a computer. The rules given to the human participants in the simulation or the computer program represent the premises of the model. Its operation produces the implications.
>
> There are many forms of simulation, and where simulation shades off into other forms of study or model-building is hard to specify and probably not too important.[6]

As compared, then, with the Tinker Toy model of a molecule, which can represent only static structure, not process, a simulation can be thought of as a *dynamic model*. Simulators, therefore, must try not only to build a model of system *structure*, but also to incorporate system *processes*. In doing so, they abstract, simplify, and aggregate, in order to introduce into the model more clarity than exists in the referent system.

## ABSTRACTION AND SIMPLIFICATION

What is abstracted? That is, which components and relationships are included in the simulation and which are not? This will depend on the purposes of the simulator; it cannot be decided in a vacuum. Relevance or irrelevance can be determined only within the framework of a particular goal. Let us take, for example, the simulation of an aircraft in flight. If the aim is to study the "lift" provided by a particular type of airframe configuration, then a wooden form shaped like the aircraft in question placed in a wind tunnel will provide the data needed. We can eliminate all the internal workings of the plane, except, perhaps, those needed to provide for the aileron and tail settings that govern its flight. Details such as radio equipment, seats, wiring, fuel tanks, and stewardesses, which, from one point of view, would make the simulation a more complete and accurate representation of an aircraft in flight—and thus more "valid"—are, in fact, only expensive and distracting rubbish. The usefulness and, thus, the "validity" of the simulation are achieved through intelligent abstraction and simplification, not through detailed and accurate representation of the entire system in question.

If, on the other hand, the aim of the simulator is to study human fatigue on an aircraft in flight, then a fairly detailed simulation of the interior of the aircraft will be needed, with its space limitations, its physical layout, its vibrations and noises, and its human occupants. The external configuration and air speed can be ignored.

So the design of the simulation is determined by the specific problem to be studied, not by general considerations of "perfect replication." In fact, the entire idea of perfect replication is nonsense. No two things can be identical in *all* respects; they have differing positions in time and/or in space, if nothing else. When we say that a model is a *representation* of something, we imply that the two differ in some respects. It is important to bear in mind that all modeling begins with *abstraction* and *simplification;* they constitute "the name of the game" rather than being inconvenient limitations that simulators could overcome if they had more funds, better facilities, more computer memory-space, or a more comprehensive theory.

It is equally important to recognize that for some purposes a very simple model is preferable to a more complicated one, if only because it is cheaper and easier to manipulate. The difficult questions that model-builders face concern *which* elements, *which* relationships, *which* processes should be included, and which can be neglected. It is to answer these questions that modelers cry for better theory. The theory regarding airfoil lift, for example, is so well worked out that the problem could probably be solved in a few minutes on a computer rather than in a wind tunnel. But the theories regarding human fatigue and its relationship to noise, space limitations, the presence or absence of other people, or the activity being engaged in, are so primitive that the simulation builder would be hard put to know just what he should include in his simulation and what he may exclude in order to obtain useful and generalizable results.

In sum, then, simulations tap into different bodies of theory about referent systems, depending on the simulation purposes. It is not possible to judge the merits of a simulation on the basis of its simplicity or complexity except in terms of its purpose. It is certainly possible, however, to judge a simulation according to the validity of the theories or part-theories that it incorporates. A simulation, for example, that attempts to represent the movement of the heavenly bodies in space would be rejected if it were based on the theory that space is filled with ether. Simulation shares the problems of all other scientific endeavors in that the usefulness and generalizability of its results depend on the adequacy and validity of the theory on which it is based. The matter of adequacy and validity is of particular concern to social scientists, as we shall see in later chapters.

There are other ways of judging the usefulness of a simulation. Simulations also may be used to *create* theory where none existed. This kind of bootstrap operation is one of the most fascinating attractions of simulations, and this, too, I shall discuss in detail later.

The essential points to be remembered so far are, first, that modeling is a special form or sub-type of theorizing, whereas simulation is a special form or sub-type of modeling; and, second, that central to the process of simulating are disciplined *abstraction* and *simplification*.

## SUBSTITUTION

A third and equally central process in simulation is *substitution*. Obviously, a model is a *substitute* for the referent system. The amount and kind of substitution, the degree to which components in the model or simulation faithfully represent their referent counterparts, is crucial. When a scientist builds a simulation of a harbor to study water currents or sand deposition, he does not, of course, try to build his simulation of the identical components of the system he wishes to study; he doesn't haul buckets of sand and sea water into his lab, or raid the docks at night for piers with which to construct his model. He *substitutes*. He uses something else to represent the components of his referent system. The rocky shore may be represented by papier-mâché, the piers by matchsticks, and the sand by silt. But the configuration of the papier-mâché must accurately represent the configuration of the harbor's rocks; particles of silt must bear the same size-relationship to the grains of sand as do his matchsticks to the piers, or his entire model to the harbor he is studying. The ocean currents may be simulated by the use of a pump, but they must accurately represent the forces he wishes to study. He must be *very* careful in his substitutions. He may have remembered size relationships, but forgotten weight, surface texture, and viscosity. Does he use water to simulate water? If so, does water flowing around a matchstick in a papier-mâché tank set up the same pattern of eddies and swirls as water flowing around a mussel-encrusted pier in a harbor? Does water flowing over a silt bed at one mile per hour affect the silt in the same way that water flowing over a sand bar at five miles an hour affects the sand? If he has a theory to tell him that it doesn't, or if his observations convince him that it doesn't, then he must find a substitute for water which a theory will tell him *does* act the same way around matchsticks and over silt as water does around piers and over sand. Perhaps he can't find a theory that will enable him to select a substitute. Then he is obligated to use a different approach.

Instead of building a mock-up of the whole harbor in miniature, perhaps he should use a very large tank, real sand, real sea water, and real piers. But if he wants to see how water acts on sand as it flows around the harbor piers, he may only need to use two piers. He has made only partial substitutions—the tank for the ocean, and two piers for the whole dock. He has miniaturized a referent system in which size, space, and force are crucial elements; it is not just a miniature *representation,* but a *model.* But he must be sure that the relations between size, space, and force are the same in his model as in his referent. Then, studying their interaction in this limited space, perhaps he can extrapolate to the larger space of the harbor. But whether he uses silt and matchsticks or real sand and piers, he must substitute, as in all cases of modeling; and what he substitutes for what can be crucial.

We come again to metaphor and analogy, for the question of what is substituted for what is the question of *analogy* and *analogue. Analogy* is defined as "resemblance in some particulars between things otherwise unlike"; and an *analogue* is something that is analogous to something else, or something *similar in function* but different in structure and origin. Metaphors produce analogies: if we think of electricity as being *like* a fluid, we are led to analogies between electric current and water in terms of rate of flow, differences of level, and force. If our metaphor is correct, the analogies will be useful.

But as we saw with the example of a harbor mock-up, the relevant properties of the analogy not only must be similar to those of the referent, but also must interact with each other and with another entity in the same way as do those of the referent. A single component may have several properties. Water, for example, has weight, viscosity, compressibility, chemical composition, and freezing point. Water interacts with sand as a function of its viscosity, among other things. Whatever is used as a substitute for sand must have properties which interact in the same way with water as does sand. If fresh water is substituted for sea water, then the modeler must be sure that the viscosity of fresh water interacts with the sand-substitute in the same way that sea water interacts with sand.

If he fails to reconstruct these relationships accurately, then he has fallen into the trap that lies in the path of all analogizers—that of false or incorrect analogy. The danger is well illustrated by the story of the American student and an Indian exchange student having lunch together on a Mid-western campus. The Indian orders tea, and when it arrives in typical American form, he carefully tears open the little bag and dumps the leaves into his cup. "You don't have to do that," explains the American; "The water will penetrate the bag." Whereupon the Indian takes a little bag of sugar from the sugar dish and drops it unopened into his cup of tea! Careless or inadequate analogizing will result in a sticky mess for the social science simulator as well.

Not all models, of course, are physical representations of a referent system. The representation may be entirely symbolic, and the substitutes may be *iconic, verbal,* or *mathematical.* A pie-chart is an *iconic* model, that is, a pictorial representation of distribution among segments of a population; a description in words of the referent is a *verbal* substitute; the representation of elements and relationships in the model by symbols and formulae is a *mathematical* substitute.

In simulations, all three types of substitutes may be used to assist in description. In the harbor mock-up example, for instance, the wave flows and force might be represented by vector arrows; some of the relationships might be set forth in mathematical formulae. But in simulations, the substitutions usually involve electronic and/or physical components as well. That is, 500 tidal ebbs and flows might by cycled on a computer, thus providing an electronic representation of the forces operating on the sand with all the replicate elements operating interactively over time. Establishing the correct relationship among all the elements can be excruciatingly difficult.

Many students of simulation describe the relationship between the referent component and its substitute in the simulation as being either *isomorphic* or *homomorphic. Homomorphic,* as used by mathematicians, refers to correspondences that may include many-to-one relationships, whereas *isomorphic* refers to punctiform or one-to-one relationships. Isomorphism also is frequently used to denote the extent to which all elements of the referent system are faithfully represented in the simulation. Both terms have counterparts in developmental biology (analogous and homologous) where the distinctions between them are subtle; but it is not clear that they can be usefully applied to describe the relationship between a simulation and its referent since their usefulness is highly sensitive to the level at which analysis is being conducted. A more useful way to distinguish between types of substitution is suggested by Robert Boguslaw:

> . . . there are only two basic kinds of models—replica and symbolic. Replica models provide a pictorial representation. They are material or tangible and look like the real thing. Examples include such things as toy automobiles or models of an interplanetary rocket. Symbolic models are intangible. They use ideas, concepts, and abstract symbols to represent objects. They don't even resemble the real thing.

> They use lines and arrows to symbolize information flow and things like diagrammatic blocks to symbolize major elements of a system.[7]

According to this distinction, the airfoil in the wind tunnel, the interior mock-up of the plane, the harbor simulation, a model railroad, or a flight trainer, are all replica models. A computer program simulating bus terminal traffic, and a system of pipes, pumps, valves, and colored liquids simulating an economic system, are symbolic models.

## WHY SIMULATE?

Why do people build simulations? The primary answers can probably be subsumed under the headings of *economy*, *visibility*, *reproducibility*, and *safety*, although there are certainly other reasons, as we shall see in later chapters.

### *Economy*

It is frequently cheaper to study a given phenomenon in a model or in a simulation than in its natural setting. So whereas constructing and operating a simulation frequently is an extremely expensive proposition, it is usually less so than the alternative of attempting to gain the desired information from the referent world. For example, to build a scale model of an air frame and place it in a wind tunnel, operate the wind tunnel, and make observations of the flow of smoke over the foil under different configurations is time consuming and expensive, but far less so than to build a full size air frame, incorporate it into an aircraft, and to fly it under the same variety of conditions. Experiments can be performed on the model much more economically than on what it models.

Furthermore, experiments performed on a model can eliminate costly mistakes that might cause waste or disaster if not caught. Assume for a moment that out intrepid simulator has been able to overcome all the difficulties we discussed in connection with the harbor simulation, and that it functions properly. Now the construction of a breakwater is contemplated. By adding a model of the proposed breakwater to his simulation of the harbor, he can determine whether its presence will set into motion any new currents or other unforeseen developments which might have undesirable consequences for the harbor as a whole. Lacking this kind of predictive device, the real breakwater might indeed reduce the chop and swell—but at the unanticipated cost of depositing a sand bar requiring monthly dredging of the navigational channel!

So there are two senses in which the use of simulation may be economical. First, because it is usually cheaper to experiment with a model than with the real thing; and second, because costly mistakes can be avoided by "running it through in advance."

*Visibility*

Using a simulation frequently increases the visibility of the phenomenon under study in two ways. First, the phenomenon may be physically more accessible, and hence more readily observed. Sitting behind a glass and watching smoke flow past an air foil in a wind tunnel is much easier than trying to measure the airflow past the wing of a plane in flight. Watching a silt deposit build up in a table top replica of a harbor is much easier than trying to measure what is occurring under 80 feet of muddy sea water. In fact, the "accessibility gap" may be so wide in some instances that observation of the phenomenon under study may be virtually impossible in nature, but extremely easy in a simulation. A working model of the solar system is one example; another example is the computer simulation of nuclear warfare that enables strategists to study the amount of destruction resulting from differences in weather conditions, weapons yield and reliability, time of warning, and extent of preparation!

A second way that simulation may increase the visibility of the phenomenon under study is by bringing it to the foreground, highlighting it, *clarifying* it. It is difficult to study the circulation of blood in a living organism, for the system of which it is a part is so complex that interference with it may radically affect the entire system. But in a *simulation* of blood circulation, it is possible to block the flow of blood at various points and observe the results.

Frequently, the phenomenon under study is so confused and chaotic that it is hard to make any sense of it. Consider the student who wishes to test the basic principles of international relations, who wants to look at world affairs in order to understand them. What does he need to look at? How shall he decide what is relevant? Where shall he start, what should he observe? The United Nations? The daily newspapers? The International Court of Justice? The flows of international trade? The national military postures? The thousands of intergovernmental and private agencies? If he tries to become *au courant* with all the elements of international politics, he will almost certainly end up confused and exhausted.

But if someone has built a simulation of international relations that incorporates most of the salient elements in simplified and explicit form, the student can study it and so gain a grasp of general outlines, an operating framework, upon which he can then elaborate the details in which he is particularly interested. For him, the simulation has functioned to *simplify* a system whose complexity obscures specific phenomena. Hydraulic models of the economic system or little plastic digital computers for children serve this same purpose of clarifying and simplifying the complex by eliminating all but the salient and relevant phenomena. So simulations aid visibility by making certain kinds of phenomena more accessible for observation and measurement, and by introducing clarity into what is otherwise complex, chaotic, or confused.

*Reproducibility*

Simulations allow scholars to reproduce chains of events that they could not otherwise observe repeatedly. There are at least two reasons for wanting to reproduce events. The first reason involves the element of *chance*. For example, suppose a researcher wants to find out how long passengers will have to wait for buses at the peak rush hour. He could station observers in the bus terminal for 360 days in a row, and through an hour-by-hour count, gain some understanding of those elements of chance which simply cannot be predicted, such as how many buses will be stopped at how many red lights, or how many passengers will not have the correct change at ticket windows. But a computer simulation of the operation of a bus terminal is not only far more economical, but also allows the researcher to build the element of chance into his simulation, run it repeatedly, and learn that the wait will be "X" minutes under given conditions with a probability of, say, .86 that it will be no more than "X plus 1" and no less than "X minus 1" minutes. These probabilities can be derived only by letting the simulation run often enough to allow all the possible outcomes to occur, and by observing the frequencies with which they do in fact occur.

Also, of course, simulations allow the student to reproduce many times a situation that might never occur again in real life; this aspect enables him to examine certain variables and relationships with respect to their influence on the outcome of the real life situation. It enables him, in effect, to play the fascinating historical game, "What might have happened if . . . ?"

In the terminology of research, simulation allows us to observe the effects of different kinds of manipulation of the input variables: it is possible to change assumptions, to alter the input parameter values, and to modify the relationships among elements of the system. For example, in the simulation of a nuclear exchange, we might want to ask, "What difference does 15 minutes' warning as opposed to 30 minutes' warning make in the amount of destruction? What difference does it make in the severity of the retaliation that will be suffered if the counterforce missiles are only 70% reliable instead of 90% reliable?" Changing input variables is closely related to the technique of allowing chance to operate in a random fashion, except that in this case we alter the variables in ways that interest us. We might ask, as another example, "What difference will it make in the international system if the chief of state of one of the major powers is highly paranoid as opposed to self-confident and trusting?"

So simulations are valuable because they allow phenomena to be reproduced, and thus (1) enable the experimenter to derive statistical probabilities when the outcome is uncertain, and/or (2) enable him to vary numerous aspects of the system in ways that yield profitable insights into how the system operates. In other words, simulations allow controlled experiments to be made that would otherwise be impossible.

### *Safety*

Frequently, propositions may be tested in simulations more safely than in the real world. There are two senses in which this is true. The first is best illustrated by the "flight trainer" for prospective pilots, or by the "reflex test" equipment sometimes used to determine whether a given person is qualified to operate certain machines safely. These are essentially training or testing simulations—laboratories for measuring or increasing human skill. The safety features of such simulations are obvious. Pilot error in the flight trainer may result in a scowl from the instructor, but it won't produce a fiery death or the smashup of a multi-million-dollar aircraft. Discovering that one's reflexes are slow may be humiliating, but it is better to discover it in a laboratory than at 70 miles per hour on a superhighway.

Not only do simulations allow us to avoid putting human beings in dangerous situations, but they also allow us to study dangerous situations themselves without actually creating them. The simulation of a thermo-nuclear exchange is one example. The computer simulation of a controlled nuclear reaction is another example; it produces information about tolerances of stability without risking the hazards of a real reactor's going "critical." So simulations are used for safety purposes, both to protect human beings while they are being trained or studied, and to produce laboratory analogues of dangerous phenomena that we need to study.

It will become obvious as we move into the chapters on simulations in research and teaching that the decision to use a simulation may be governed by one or another of these features of economy, visibility, reproducibility, and safety, depending on the research situation. Still other reasons for using simulations are that participation in a simulation deepens the involvement of the subjects, and that simulations offer an opportunity to stage "future events" so that they may be analyzed and "played through." These other reasons for simulating will be elaborated more fully in the context in which they occur.

So far, we have discussed simulations without drawing a distinction between those used in the physical sciences and those used by social scientists. In many cases, the distinction is not clear cut—the computer simulation of a bus terminal is an example—for both physical and human behavioral factors must be built into the model. However, most of the examples given so far have been drawn from the physical sciences and from engineering, because in many ways the problems are more straight-forward and the examples clearer. In a sense, I have attempted to use a principle of simulation in this chapter, by using the more simple to provide a model for understanding the more abstract and complex. The following chapter deals with the special problems and promises of simulation and games in the social sciences.

## FOOTNOTES

1. KARL W. DEUTSCH, "On Theories, Taxonomies, and Models as Communication Codes for Organizing Information," *Behavioral Science*, XI, No. 1 (1966), 3.
2. ABRAHAM KAPLAN, *The Conduct of Inquiry: Methodology for Behavioral Science* (San Francisco: Chandler Publishing Co., 1964), pp. 264–265.
3. JAMES G. MILLER, "Living Systems: Basis Concepts," *Behavioral Science*, X, No. 3 (1965), 209.
4. WAYMAN J. CROW, "The Role of Simulation-Model Construction in Social Research on Post-Nuclear Attack Events" (La Jolla, California: Western Behavioral Sciences Institute, 1967), pp. 11–12.
5. RICHARD E. DAWSON, "Simulation in the Social Sciences," in *Simulation in Social Science: Readings*, ed. HAROLD GUETZKOW (Englewood Cliffs, N.J.: Prentice-Hall, 1962), p. 3.
6. SIDNEY VERBA, "Simulation, Reality, and Theory in International Relations," *World Politics*, XVI, No. 3 (1964), 491.
7. ROBERT BOGUSLAW, *op. cit.*

# 2

# SIMULATING SOCIAL SYSTEMS: PHILOSOPHICAL AND METHODOLOGICAL CONSIDERATIONS

> . . . both scientific knowledge and ordinary knowledge of the common-sense objects of the external world are recognized as analytically unjustified, highly presumptuous, and fallible.[1]

The previous chapter was intended to give the reader a "feel" for simulations in general. This chapter is intended to introduce simulations of social systems, to demonstrate that they differ in degree but not in kind from their cousins in the physical sciences, and to distinguish between simulations and "games." The discussion in this chapter is more technical than in the last, for it deals with intricate questions of scientific methodology. At the heart of these considerations is the concept of *pattern*, as a way of viewing the organization of systems, as an epistemological tool, as a guide in designing social science research, and as a justification for using simulations and games to study human behavior.

## INFORMATION AND ENTROPY IN SYSTEMS

Simulations of social systems are more primitive than simulations of physical systems. To see why this is necessarily so, we must look more closely at the term *system*, using the twin concepts of *information* and *entropy* as a way of characterizing a system of any kind. *Information* is not being used here in the familiar sense of knowledge gained about something; it is used in the more technical sense of the *amount of formal patterning or complexity in a system*, the degree of order or structure, the predictability; in short, the more *information* there is in the system, the more *certainty* it contains. *Entropy* is lack of information, randomness, and unpredictability. It is the opposite of *information* and is therefore sometimes called *neginformation*. (Similarly, information may be termed *negentropy*.) To understand information and entropy better, consider the three following types of systems:

1.
2.
3.

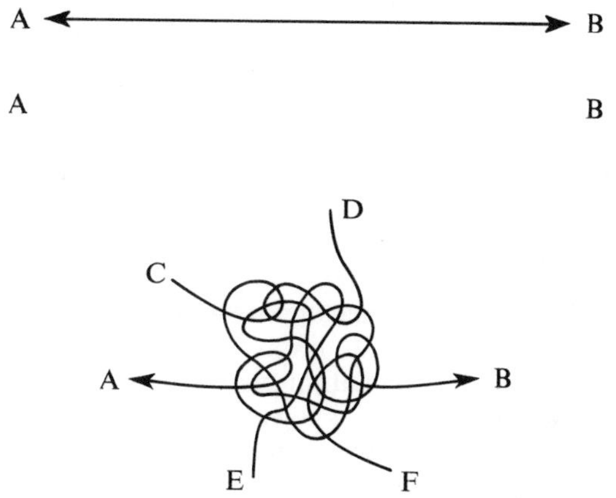


Number (1) is a system comprised of two units, (A) and (B), which have a known relationship to one another. If we know the state of (A), this tells us the state of (B). In other words, the two units are completely interdependent. It is a perfect information system. It contains no entropy (randomness, uncertainty, or unpredictability). This is, of course, an "ideal type" in the Weberian sense; that is, no such system could actually exist, because there would always be some uncertainty or "play" in the system—at the atomic or molecular level, if not elsewhere. Nevertheless, many physical entities are very high-information systems and thus approximate such an "ideal." An internal combustion engine is a good example. If we know the position of one piston, then we can state with a high degree of confidence the position of every other part of the engine; given the state of only one part, the state of the whole system is known.

The units of a high-information system need not, however, have quite this kind of relationship. The state of one unit does not necessarily disclose the states of all others. But if the *relationship* among the units is known, and given the states of all but one, the state of that one unit can be determined. For the purposes of study, for example, we can regard water-and-environment as a system. If we know the state of the water—how pure it is, how much pressure it is under, and how much it is being "jiggled"—we can determine the exact temperature at which it will freeze. Such statements of the type "If A is X, then B is Y" are the stuff of which the "laws" of science are constructed. And as implied by both examples, it is not necessary to limit ourselves to A and B. We can also add C, D, E, F, G, and so on.

Simulating such strictly-patterned systems is straightforward. It is simply a matter of calculation and of finding analogues. This can be complicated and difficult, but it is essentially an engineering problem.

Now consider system (2):

2. A B

More accurately, we should refer to this as a "non-system," since there is no relation between (A) and (B). Knowing the state of (A) tells us nothing about the state of (B); there is no pattern or information. Such a *non-system* (or *negsystem*) is characterized by randomness, lack of organization, and unpredictability—it represents complete entropy. The "ideal type" of such a condition would be a totally disordered universe in which there was no relation between any of its particles and hence no structure (information); knowing the position or state of any given particle in the universe would tell us nothing about the position or state of any other particle. It is entirely possible that no such condition exists in the universe; it may be that *everything* is at least partially determined, but that we simply don't know in what way. Still, we live in the midst of what *seem* to be myriads of non-systems characterized, from *our* observational viewpoint, by a high degree of entropy. There is no apparent relationship between the number of books on my shelf and coffee production in Brazil—although a clever metaphysician might be able to find one. The connection, if any, between Saturday afternoon football scores and the Monday morning stock market is not self-evident. On the other hand, Saturday afternoon football scores and Monday morning class attendance *may* be related—intuitively, we would suspect that they might be. But we have no evidence to demonstrate that they are, and unless we had, we simply could not simulate this kind of system, or "non-system."

This brings us to the third kind of system:

3.

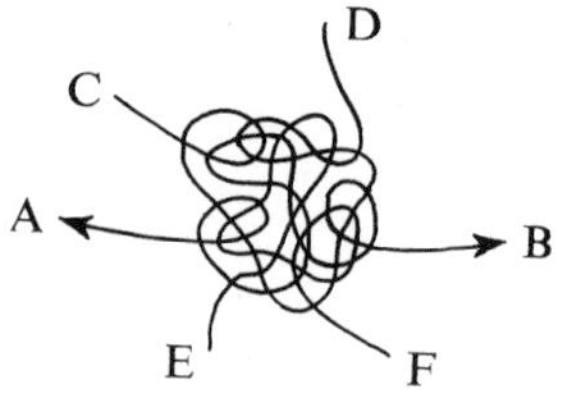


In this sytem, we have reason to believe that there is information, order, and predictability, but the unknowns are multitudinous and the connections ("linkages") between (A) and (B) are so tangled that we cannot predict much about (B) from knowing a good deal about (A). This is the situation of most social science, and our social-behavioral world probably constitutes such a system. John Madge says:

> One point on which all social scientists from Comte and Spencer to the present day have been agreed is that human behavior is less predictable than the events with which most previous scientists have had to deal. This has been interpreted to mean either of two things. Some people conclude that human and social behavior is not wholly subject to determining factors, but that every individual has some capacity of choice which enables him to vary his conduct in partial independence of the forces operating upon him. Others believe that, although human behavior is fully determined by circumstances, these circumstances in all their ramifications are so numerous and unknowable that we can never hope to predict how any individual or group will respond to a given situation.[2]

We are almost certain, for instance, that there is some relationship between a man's personality and his political beliefs, but the variables are so poorly defined, the relationship is so complex and is mediated by so many other factors, that it is virtually impossible to say what that relationship is. For most practical purposes, we therefore can nearly consider it an instance of system (2)—a non-system. This is true of most problems that social scientists try to study. The questions are too complicated and fraught with too many uncertainties to make accurate prediction feasible. The social-behavioral "universe" is almost certainly not random, but as far as our ability to understand it is concerned, it frequently might as well be. And it is then impossible to simulate—unless we want to build a random-events generator. Even such a "sub-universe" as the operation of an entire national political system could not be simulated in the present state of our knowledge.

Nevertheless, all is not "blooming, buzzing confusion" and our prospects are not as bleak as the foregoing might seem to imply. There is a slowly growing body of empirical knowledge that does disclose relations among some of the "particles" in the system, that does demonstrate that the complex "universe" of human social behavior and societal functioning is *not* random but rather is characterized by a whole spectrum of states of determination, ranging from complete disjointedness through negligible, partial, or substantial, to nearly complete determination. The degree of apparent entropy is decreasing as our ability to "tap in" to the information in the system grows greater. And just as we have been able to derive laws about the physical universe, it is becoming possible to posit "laws" of individual and social behavior—but as yet only in an often *primitive* and *probabilistic* way.

## PRIMITIVE AND PROBABILISTIC SYSTEMS

I put the word "laws" in quotes and use the word "primitive" because most of the "laws" pertaining to human behavior can be stated only in terms of rough relationships indicating direction or "trend" or "tendency," but not in terms of degree or causality. For example, we can say with some certainty that raising the educational level of the population will increase, rather than decrease, general citizen involvement in political matters. But we cannot determine *by how much* political involvement will increase, nor can we say with certainty that the raised educational level in itself *directly causes* increased political involvement. Our difficulties arise partly because there are so many intervening factors that we cannot control in order to test the hypothesis, and partly because we have neither the resources nor the tools to measure, in a meaningful way, either "educational level" or "political involvement."

I used the word "probabilistic" because most of our laws are based on statistical probability and therefore must be qualified. There are many reasons for such qualification. In the first place, even in studying purely physical events, the mere taking of measurements changes the phenomenon to some degree, however slight. This "distortion by measurement" occurs to a far greater extent in dealing with social and behavioral events—to such an extent, in fact, that the researcher may be in danger of creating self-fulfilling or self-denying prophecies. The mere enunciation of a principle—such as, "the higher the educational level, the greater the political involvement"—may change the behavior with which we are dealing. Also, as Madge suggests, there may simply be more randomness in social systems and in human behavior than there is in physical systems. In any case, we cannot (yet?) systematically account for such randomness in the social-behavioral universe as we can, for instance, in the case of the laws describing the behavior of gases.

The best we can do is to state that some relationship in the social world holds "most of the time," or "if all other things are equal," or "allowing for the way we have made the concepts or entities operational in our study, it holds—but of course one cannot be certain that these results can be generalized . . ." and so on. We state our conclusions with a given level of confidence, not with certainty. There are too many unknowns.

The point, however, is that we do achieve something better than sheer guesswork. A sociologist may conduct a study and find that middle-class white juveniles have a lower incidence of arrests than do white juveniles in the slums of the same city. He may repeat the study enough times and in enough cities to become confident that this is generally true—even though there may be exceptions. Now he knows something. He knows that there is a relationship of a certain kind between (A), the class background of white juveniles, and (B) the arrest records of white juveniles. He has a law. He may even make gross predictions, even though he may have no theory to explain his predictions. He may find that the law frequently does not hold true, and he may know little about the other factors that determine whether or not it holds, but he is not simply shooting in the dark. He is in system (3) rather than in non-system (2). This is the condition of most social science.

*Despite the extreme complexity of human behavior and of societal structure, we have reason to assume, then, that there are identifiable patterns, regularities, and laws. It is upon this assumption that social science simulations are constructed.* These laws are different in degree, not in kind, from those that physical engineers use in the construction of their simulations. B. F. Skinner illustrates both the problem and the assumption regarding its solution by reference to the British physicist Sir Oliver Lodge, who once asserted:

> "though an astronomer can calculate the orbit of a planet or comet or even a meteor, although a physicist can deal with the structure of atoms, and a chemist with their possible combinations, neither a biologist nor any scientific man can calculate the orbit of a common fly." This is a statement about the limitations of scientists or their aspirations, not about the suitability of a subject matter. Even so, it is wrong. It may be said with some assurance that if no one has calculated the orbit of a fly, it is only because no one has been sufficiently interested in doing so. The tropistic movements of many insects are now fairly well understood, but the instrumentation needed to record the flight of a fly and to give account of all the conditions affecting it would cost more than the importance of the subject justifies. There is, therefore, no reason to conclude, as the author does, that "an incalculable element of self-determination thus makes its appearance quite low down the animal scale." Self-determination does not follow from complexity.[3]

In addition to the problem of sheer complexity, social scientists may be confounded by a host of other difficulties. For instance, there is the problem of the self-fulfilling or self-denying prophecy—the problem that changes in society or in individuals often come about as a result of statements about that society or those individuals. To illustrate: one of the surest ways to turn a person into the leader in a small group is to tell him (even if it is not true) that tests show he is fitted for leadership.[4] Or note that the mere publication of income statistics will push the average income upward, for all those whose income is below average will exert the pressures at their command to increase their income.

Another difficulty for the social scientist is that there are so many pseudo-laws of human behavior—bits of conventional wisdom that often are not true. For example, there was a widespread belief a few years ago that if people were thrifty and built up savings accounts instead of spending for "luxuries," national prosperity would follow on the heels of individual prosperity. All the developments of recent economic experience and theory tell us that this is nonsense, or at least naïve, since mere blind thrift could result in idle cash deposits, idle men and resources, and a spiral of deflation and depression.

But despite these problems of complexity, inadequate measures and concepts, self-fulfilling or self-denying prophecy, and the blinders of conventional wisdom, simulators in the social sciences believe that they are dealing with a true system containing information, rather than with a non-system or a state of entropy; their scientific problems are the same as those of physical scientists—merely more difficult. But their practical problems are enormous. It is impossible to simulate a system unless one has an adequate understanding of how it operates. If simulation is defined, as in Chapter 1, as the simplified replication in another medium of observed phenomena, then it is clear that such phenomena cannot be fully replicated until social scientists fully observe and describe them. So our inability to replicate is due less to limited simulation engineering skills than to the lack of adequate social science theory and data. But despite incomplete understanding of the phenomena they are trying to model, and because they are convinced that trying to simulate the phenomena is worthwhile for a variety of reasons, scholars "take a stab at it." They turn to *piecemeal* and *skeletal* simulations and games.

## PIECEMEAL SIMULATIONS

A *piecemeal* simulation is one in which the researcher attempts to simulate a small segment of social behavior and study it intensively. The choice of the segment is usually based on a conviction that the nature of the units composing this segment, and the relationships among them, are fairly well established; that is, that there is an "island of theory" or a "micro-theory," which describes this particular segment of social interaction with a fairly high degree of confidence. For example, certain types of economic behavior, such as those simulated by Orcutt, Greenberger, Korbel, and Rivlin,[5] are reliably described by theory; so is the behavior of committees faced with political decisions,[6] or the conflict and cooperation behavior of two persons in a prisoner's dilemma game or one of its variants.[7] These are only a few examples of those segments of behavior which *could* be simulated; Berelson and Steiner[8] have documented several hundred reasonably well-established principles of human behavior, most of which would lend themselves to simulation treatment.

For example, Hovland, Janis, and Kelley[9] have explored the relationship between communications and human behavior—specifically, the conditions under which a persuasive communication is or is not effective in modifying beliefs. Just as in the harbor simulation described earlier, in which the location of a proposed breakwater can be varied to study the impact of different placements on sand bar formation, so the principles governing persuasive communication can be further analyzed through the use of simulations. Parameters such as personality characteristics, group structure, and communication flow can be systematically varied to study the impact of various configurations on the communication outcomes.

There is a difficulty with such piecemeal studies, however. Scientific knowledge of the sort I have described usually has been purchased at the price of narrow encapsulation. That is, experiments are performed in a laboratory under essentially sterile conditions, with all other factors besides the one under study presumably being "held equal." But the principles derived under such conditions may not hold in the non-sterile and richly complicated world to which we wish to generalize them. We may establish in a laboratory, for instance, that in a two-person prisoner's dilemma game, women are more competitive than men; but we can never be certain that it isn't the nature of the laboratory situation itself that creates this effect. Outside the laboratory in the world of "real life," something different may be true. We are probably entitled to assume that findings in one setting are more apt to hold in another than their *opposites*, but this probability is little comfort if we have reason to believe that the fact of extreme simplification of the situation, of holding other things equal, may produce an effect that confounds—even if probably not reverses—the results of the experiment. The "unreality" of the laboratory, the fact that behavior in the laboratory has no "real life" consequences, also may vitiate the usefulness of knowledge gained in such "piecemeal" simulations. The problem is inherent in more intricate and complex laboratory games and simulations as well. There is reason to believe, however, that the problem is less severe because the subjects, or "participants," become deeply involved, are subjected to more complex stimuli, and are given more avenues of response.

It should be noted at this point, however, that the assumption that a richer environment and greater involvement decreases the disparity between human "laboratory behavior" and "natural behavior" is just that—an assumption based on the impressionistic observations of social scientists and fortified by growing evidence as to the discrepancies between laboratory and field observations of animals. Systematic evidence about human beings has yet to be gathered. This whole problem is discussed at greater length in the chapter on "Validity."

## SKELETAL SIMULATIONS

Another approach is to use a *skeletal* simulation. The researcher does not try to narrow his focus to one small segment or aspect of human social behavior; instead he tries to simulate a large and complex system, such as "international relations." But he knows that he cannot identify all the units of the international system, much less the nature of the relationships among them. So he selects those units and those relationships about which his information is greatest and, using them as a framework—as the "bones"—he builds a skeleton of international relations. He hopes that by continually gathering more data in the field, by operating the simulation over and over and thus learning what is pertinent, he slowly will be able to flesh out the bones of his skeleton until someday he has a more complete simulation of the system in which he is interested. In the meantime, he must be aware that he has abstracted and cruelly abbreviated, that his simulation is to real life what a skeleton is to a living man.

It is here, in the abstraction and abbreviation, that danger lies. The skeletal simulation is particularly vulnerable to the danger that I might call the "excluded variable." In Chapter 1, we saw that the very core of simulation is abstraction. But *what* to abstract from reality and include in the simulation must be determined by an intelligent evaluation of what is crucial to the operation of the system. And when the scholar is under social, financial, and intellectual pressures to "create a product"—that is, to devise an operating simulation—his rules for abstraction may become less rigorous. The variables embodied in the simulation are likely to be those about which he knows the most, rather than those he has determined to be most crucial. Thus, availability of information is apt to be a more powerful selection criterion than appropriateness.

Assume that you are trying to construct a simulation of international relations. You have detailed information about the comparative military hardware levels of two nations in the system. You know nothing about the personalities of the two chiefs of state. So the temptation to ignore decision-maker personality-variables and to include the military variables in detail is almost overwhelming—simply because the information is available, and *not* because you have assessed the relative importance of the two variables as determinants of the relations between those states. Such errors arise, not because the scientific process is weak, but simply because the human and social pressures to take the easier path are great. One advantage of using simulations in research, however, is that if you have neglected important variables, the outcomes of your simulation are apt to be absurd. This is why simulation plays so important a role in theory-building, as will be discussed more fully later on.

A second danger applies to piecemeal as well as to skeletal simulations, and like the first, arises from human frailty rather than from any weakness of the scientific process. It is often heuristically useful to operate an admittedly inadequate simulation based on a limited or erroneous model; the danger lies in forgetting that the outcomes also are likely to be inadequate. Since a simulation has "face validity"—that is, since it is *called* a simulation of human conflict, committee decision-making, or international relations—it is easy to forget that it may not simulate any of those things and then to be tempted to give more weight to the results than they deserve.

In his book *Deadly Logic*, Philip Green discusses this danger in detail[10] by arguing that game theorists have fallen into just this trap. Game theorists, says Green, begin by suggesting that international strategic interaction contains certain elements of game theory. The theorists then list the assumptions and limitations essential to a game-theoretic analysis, such as known utilities, rationality of decision-makers, and the ability to predict the particular outcomes of particular behaviors. They proceed to explore the game-theoretic model and then arrive at a set of "heuristic" recommendations based on the model. But the theorists conscientiously point out that these recommendations cannot be applied to real international strategic problems, for since real world decision-makers are not necessarily rational, since utilities are not known, and so forth, the assumptions necessary for the game-theoretic analysis are false when applied to international politics.

So far, so good. But Green goes on to demonstrate that all too often, when one reads the non-technical writings of some game-theorists —the policy recommendations they put forth as "experts" on strategy, rather than as game-theory analysis—one finds that their "real life" recommendations are identical to those derived from their game-theory work. The game theorists seem to have been insidiously convinced by results obtained from a model admittedly based on false assumptions, even though they have verbally recognized the danger. This is the error of placing more stock in findings derived from a model than the quality of the model warrants. It is an error to which any model designed to look like the "real thing" makes a researcher as susceptible as does armchair philosophizing! But this question of the proper use of results from incomplete simulations is extremely complicated, so we shall return to it later.

## THE GAMING APPROACH TO SIMULATION

We saw that due to lack of theory and supporting data, social science simulators are limited in their ability to construct adequate simulations of the systems in which they are interested. Consequently, they often have recourse to piecemeal and skeletal simulations, with their attendant dangers. Another, and many think more profitable, approach is to drop the idea of "simulating" in the strict sense, and to turn to "games."

What is a "game?" I implied one definition in the introduction to this volume by indicating that when human players enter a simulated system (such as the simulation of medieval warfare called "chess") and begin to manipulate the units and relationships in the structure, the simulation acquires the characteristics of a game. Other definitions are more elaborate, but do not essentially alter this definition. Combining the definitions of E.W. Martin, Jr., Martin Shubik, J. M. Kibbee, and Richard Dawson suggests that the term *gaming* can be applied to simulations in which human actors participate in the simulated system, generally in a competitive situation.[11]

A more formal and at the same time more general distinction between simulation and gaming is one I have derived from sociologist Erving Goffman's analysis.[12] In a simulation, the rules for translating external variables into simulation variables are highly formal; in more colloquial language, the rules are tight and tough. All substitutions and analogies must be defended; the relations between variables must be carefully specified; the operation of the simulation must be governed by mathematical rules. Clearly, then, the translation of variables must be based on adequate theory and data.

In a "game," according to my definition, there is more leeway with respect to analogical consistency and strictness. The rules for translating "real life" variables into simulation variables are less demanding, so it is possible to "play around" a bit and "make do," as we shall see in the illustration below. On the surface, it does not seem that my distinction, based on the amount of strict and formal resemblance between simulation and referrent, is related to the distinction suggested earlier, which is based on the insertion of human players. As we shall see, however, the use of human players is only one example of the "informality" that defines a game in terms of my general statement, for human players can serve as a *surrogate* for a missing or inadequate variable.

To illuminate the difference in formality between a simulation and a game, let us see how a researcher might go about building a game. His thinking goes something like this.

"I want to construct a simulation of a social system—international politics. But I don't know enough about this system to build an accurate analogue, so I am not going to claim that I can simulate it. I may be able to build good simulations of small sub-parts of the international political system, or I may be able to include some of the major variables and relationships pretty adequately; but there are immense gaps in my knowledge, and there may even be gaps I don't know enough to know are there. So I'll do the best I can. I'll use the best theory and data at my disposal and see what I come up with. Where there are gaps—missing variables, or ill-defined relationships between the variables I've included—I'll admit it, and I'll leave the space empty or the linkages open. In some cases, however, I do have a rough idea of what should go in the space, but I don't know enough about it to simulate it. So I'll either use the thing itself—put it into the simulation bodily—or I'll use the closest substitute for it that I can get, even though I don't know much about the substitute either. I'll consider the substitute a 'black box' to be studied as I operate the game.

"For example, in this game of international politics I'm building, I know that culture (whatever that means) must have an important impact on the behavior of national decision-makers, but I don't know just what impact. So I'll leave an open space, and plug in culture when we know more about it. In the meantime, I'll see what difference it seems to make if I leave culture out. Perhaps the game will operate as our observations of the real world suggest it should. In that case, I can conclude either that (1) culture is not an important variable and I can afford to ignore it, or that (2) the cultural effect is being cancelled out in the real world by another variable I've also left out; in this latter case I can continue to ignore both culture and the other variable, or worry about culture again when I get that other variable built in.

"On the other hand (3), I can conclude that even though the game *seems* to operate as I think it should and its outcomes are not clearly absurd, I don't know enough about the "real world" to make an adequate comparison, and so I can't come to any conclusion about the culture variable. In this case, I'm better off with a game than with the real world. I can't study culture very well in the real world; I can't get access to decision-makers; and even if I could, I can't impose experimental controls on their behavior. With a game, however, I can use surrogate decision-makers, such as college students of different nationalities. I know they're not really analogues of national decision-makers, but they do give me a way of finding out something about the impact of culture on decision-making behavior. I can study the behavior of American students in a simulation and compare it with that of Mexican, Japanese, and Norwegian students in the same simulation. At least the decisions of these students from different cultures will be more like those of their national leaders than are the *a priori* decisions fed into a computer.

"From what I learn about the decision-making behavior of real people with different cultural backgrounds, perhaps I can start to build a *theory* about the culture-variable in international decision-making. So I can use my 'soft' game as a laboratory: I can study certain important aspects of human behavior, and at the same time I can work towards the day when I can explicate the cultural variable with confidence, build it into my game, and take another step towards having a true, 'hard,' simulation."

This is not a hypothetical conversation, by the way; it is one I once had with myself that partially determined the direction of my current research. Note that in this illustration, I translated the external variable, culture, and its linkage with decision-making into a simulation analogue in a "loose" or makeshift way; the transformation rules were extremely informal. Thus, when good theory and reliable data are available for all the relevant variables, we can translate the variables according to strict rules for analogizing, and construct a "simulation." But where theory is weak or data scanty, we can either leave the space open (omit the variable) or *fill the space with a substitute that will, itself, then become an object of study* so that, eventually, the space can be filled accurately.

Thus, *the game can serve as a "pre-simulation," to be used both as a laboratory for studying basic principles of human behavior and as an admittedly inadequate framework for conducting research leading to improvement of the framework itself.*

This "gaming" approach to simulation building is one that a colleague refers to as "messing around" in science. This is not a disparaging phrase; "messing around" is a legitimate way to increase knowledge. In fact, some philosophers of science have argued that this approach to building a body of knowledge about human social behavior is sounder and more productive than the more traditional methods. To understand why this is so, we must turn our attention directly to some questions of scientific method, about which we have been hinting for several pages.

## PATTERN MATCHING VERSUS THE QUEST FOR PUNCTIFORM CERTAINTY

"Truth is found more often through error than through confusion."
Sir Francis Bacon

The "gaming" approach to simulation-construction is similar to lifting oneself up by one's bootstraps or, perhaps more accurately, to rebuilding an airplane while it is in flight. Although this may at first seem like an exercise in absurdity, there are sound reasons for advocating it as a research strategy. But whether we turn to games as "pre-simulations"—as a means of elaborating and refining theory that can then be embodied in a simulation devoid of human participants—or whether we use games as a laboratory for studying the behavior of human subjects, we confront certain basic epistemological questions.

Let us first consider simulation-construction and the elaboration, testing, and refining of theory. It is basic to science that tests of a theory or a hypothesis do not prove it true, but improve its credibility by *failing to prove that it is false*. One way of going about this is to state the theory explicitly, establish some hypotheses about the phenomenon that should occur if the theory is correct, and then determine whether the predicted phenomenon does in fact occur. If, in repeated observations, the predicted phenomenon does not occur, then we doubt the validity of the theory; if it does occur, then confidence in the theory is increased. To take an absurdly simple example, we may state explicitly the theory: "The world is flat, not round." We then establish an hypothesis about what will occur if our theory is correct: "If the world is flat, not round, then any object traveling in a continuing straight line in any direction will eventually fall off." If it cannot be shown, through adequate observation, that an object does *not* fall off, this constitutes *failure to prove the hypothesis false*, and confidence in the theory is increased. If, on the other hand, it *can* be shown that an object does not fall off the earth, the hypothesis is disproved, and confidence in the theory is shaken. The more tests of this kind that the theory passes, the more confidence we have in it.

Confidence in a theory is further increased if we can devise "competing" or alternative theories to explain a phenomenon, extract hypotheses from them, test these hypotheses, and find that they fail. By disproving the alternative theories, we increase confidence in the original theory. An illustration may be helpful. Suppose I notice that when I am getting dressed I always put on my right shoe first; I see that my wife does the same, and I begin to wonder why. Then I realize that we are both right-handed, and I tentatively set up the theory that "shoe-priority" is a physiological phenomenon related to right- or left-handedness. I establish the hypothesis that "Right-handed people will put the right shoe on first; left-handed people will put the left shoe on first." I then devise an experiment, or "test" of the theory, by surveying many right- and left-handed people to determine the order in which they put on their shoes. My studies show that in a very large percentage of the cases, shoe-priority is indeed related to handedness—a high enough percentage to give me confidence that my findings are not just chance. Confidence in my theory is increased, since the hypothesis was confirmed.

However, there may be another explanation. Perhaps right- or left-handedness is not a physiological but a cultural prenomenon; if this is the case, my theory that "shoe-priority is physiologically determined" is wrong. So I study many cultures. I find that right-handedness predominates in approximately the same proportions in each of them, and that the relation between shoe-priority and right- or left-handedness prevails in their cultures as it does in mine. So my confidence in the theory is further increased. Now I discover that some primitives, such as the Onges of Little Andaman Island, are completely ambidextrous; so again I question the physiological basis of handedness; (of course, since it never occurred to the Onges to wear shoes, it will be somewhat difficult to add them to my sample). Additional challenges can be put to my theory; there is no point at which I can say for certain that I have eliminated *all possible* alternative explanations for what I have observed. But as the challenges become more and more "far fetched," the confidence I have in my theory increases. This is the process of science.[13]

I have intentionally used the term "far fetched," since it is precisely in the decision as to what is a "far fetched" and what is a "reasonable" explanation or theory that a difficult epistemological question arises. In simple terms, a theory is judged reasonable to the extent that it *fits in with other theories that have also inspired a high degree of confidence.* The more complex the "network of theory" into which any given theory fits, the less evidence we think we need for accepting the given theory as valid. In other words, the more a given theory is consistent with what we already know, the more confidence we have in the theory. Conversely, the better that *new* bodies of data-supported theory fit into the existing network, the more confidence we have in the web. And the more complete and rich is the "known," the more completely are we able to judge whether the theory in question is compatible with it. In short, as the network of explanations about phenomena grows more detailed, internally consistent, and complex, the more confidence we have that the explanations are accurate—even without added "data" to support any given single explanation.

The internal logic of the network itself is a kind of "proof" of the validity of any given section of it. Thus a number of theories have been put forth to explain the path of the planets around the sun. But since only one theory is consistent with all the other theories explaining phenomena that are part of the system such as gravity, and the age of the solar system, we place our confidence in that theory and reject the others. We look at the whole network or "pattern," and to the degree that bits of data or theories "match" the pattern, our confidence in the accuracy of data, theory, and pattern is increased. "Pattern matching" has become a powerful epistemological tool in dealing, first, with discrete, "punctiform," or "proximal" bits of isolated data whose significance is not evident; and second, with problems of measurement-error.

The conventional, logical positivist, inductive approach to science involves gathering isolated, punctiform bits of data in a specific area of interest, fitting them together into part-theories and, in one-step-at-a-time fashion, trying to construct more comprehensive theory. In an illuminating discussion of pattern-matching as a scientific approach, Donald Campbell contrasts the "quest for punctiform certainty" with "distal" knowledge derived from "a prior identification of the whole." "Both psychology and philosophy," says Campbell,

> are emerging from an epoch in which the quest for punctiform certainty seemed the optimal approach to knowledge. To both Pavlov and Watson, single retinal cell activation and single muscle activations [punctiform data] seemed more certainly reidentifiable and specifiable than perceptions of objects or adaptive acts.[14]

But, says Campbell, we can identify any single "particle," or bit of data only because we have previously identified the complex "whole." As he implies, we can single out and identify single retinal-cell activation only because we have previously identified the complex phenomenon, "perception." Rather than recognizing and identifying the complex whole through identification of its particles and establishment of their relationships, it is the complex whole about which we can have the more certain knowledge, and that enables us to know something about elements or particles of which it is composed. As another example:

> Imagine the task of identifying "the same" dot of ink in two newspaper prints of the same photograph. The task is impossible if the photographs are examined by exposing only one dot at a time. It becomes more possible the larger the area of each print exposed. *Insofar as any certainty in the identification of the single particle is achieved, it is because a prior identification of the whole has been achieved. Rather than the identification of the whole being achieved through the firm establishment of particles, the reverse is the case, the complex being more certainly known than the elements, neither of course, being known incorrigibly.* [Emphasis added.][15]

Campbell's contention is clearer if we think of the difficulty of identifying a particular star on a clear summer night. No single star is identifiable by itself without the pattern of stars around it to give it its identifying context. The frame of other stars, each of them also unidentifiable in isolation, provides the information necessary to give meaning to what would otherwise be uninterpretable.

This point is further demonstrated in the recent work of Nobel laureate H. K. Hartline, in his studies of primary chemical and physiological visual processes in the eye. He "devised methods for recording the nerve impulses from single cells of the eye of the horseshoe crab and cold-blooded vertebrates." He and his associates demonstrated that "individual nerve cells in the retina never act independently, it is the integrated action of all units of the visual system that give rise to vision."[16]

Kepler's attempt to chart the orbits of the planets by using musical intervals as the basis is an approach based on an assumption of "natural order" and all things fitting together.

Again, research into basic cognitive processes mathematically demonstrates that at the most primary level of perception and cognition, no sense impression can be understood without a pre-established frame of reference—a set of rules for translating that sense impression into a meaningful message. This is the pattern a child's learning follows. He slowly builds an interpretive structure—a context for evaluating information—which is elaborated and modified with each new perception.

This kind of "knowing," which comes from the recognition of patterns and thus of the sub-units of those patterns, is called *distal* knowledge. We confront a collection of fragments—bits of punctiform data, each of which is uninterpretable—and suddenly we see the entire pattern or context. Common expressions used to describe this experience include "insight," "revelation," "seeing how it all fits together," and "having it suddenly all make sense." They all express the recognition that when an entire context or pattern is grasped, *each part of the pattern* is also more clearly apprehended. In a sense, we may say that the whole is greater than the sum of its parts.

Pattern-matching, then, enables us to make sense of punctiform data. It also enables us, as Campbell further points out, to cope with the problem of measurement-error—the fallibility of meters—and with the associated problem of explicitly relating theory to experimental data.

A fundamental problem of epistemology revolves around the argument that, in essence, all knowledge is indirect, all sense data "incorrigible" and all "meters" or measuring instruments, are fallible. We can never hope to purify knowledge of all faults, errors, and deviations. Since any meter involves "many physical laws other than the construct-relevant one, . . . (e.g. inertial forces in a galvanometer)," Campbell argues, we can never completely or specifically compensate for these sources of meter-fallibility. A certain amount of error is inevitable. Hence, says Campbell, we must reject a "purely 'proximal' science in which scientific constructs [are] defined in terms of (exhaustively known through) specific meter readings."[17] Punctiform certainty is a mirage.

But the inevitability of measurement-error or observation-error implies that there cannot be a perfect fit between theory and data. For example, says Campbell, take the case in which we

> graph together a set of empirical points and a theoretically derived curve and achieve a good correspondence. Some of the points lie above the line, others below, but in general they fit well, and some lie "exactly" on the line. If there is no systematic deviation, we interpret the point by point deviation where they occur as error, and would expect such error to occur on some of the "perfectly fitting" points were the experiment to be replicated. While an over-all fit has been required, no single observation point has been taken as an infallible operational *definition* of a theoretical value. . . .[18]

Thus, the points graphed together give us a *pattern* by which we can match theory to data and can "distribute the fringe of error over all of the observational points, potentially. . . . *A priori* . . . any of the points could be wrong." It is through a process of this sort, says Campbell, "that physicists can throw away 'wild observations'." At any period, physicists have assumed that *most* of their knowledge is correct, and paradoxically, it is from "this floating platform of over-all pattern," that they have been able to question and re-examine a particular measurement process and refine their measurement instruments. "The 'anchoring' of theory to data," says Campbell, has not at all been achieved through a *perfect* correspondence at any particular point, but rather through a pattern matching of the two in some over-all ways.[19] Furthermore, a network or pattern of theory, even if it is not absolutely accurate, provides a standard—Campbell's "floating platform of pattern"—against which to check given observations that are always subject to measurement error.

We have seen the importance of looking at the "whole" in order to better understand its parts, instead of trying to understand each part in isolation, and then from piecemeal understanding to build up a whole. We have seen that to the degree a theory fits ("matches") a network of theory (a "pattern"), we may have confidence in the theory. And we have seen that because the measurement of any single phenomenon is subject to error, the pattern-matching model of relating theory to data allows us to assume that any "meter reading" is in error without requiring us to impeach the theory. Moreover, and even more important, it is extremely difficult to *interpret* the measurements in the absence of an over-all framework or pattern.

Now we can use pattern-recognition not only in understanding concrete physical phenomena, but also in handling abstractions—in testing concepts and in building theory. An idea acquires new meaning when it is set in the context of other ideas; then, both idea and context enrich and illuminate each other. Scientists increasingly recognize that the inclusion of theories and part-theories in a larger construct is a powerful technique for enhancing data-gathering and theory-testing, *even though the scientists may lack confidence in the absolute validity of many of the theories included in the construct.* As Campbell observes, the certainty of identifying any single part is facilitated by a prior identification of the whole, even if the prior identification is uncertain and partially erroneous.

We are now back to our starting point; this is the process in science we referred to earlier as "messing around." It is the process involved in constructing a "game" that you hope eventually to develop into a simulation. Instead of waiting to build a construct (simulation) until you are certain of the nature of all its elements, you build a game that requires tentatively postulating the entire model. By watching the behavior of the operating sub-parts of the tentative model and by noting how they "fit" with its other parts, you can check and refine both the sub-parts and the model as a whole.Thus, as Bacon implies and Campbell argues, establishing an uncertain and partially erroneous framework may be a way of generating the sub-theory and data from which complete and well-validated theoretical constructs can eventually emerge.

## REPRESENTATIVE SAMPLING: GAMES AS COMPLEX LABORATORIES

The second sound rationale for constructing a tentative but "complete" model for study rather than waiting until all information is available for each sub-part is that such a model can be a "man-machine game" providing a rich laboratory for the study of human behavior. By building a game that incorporates the central features of what we wish to study, even if those features are only rough approximations of the "real world," we can provide a wide range of stimuli for the human subjects, thereby offering the subjects opportunity for a wide range of possible behaviors. In such a game situation, as in the real world, everything is complicated, messy, and tangled.

Despite the assumption to the contrary, the complex laboratory that a game can provide is superior to a more simple laboratory, such as a study of decision-making in which the subject simply manipulates two sets of lights. My argument for the superiority of a complex laboratory is based on Spinoza's dictum that the pattern of research should be the same as the pattern of what is being studied. This dictum may be applied to the design of research, the organization of data analysis, or the search for theory; it also may be applied to the design of laboratory experiments. This dictum is pattern-matching of a different sort and in a different context.

The argument for matching the pattern of the research design or laboratory experiment with the pattern of that being studied is based on some assumptions about the "uniformity of experience."

One way of gaining information about the world is by inference. Under controlled conditions, we measure the behavior of some sample of a population. We then infer that the findings about the sample can be applied to the whole population, subject, of course, to the limitations imposed by the sampling techniques. For example, public opinion pollsters question only about 1500 persons in the United States, carefully selected so that the composition of this sample closely resembles the composition of the population as a whole in regard to relevant characteristics. It is then inferred that the responses of the total population would be similar to the responses of those in the sample—with, incidentally, extremely reliable results.

Alternatively, we may measure the behavior of some *entity* (not an actual sample) thought to *resemble* the population in question, and then infer that the behavior of the entity tells us about the behavior of the population. For this reason, comparative psychologists study the learning behavior of rats in cages and mazes. From their studies, the psychologists draw inferences about the learning process in humans. In this kind of study, the psychologists are using substitute entities, or "surrogates."

It is generally assumed that the more closely the surrogate resembles the population of interest, the more confidently inference can be made. The experimental psychologist more confidently extrapolates from primate behavior to human behavior than from rat or fish behavior. The game approach we are considering here goes a step further: it suggests that the more closely the *laboratory* used in the study resembles the *situation* to which inferences are made, the more valid the inferences.

*The technique of representative sampling of subjects is extended to representative sampling of situations.*

To illustrate the reasoning, a basic tenet of Freudian theory may be false and is at least suspect because Freud failed to take the nature of his laboratory into account and ignored the interaction between behavior and environment. Freud studied apes in the London zoo, concluded from their behavior that they are primarily dominated by sexual drives, and extrapolated to human beings. Even though he argued that his surrogates (the apes) were similar to the population in which he was interested (human beings) and thus showed awareness of the first technique for narrowing the inferential gap, he ignored the situational context—in this case the problem of environmental contamination. Recent field studies of apes have demonstrated that in the natural environment, their sexual activity is far below the level displayed in the zoo, where most activities that dominate their normal existence are impossible. Similar findings could be cited for rats, wild mice, and other common laboratory animals. Freud's inference were incorrect because the nature of his laboratory distorted the behavior of his subjects. The same problem arises when human subjects are placed in a laboratory setting that severely restricts their range of behavior.

If, for example, one is interested in learning about the decision-making behavior of chiefs of state as a function of personality, but cannot study them directly and must use surrogates, two rules should be followed:

(1) The surrogates should be as much like chiefs of state as possible;
(2) The situation in which each surrogate is placed should be as much as possible like that in which the chief of state operates.

Both rules are often broken for a good reason. Understandably, given the limits on resources, research subjects must be chosen on the basis of availability, not suitability. And laboratory environments are usually made as austere and simple as possible: first, because such simplicity makes data-gathering easier; second, because social scientists often do not know enough about the characteristics of the environment to which they wish to generalize to recreate it with fidelity in the laboratory; and third, because they have accepted as an article of faith that the physical science paradigm applies to social sceince; hence they believe that results are more reliable if all variables but the particular one under study are not allowed to vary except in exactly known ways.

The result of such studies, however, is a repetition of Freud's error. The studies neglect the fact that our subjects are human. In the stilted and restricted laboratory environment, the situation of the human subjects is like that of Freud's apes: they have little opportunity to display the richness and complexity of behavior that characterizes their normal existence. The laboratory does not sufficiently resemble the referent situation. Thus, for example, in studying the relation between personality traits and decision-making behavior, we are justified in generalizing our laboratory results to real-life chiefs of state according to the degree that:

(1) the subjects can become intellectually and emotionally involved in the situation
(2) they can become goal-oriented
(3) they can have at their disposal a variety of means as much as possible like those available to chiefs of state for reaching their goals
(4) the communication system in which they are enmeshed has the same characteristics of overload and uncertainty as does that of a chief of state; and
(5) they are operating in ambiguous, threatening, and probabilistic situations.

In brief, the greater the extent to which the laboratory provides a physical, social, and psychological environment identical to that in which a chief of state operates, the greater the extent to which we are justified in inferring that these laboratory results are "valid" with respect to chiefs of state. Perhaps the clearest available statement of these issues is made by Donald Campbell in an unpublished paper called "The Principle of Proximal Similarity in the Application of Science," which I shall quote nearly in full.[20]

> These paragraphs are an attempt to make explicit an advantage which the experimental use of manned simulation has over simpler small group research when one's goal is the development of principles to be applied to a complex social situation. This advantage has no doubt motivated the development of manned simulation, but is apt to be overlooked because it is not made explicit in current philosophies of science.
>
> **PROXIMAL SIMILARITY**
>
> Whatever epistemology we may choose in interpreting the laws of science—even if as realists we regard science as iteratively asymptoting on truth—we recognize that the science we have today is only approximate. . . .
>
> This predicament is well known, and gives rise to the caution scientists show in applying their knowledge to new situations. It is one aspect of that caution which is central here—there is more caution the greater the extrapolation required, or the more dissimilar the situation of application from the laboratory of generation, for the greater the dissimilarity, the more likely are these as yet unknown variables to affect the outcome . . .
>
> **EXTRAPOLATING ABOUT EXTRAPOLATIONS**
>
> The process of science consists in positing totally general laws and then qualifying them as our experience in extrapolating them to

new situations shows the qualifications and exceptions to be needed. In each new application we are again going in some degree beyond the conditions under which the law has been tested. The confidence with which we do this depends upon our previous experience with this particular law and with the general domain of laws. In some domains of physics and astronomy, the experience in extrapolation has been remarkably sanguine, general laws holding without qualification in wide ranges of application. Such a background lends credence to any specific new application of one law from such a domain.

Our experience in extrapolating social-pyschological principles from the experimental laboratory of undergraduate psychology courses is much poorer. Repeatedly, efforts to replicate experimental findings fail, although our publication policies (both the self-policing of authors and the preferences of journal editors) are such as to cover over a good part of this failure. Some of the failure is due, no doubt, to sampling vagaries. But a good deal of it is probably due to supposedly irrelevant differences in the experimental procedures, topics, or populations. Such failures warn us that we do not have a law which can effectively be generalized in disregard of the specific conditions on innumerable other variables.

More direct evidence comes from the usual presence of significant interaction effects in complex experiments. If in experiments in which there were two or more treatment dimensions we regularly got significant main effects with no interactions, our experience would encourage extrapolation. We would have found, for example, that the relationship between A and B was constant over all levels of C, that an A-B law unqualified with regard to C could be stated. Instead, it is our usual experience that the A-B relationship is different for levels of C, occasionally to the point of a reversal in direction. If such multiple factorial experiments be regarded as experiments in generalization, they give us great grounds for caution, particularly when we generalize the expectation that had we included in our experiment dimensions F, G, and H, or X, Y, and Z, the A-B relationship might well have shown interactions with all or some of them too. The high rate of interactions on the variables we have explored must make us expect such for the many unexplored ones . . .

### CLEAR-CUT PURE-VARIABLE SMALL GROUP EXPERIMENTS VS. MANNED SIMULATION AS A BASIS FOR GENERALIZATION TO INTERNATIONAL NEGOTIATION

There is at present a tendency on the part of some to regard the results of laboratory social psychology utilizing plain settings, simple tasks and treatment differences which vary in only one pure dimension, as superior in generalizability to the products of manned simulation. For example, an early draft of a most competent review of simulation in the social sciences stated: "In this light, inter-nation simulation is not a new technique, but a very ambitious extrapolation of the usual techniques of the social psychological experiment. There are hazards in generalizing to the real world even the simplest behaviors of small laboratory groups, and these hazards clearly increase when laboratory subjects are required to play unfamiliar elite institutional roles." The implications of the principle of proximal similarity exactly contradicts this: a complex simulation is a better base for generalizing to a specific natural situation than a simple experiment if the greater complexity provides greater similarity to the natural situation in question. . . .

**VARIABLES HELD CONSTANT**

The differences between simple small group experimentation and simulation may be discussed under these two aspects: 1. variables held constant, 2. variables experimentally manipulated, if any. It will be argued that the main difference is, or should be, in the variables held constant. Any experiment or simulation manipulates at most three or four variables. All the other conceivable variables are held constant at some one level. This is just as much so for the "simple" experiment in which they are totally neglected as in the manned simulation in which the elaborate scenario and non-experimental inputs build up specific common values for at least a number of them. Insofar as the background, held constant, values achieved in simulation, however "artificially" established, are closer to the setting of application than are the settings of the "simple" experiment, the simulation is the better basis for generalization. Such greater similarity probably exists for these variables: degree of involvement, group-identification, future responsibility for outcomes of decisions, type of tasks and problems faced, time spent in role, etc. When we look at the task of generalization in this light, we are overwhelmed with the petty degree of similarity achieved on these variables, and the innumerable other variables neglected entirely. Surely this is a sorry base for generalization, better only by contrast with the "simple" and "pure" small group experiment. The absolute degree of similarity will not be argued. All that is claimed is that given our many poor bases for making generalizations into the important arena of application, this is a better one. From this stance, the error of the quotation above is not its disparagement of the manned simulation, but its naïve faith in the still more irrelevant simple small groups experiment. In our predicament, we must work with the best of those poor tools available to us, and manned simulation . . . seems one of them.

There is another way in which manned games narrow the gap between the data we gather and the processes to which we are interested in inferring. In the behavioral sciences we often attempt to learn about an individual by obtaining his verbal responses to a questionnaire. That is, a psychologist will infer aspects of personality from a subject's verbal reports or interpretations of a projective test. A sociologist will infer real attitudes from attitudes expressed on paper or in an interview. A political scientist or pollster will infer political beliefs and predict political behavior on the same grounds. But the inferential road is filled with pitfalls. There is a wealth of evidence that there may be little relationship between expressed feelings and true feelings, that the analysis of projective tests may be more dependent on the personality of the analyst than of the subject, that opinion and attitude surveys have little value in predicting behavior.

Gaming enables us to shorten that inferential road for some types of behavior. If we are interested in subjects' bargaining strategies, orientation towards competition as opposed to cooperation, reaction to stress, and other basic personal and interpersonal processes, these can be studied *directly* in a game—without the possibly contaminating intermediary of a questionnaire. In addition, if we are interested in individual qualities, such as political, social, economic, and military philosophy, concepts of role and status, or overall ideology, we can study this also in a game—not as directly as more basic process—yet a good deal more directly than by interviewing a subject or asking him to respond to a questionnaire. The written messages and the minute-by-minute recorded decisions he produces as he acts within his particular simulated social system provide a detailed record of his behavior that is more illuminating than a less direct method could possibly be.

There is still the problem of analyzing these data, and this can be more difficult than analysis of a structured questionnaire, though probably not more difficult than analyzing an open-ended questionnaire, an interview, or a projective test. (Some have even gone so far as to say that a game is indeed just that—a very elaborate, rich, and unstructured projective test.) There also is the problem that whereas we can argue the greater accuracy of games as an indicator of those behaviors that are usually measured by test or interview techniques, it is virtually impossible to prove or disprove. Even though we can compare behavior in a game with responses on a test, it is usually far less feasible to compare either of these with behavior in a completely natural setting. We cannot get access to the "natural behavior" because we have no control over time and events and no adequate observational techniques. In short, demonstrating the validity of either tests or games is terribly difficult, whereas examining the inter-method reliability might be quite easy. I am currently undertaking just such an effort by comparing the responses of American, Mexican, Japanese, and Norwegian students on a "Modes of Strategic Thinking" questionnaire with their behavior in an Inter-Nation Simulation on political, military, and economic matters. At this point, it is too early to give results. However, the predilection of most who have used both games and verbal response tests extensively would be, I believe, to place greater faith in the validity of game responses should there prove to be a discrepancy between the two measures.

These arguments point directly to "games" as ideal laboratory environments, if we are interested in the interaction between a human being and the system of which he is a part. Games provide a powerful research tool for generating information. As knowledge about basic human behavior increases, the game evolves towards its end point—simulation.

In Chapter 1, I discussed simulations in general, their uses, and limitations. In this chapter, I have focused on the philosophy underlying attempts to simulate, pointing out some of the dangers inherent in trying to simulate a social system when we have very limited knowledge about that system. I have distinguished between *simulations* as the complete and accurate representation of a referent and *games* as an initial postulation providing the framework for further building. I have presented some epistemological bases for using such games as frameworks for the generation of new data and theories. Finally, I have argued that in the study of human behavior, games can provide a laboratory that is superior to the more traditional laboratory setting because the games laboratory is more richly representative of the referent world to which we wish to generalize. In these considerations, the underlying concept of patterning as crucial to knowledge has been stressed.

## FOOTNOTES

1. Donald T. Campbell, "Pattern Matching as an Essential in Distal-Knowing," in *The Psychology of Egon Brunswick*, ed. K. R. Hammond (New York:Holt, Rinehart & Winston, 1966), p. 81,
2. John Madge, *The Tools of Social Science* (London: Longmans, Green and Co., 1953).
3. B. F. Skinner, "Is a Science of Human Behavior Possible?" in *Philosophical Problems of the Social Sciences*, ed. D. Braybrooke (New York: Macmillan Co., 1965), p. 24.
4. Richard E. Farson, James Johannson, and Lawrence Solomon, "Studies in Group Leadership" (La Jolla, California: Western Behavioral Sciences Institute, 1965).
5. Orcutt, *et. al., op. cit.*
6. James Barber, "Government Committees in the Small Group Laboratory," prepared for delivery at the 1963 Annual Meeting of the American Political Science Association, New York, September 4–7, mimeographed, Yale University. Or, Wayman J. Crow and Robert Noel, "The Valid Use of Simulation Results" (La Jolla, California: Western Behavioral Sciences Institute, June, 1965).
7. Morton Deutsch and Robert M. Krauss, "Studies of Interpersonal Bargaining," *Journal of Conflict Resolution*, VI, No. 1 (1962), 52–76. Anatol Rapoport and Carol Orwant, "Experimental Games: A Review," *Behavioral Science*, VII, No. 1 (1962), 1–37.

8. BERNARD BERELSON and GARY STEINER, *Human Behavior: An Inventory of Scientific Findings* (New York: Harcourt, Brace and World, Inc., 1964).

9. CARL I. HOVLAND, IRVING L. JANIS, and HAROLD H. KELLEY, *Communication and Persuasion: Psychological Studies of Opinion Change* (New Haven: Yale University Press, 1953).

10. PHILIP GREEN, *Deadly Logic: The Theory of Nuclear Deterrence* (Columbus, Ohio: Ohio State University Press, 1966).

11. DAWSON, *op. cit.*, p. 9.

12. ERVING GOFFMAN, *Encounters: Two Studies in the Sociology of Interaction* (Indianapolis: Bobbs-Merrill, 1961).

13. cf. discussion by KARL POPPER, "Unity of Method in the Natural and Social Sciences," in Braybrooke, *op. cit.*, pp. 33–41.

14. DONALD T. CAMPBELL, *op. cit.*, p. 83.

15. *loc. cit.*

16. "Science and the Citizen," *Scientific American*, December 1967, p. 48.

17. CAMPBELL, *op. cit.*, pp. 99–102.

18. *Ibid.*, pp. 100–102.

19. Preliminary Research Memorandum, JWGA/ARPA/NU, Advanced Research Projects Agency, SD-260, Northwestern University, July 1966.

20. For another compelling statement of this position, see WAYMAN J. CROW, "Simulation: The Construction and Use of Functioning Models in International Relations," in Hammond, *op. cit.*, pp. 341–358.

# 3

# INTELLECTUAL AND HISTORICAL ROOTS OF SOCIAL SCIENCE SIMULATIONS

> . . . the domain of truth has no fixed boundaries within it. In the one world of ideas there are no barriers to trade or to travel. Each discipline may take from others techniques, concepts, laws, data, models, theories, or explanations—in short, whatever it finds useful for its own inquiries.[1]

In 1908, Farrand Sayre published *Map Maneuvers and Tactical Rides*,[2] a discussion of the use of war games to train military officers in tactics. War games were played with maps and wooden soldiers; the map-scale was based on the "distance a modern cavalry brigade can gallop in one minute." Sayre argued that such games were useful, because in learning how to conduct wars, "the cost of permitting [an officer] to learn by experience derived from his own blunders is too great to be considered." Sayre's argument highlights one of the main points of this chapter: the historical roots of modern social simulation and gaming techniques are deeply embedded in war games. But the current potency of the technique depends primarily on the infusion of intellectual vigor from small-group experimentation, decision theory, and systems analysis. We shall examine each of these social science methodologies in the light of its distinctive contribution.

## WAR GAMES

The genesis and evolution of war games are obscure, but they are closely related to, and perhaps a direct outgrowth of chess and similar board games played for pleasure. Such games originally served as symbolic equivalents of warfare and probably were used for training purposes and as adjuncts to planning.[3] In 1798, the "Neue Kriegspiel," a true war game, was developed at Schleswig. However, it was criticized for presenting so complicated a model of warfare that an officer would be overwhelmed by the difficulties of making a decision under battle conditions and thereby rendered incapable of action. Instead of a board, the game used a map divided into 3,600 squares, each with distinctive topographical features, on which game pieces were moved to represent troop and cavalry maneuvers.

A century later, the war game had split into two types, the "rigid

Kriegspiel" and the "free Kriegspiel." In the "rigid" version, a game was controlled by very formal rules, charts, maps, tables, and pre-programmed calculation routines, and dice were used to generate random effects. In the "free" version, most of this paraphernalia was replaced with human referees, a "control team" who ruled on the permissibility of given moves. Popular in the military academies in Prussia, both types of game spread rapidly to other countries, including Britain and the United States. The games were used extensively at West Point in the last quarter of the nineteenth century. In most of these settings, the free variety was more popular than the rigid, since the flexibility of using a control team made it easier to administer than the rigid version, which required extensive calculations and data support.

Since the beginning of World War II, versions of the "Kriegspiel" have been widely used, particularly by the Japanese and Germans who employed them heavily during the War. Most versions combined the "rigid" and "free" forms, embodying richly programmed environments and data bases but with the addition of human judges as a check on the pre-set calculation routines.

Here are several descriptions of these modern versions. The first description refers to the games played at the Total War Research Institute and Naval War College of Japan:

> Here military services and the government joined in gaming Japan's future actions: internal and external, military and diplomatic. In August 1941 a game was written up in which the two year period from mid-August 1941 through the middle of 1943 was gamed, was "lived through" in advance, and, of course, at an accelerated pace. Players represented the Italo-German Axis, Russia, United States, England, Thailand, Netherlands, East Indies, China, Korea, Manchuria, and French Indochina. Japan was played, not as a single force, but as an uneasy coalition of Army, Navy, and Cabinet, with the military and the government versus those of heavy industry, and so on. Disagreements arose and were settled in the course of an afternoon, at the pace of this game—with the military group, by the way, as the more aggressive one, winning arguments.
>
> Measures to be taken within Japan were gamed in detail and included economic, educational, financial, and psychological factors. The game even included plans for the control of consumer-goods, plans, incidentally, which were identical with those actually put into effect on December 8, 1941.[4]

The following quotation describes war gaming in Germany, the Soviet Union, and the United States:

> Before Hitler assumed power in 1933, the leaders of the German Reichswehr were much concerned about Polish military strength and political designs. The German armed forces were then restricted to 100,000 men in strength. In 1929, a young staff officer, the later General Erich von Manstein, charged with the responsibility for the

organization of a war game involving German defense against a Polish attack on East Prussia or Upper Silesia, realized that the outbreak of war would be preceded by mounting political conflict. In that conflict, he thought, Germany would have to avoid giving France and Czechoslovakia cause for entering the war as Poland's allies and the League of Nations a pretext for not declaring Poland the aggressor. Manstein proposed that the strictly military exercise be introduced by a political game in order to let political and military leaders learn from each other. High-ranking members of the Foreign Office played the roles of the president of the League of Nations Council and of the Polish and German Foreign Ministers. In his recently published memoirs, Manstein writes that the inventiveness of the player representing Poland in alleging German provocations left his German counterpart "completely speechless" and that the skillfully simulated procrastination of the League was grimly appreciated by all participants. "We had the impression also," Manstein reports, "that the gentlemen from the Foreign Office, to whom such a playing-through of possible conflicts seemed to be completely novel, were thoroughly convinced of the value of the game . . ."

From an article in the Sunday *Times* (London), December 9, 1956, it appears that the Soviets may have made use of a similar procedure. Alexandre Metaxas, who is identified as a Russian-speaking French journalist, reports that Soviet political specialists try to anticipate the results of international political moves by putting themselves in the role of each interested party in turn. Metaxas claims that the course to be followed by the Soviet Foreign Office is determined in part by the results of this simulated interaction. It is not clear from his account whether actual gaming procedures are involved.

RAND's interest in political gaming grew out of work in political analysis and previous experimentation with the use of gaming techniques for other purposes. For several years RAND has worked extensively with various sorts of highly formalized war games. At one point an attempt was made to devise a "cold war game": in which a few political and economic factors were assigned numerical values so that the relative worth of alternative strategies could be assessed quantitatively. Players were allowed only a limited choice of specified moves. This experiment was abandoned when it became clear that the simplification imposed in order to permit quantification made the game of doubtful value for the assessment of political strategies and tactics in the real world.[5]

Nevertheless, until about 1960, RAND continued to use these war games as political-military exercises to test strategies and permit contingency planning. By 1957, the Massachusetts Institute of Technology had begun similar exercises; since then, it has conducted about ten major strategy games using "real life" high level military and other government personnel as "decision-makers." These games are designed to give the player experience in handling potential crises and thus are adjuncts to other planning tools.[6]

This summary of war gaming exercises is not exhaustive, but it does indicate that when gamers venture outside the confines of the battlefield, with its purely tactical problems, in order to solve strategic questions, they have necessarily entered the broad domain of social and political gaming.

The most contemporary attempt at war gaming with which we are familiar, the United States Joint Chiefs of Staff Joint War Games Agency, explicitly recognizes this necessity. The title of the game, *Technological, Economic, Military and Political Evaluation Routine* (TEMPER), reveals its designers' awareness that to be meaningful, a war game must be set in the larger social context. Evaluations of the game[7] show that its users are decidedly concerned with the adequacy of the economic, sociological, and psychological theory incorporated in the game. Thus war gaming, an ancient technique, has evolved to the point that it is indistinguishable from any other kind of large-scale social gaming.

At the same time, the distinction between "rigid" and "free" games has broken down. By using computations and data banks at some points, and human referees at others, it has become possible to combine the best features of both. As Weiner reports:

> At the present time the two major forms of war games, the free play and the rigid play, still exist. Both have been employed as techniques for analyzing and evaluating military tactics, equipment, procedures, etc. The free play game has received support because of its versatility in dealing with complex problems of tactics and strategy and because of the ease with which it can be adapted to various training, planning, and evaluation ends. The rigid play game has received support because of the consistency and detail of its rule structure and its computational rigor. In addition, the development of large capacity computing machines has made it possible to carry out detailed computations with great rapidity and made it possible to go through many different plays of a game. With these developments the number and types of war games have increased.[8]

It is fortunate that chess, as a simulation of warfare, reached its final form before the social sciences invaded the once relatively simple world of the military tactician and strategist, else its complexity might have been the death of it! In any case, this brief history is intended merely to show that gaming has a venerable history in the military arena and that social science gamesmen owe a sizeable debt to the ingenuity of their martial precursors. Now, we should consider the other intellectual tributaries that have fed the main stream of contemporary gaming.

## SMALL GROUP EXPERIMENTATION

Experimental social psychologists and sociologists have been interested in "small group" phenomena since the mid-1930's. By putting a small group of people in a laboratory setting and assigning them an appropriate task, the experimenter can study communication patterns, interaction modes, perceptions, evolvement of leader and follower roles, problem solving, and other group processes. The literature in this flourishing branch of social psychology is so vast it cannot even be sampled in a meaningful way. Even though small groups have been used for many purposes, the basic format of each experiment is usually the same. Laboratory "conditions" are established—that is, persons are selected for group membership according to relevant criteria of personal characteristics, the group is structured in any of several ways, and the environment in which the group operates is altered at some time during the life of the group. One or more of the conditions will constitute the independent variable, and the final state of the group, or its "output," is the dependent variable.

At one end of the "small group" spectrum are therapy groups and sensitivity training groups. Both groups are almost entirely unstructured in terms of personnel or scheduling of group activity. Their goals are to increase the involvement and heighten the sensitivity of their members to their own and others' veiled psychic states. At the other end of the spectrum are the sets of laboratory-research groups, whose members are carefully chosen and matched within the groups on the basis of their personal traits. The members of these groups are forced to operate in a highly controlling structure and are given a highly specified task to perform. Somewhere along this spectrum, though it is hard to say where, one crosses the line beween small group experimentation and elementary gaming.

Small group experimentation has vitalized gaming in two ways. First, group research has served to develop many well-established principles of social interaction that can be incorporated into games and simulations as verbal or mathematical statements. These statements include principles regarding the efficacy and reliability of different kinds of communication nets, the development of group loyalty or ethnocentrism, the cohesion of groups as a function of outside threat, and the impact of shared responsibility for a decision on the kind of decision that will be made.[9] These and other principles of group interaction may be included in modern simulation efforts.

The second way that small group experimentation has stimulated gaming work derives from the success of small group experiments as a laboratory technique. It has become apparent that if one wishes to analyze a social system of almost any size or complexity, the small face-to-face group must be considered as a major component of the system. It is therefore assumed that much can be learned about social systems by studying groups, both because small groups are sub-parts of all social systems, no matter how large and complex, and because the small group can be considered an analogue to a more complex social system, enabling us to generalize from one to the other. It is a small step to assume that one can learn *more* if he places the small group in an environment similar to that of the social system he wishes to study, gives the small group similar resources, and faces it with similar tasks. (See the discussion of the Inter-Nation Simulation and similar games in the latter part of this chapter.) Thus, small group experimentation would probably have evolved into gaming and thence into simulation without the antecedent paradigm of war gaming. Of course, those who use the enriched small-group laboratory to study other social systems are aware of the dangers of too facile generalization, but they argue that some of the difficulties may be overstated. Harold Guetzkow, one of the originators of Inter-Nation Simulation, defends such generalization as follows:

> There will be those who question the validity of my interchanging the terms "group" and "nation" and of applying concepts developed in the study of groups to nation-states. It has sometimes been argued that the sovereignty of nation-states is a unique characteristic, not possessed by others . . . Such assertions seem to me to be over-statements, resulting from careless conceptualization and the extravagant nurturing of the original sovereignty concept by eighteenth and nineteenth-century nationalisms. The facts of international life indicate that states, like other groups, are circumscribed in their behavior by political, social, cultural, and economic realities both within themselves and in their external environment. The leaders of nations, just like the leaders of other groups, are dependent for their positions upon a complex structure of power within the group . . .
>
> In this sense, nations share common features with less comprehensive and less powerful groups . . . My model endeavors to help cross . . . artificial academic barriers by developing a general theory of intergroup relations applicable to nations. Even as the model applies concepts about groups to nations, it, in turn, should be applicable not only to nations, but to all groups, political parties, cities, states, and both regional and international organizations. By identifying a basic similarity among all these units, it may help to refocus thinking and research in them all.[10]

Small group experimentation, then, has provided basic data and furnished a research model that almost inevitably has led to gaming and simulation.

## DECISION THEORY

Decision theory, which is derived from the study of human decision-making, offers a "way of thinking about" social systems, ranging from small groups through formal and informal medium-level organizations, to nation-states. The most intense early work was undertaking in the late 1940's by Herbert Simon and his colleagues who used a "decision-making" approach to study public administration and private organizations.[11] Later, Richard C. Snyder and his colleagues elaborated the decision-making perspective to the study of national and international political situations.[12] The decision theory approach assumes that to understand how an organization operates, one must understand the roles and personal traits of its decision-makers and the environment in which they carry out their primary task. In its simplest form, the decision-making paradigm may be expressed somwhat as follows:

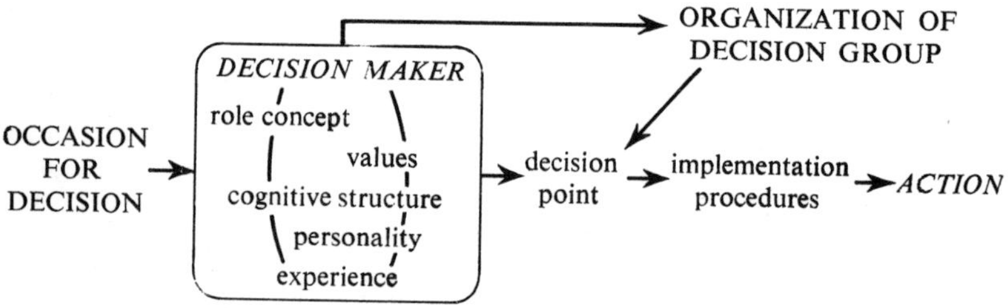


This model could be expressed in many different ways; it is not intended to represent all the various concerns of decision theorists. It merely indicates their belief that to produce decision outcomes, *environmental* characteristics, such as the occasion for decision, the organization of the information processing and decision-making groups interact with *personal* characteristics of the decision-maker, such as his values, cognitive structure, personality, and experience.

Once such a model is accepted, the real question becomes apparent: Just *how* do each of these various environmental and personal characteristics interact with each other to affect the decision? Research-minded individuals immediately try to design experiments that will allow factors such as role concept, personality, and organization of the decision-making group to be individually varied; and once again, the path leads to gaming. Mathematical game theory, which is simply a formalized set of statements about decision-maker values or "utilities" and the logical consequences of basing decisions on these utilities, is a source of ideas for varying the research parameters, as is the rich literature on role, personality, values and cognitive structure.

## SYSTEMS ANALYSIS

Social technologies such as operations research, cybernetics, information theory, and general systems theory, all of which refer to new ways of viewing complex systems, can be classified in the general category of *systems analysis*. In Chapter 2, which dealt with the general philosophical basis of simulation efforts, I have discussed one contribution of general systems theory—viewing the organization of any particular "universe" from the standpoint of the amount of information or entropy it exhibits. Some of the other systems-analysis technologies, such as cybernetics, have evolved to the point that they can be expressed in precise mathematical formulations. Other technologies are expressed only in general verbal statements and in the thought-models of those who use them. Each technology, however, has made its own particular contribution to simulation and gaming.

*Operations research* grew out of the logistical problems of large-scale military operations during World War II. Used as an aid to planning, for example, how much ammunition of various types would be required by a landing force, it was quickly appropriated by industry and government. Both institutions comprise a number of highly complex organizations. The organizations are responsible for a wide range of operations in which decision-making is widely diffused, often at different organizational levels, rather than resting with any one individual.

In complex organizations, each component that is responsible for accomplishing an over-all goal develops its own dynamics and objectives that conflict with those of the other components. By systematic analysis of the components, their functions, their objectives, and the relationships among them, operations research enables a complex balance to be attained in which friction is reduced and component-objectives and behavior contribute to, rather than detract from, the over-all organization goals. Thus, operations research is a highly sophisticated application of decision theory to complex bureaucracies.

The primary purpose of operations research is to provide managers with a scientific basis for solving problems in the organization. In its analysis, operations research examines the physical, biological, psychological, and sociological aspects of the organization's functioning. Thus, both in its way of thinking about a problem and in the kinds of data it utilizes, operations research provides a basis for gaming and simulation construction.

*Information theory* and *cybernetics* are outgrowths of technological progress and the concommitant increase in the complexity of communications. These technologies enable us to understand both communication as a "system within a system," or as the nerves of a system, and information feedback as a control mechanism. Such concepts are essential for contemporary computer technology. They have enabled scientists to progress in quantifying intangibles such as "purpose" and "goal-seeking." Thus, we are able to represent, in part, at least, such difficult abstractions in simulations.

The current vigor in simulation and gaming stems from an equal vigor in the technologies discussed above as well as in the institutions and enterprises to which their uses are relevant. In the contemporary economic, social, and political setting, which encourages innovation, education, and research, gaming and simulation have invaded most fields in which an understanding of human and societal behavior is a desideratum. Thus not only in war and military operations, but also in management and business, economics, political science and international relations, sociology, education, and psychology—independently of each other and for varying purposes—considerable effort has been put into devising new games and simulations or adapting existing ones. The next portion of this chapter is a brief survey of the history of gaming in each of these enterprises.

## MANAGEMENT AND BUSINESS GAMES

The American Management Association developed the first widely used management game in 1956 after its members visited the Naval War College.[13] The managers concluded, if I may paraphrase Charles Wilson's famous statement about General Motors, that what was good for the Navy should be good for business! The AMA game consists of five teams of five players each; each team represents the officers of a different firm manufacturing a similar product, competitively sold in a common market. Each play period represents three months and involves six basic decisions regarding selling prices, marketing budgets, research and development expenditures, rates of production, plant capacity, and the purchase of information about competitors' behavior. All financial transactions are represented by cash flow, and budgets can be changed only within a limited range, to simulate the difficulty of sudden drastic switches in management policy. Computations are performed either with desk calculators or on a computer. Clearly, the development of this first game depended on advances in operations research and electronic computation equipment.

The game was enthusiastically received among business executives and educators. The notion of management gaming spread so rapidly that by 1958, a host of games had been devised, ranging from the very simple "In-basket"* type games to extensive computer simulations of an entire industry. Most of these games utilize computers as well as human participants and include stochastic, or random, elements.

Two immediate entries to the field were the UCLA business game,

* An "In-basket game is one in which a management trainee is given a desk with an "in" basket and an "out" basket. Every few minutes he is presented with memoranda requiring that he make decisions on a variety of matters. At the end of the session, there is a discussion of his decisions and their probable ramifications.

similar to the AMA game, and a much more intricate IBM management game. Games developed by McKinsey and Company, Boeing's "Operation Interlock," Esso's "Petroleum Industry Simulation," Herron's "Executive Action Simulation," and Vance's "Management Decison Simulation" require no computer aids. Among the more complex "man-machine" games utilizing computers or all-computer simulations are those developed by Westinghouse Electric Corporation, the University of Washington, Pillsbury Mills, and Univeristy of Oklahoma, Indiana University, and—most intricate of all—the computer-simulation devised by the Carnegie Institute of Technology.

More recently, games have been used in graduate level business schools—notably at Harvard—as an adjunct to the more traditional "case study method" of training potential business executives. Reactions among both business executives and educators range from intense enthusiasm to equally intense skepticism, though if frequency of use is any indicator, enthusiasts far outnumber skeptics. Many firms currently use variations of such games as a routine part of their executive training and retraining programs, often combining them with such related activities as sensitivity training and studies in decision theory.

## ECONOMIC SIMULATIONS

The idea of modeling is as familiar to every graduate student in economics, as is the story of the economics professor who built a basement model of the economic system made up of pipes and fluids, complete with valves, pumps, and motors. Certainly, modeling portions of the economic system, including the use of such physical representations as the pipe-and-fluid simulation, has been profitable in economics for a long time. In part, this is because economists have been so successful in gathering data and specifying relationships among variables, and in part it is because modeling has aided data-gathering and the specification of relationships. Until recently, however, there have been no large-scale dynamic simulations of economic systems, as distinct from physical, iconic, or other representations.

Although the problems involved in creating a dynamic similation adaptable to an analogue computer are enormous, Tustin[14] showed, as early as 1953, that existing analytic techniques—including time-series analysis—could be used as the bases for such simulations. Only with the advent of high-speed digital and analogue computers, and by virtue of recent advances in theoretical formulations, statistical methodology, and sample-survey techniques, have the problems become manageable.

The first serious effort to simulate a large-scale economic system by building up the model from simulations of its sub-parts was initiated in

1957. When the first detailed report of the study was made in 1961,[15] the authors stated that the work had just begun. This work continues, using the "household" as the decisional unit. On the basis of theory about household economic behavior combined with statistical information on economic trends, the designers of this model hope to make it sophisticated and accurate enough to generate long-range predictions. Similar efforts to use simulation techniques for large-scale economic prediction are being made by several other researchers,[16] among them inventors of a new discipline called "regional science." The researchers are attempting to study a limited geographic area by combining input-output analysis for the region with a computer simulation of its economic system in order to forecast the region's industrial development, resource use, and demographic characteristics.[17]

According to a 1965 estimate, between 100 and 200 man-years are spent annually in the United States on 28 to 30 economic simulations, at a cost of between $2,000,000 and $4,000,000 per year.[18] To a greater extent than with other science games, these economic simulations are used for policy planning. They are firmly grounded in data and theory, in which their builders have high confidence, and they rely heavily on the use of multivariate analysis of aggregate data. For this reason, we refer to these economic simulations as models or simulations rather than as games. They are quite complete and useful for prediction. Whereas the economists complain that their simulations now can make accurate predictions for only six months to a year in advance, most other social science gamers (with one outstanding exception mentioned below) believe that their games are now of almost no use for prediction at *any* level!

## POLITICAL SCIENCE AND INTERNATIONAL RELATIONS GAMES

As I indicated earlier, the first uses of games in political science were the "political military" exercises, which grew out of RAND's war-gaming activities and were carried on by RAND until about 1960. At M.I.T., where similar exercises were begun in 1957, they flourished into the mid-1960's. But in both cases, the games were used as adjuncts to planning, rather than as research tools. The first serious attempt to build a computer simulation of a political system was made at the University of Oklahoma by Oliver Benson, who constructed a "simple diplomatic game."[19] Benson's game was a model that geared together war potential, aggressiveness, atomic capability, coalition membership, possession of bases abroad, geographic location, and trade among eighteen countries. In cycling this model on the computer, he derived "actions and counteractions" that would change the state-of-the-system power relationships in ways that conform to international relations theory.

Meanwhile, an audacious group at Northwestern University began to work on what was to become the most ambitious, widely used, and well-publicized simulation project in the field of international relations. Professors Harold Guetzkow, Richard Snyder, and Chadwick Alger joined forces with graduate students Denis Sullivan and Robert Noel in an attempt to build a comprehensive man-machine simulation of the international system. The Inter-Nation Simulation (usually called simply "the INS") was designed as a generalized model of national and international politics. Human decision-makers or players acting as national leaders operate their nations, worry about consumer-goods levels, national defense, public opinion, elections, revolutions, and democratic values, and at the same time engage in the international politics of trade, negotiation, threat and counter-threat, alliances, war, and other military activities. The internal model of the nations is explicitly formalized in a series of equations, but the relationships among nations are left almost entirely to the players. This game was heavily used during the early 1960's: by Brody for research on the effect of spreading nuclear weapons capability;[20] by Robinson and others as a teaching tool;[21] and by Raser and Crow for the study of the impact of nuclear invulnerability,[22] to name only the three largest of approximately thirty studies conducted with this vehicle. Several of these studies will be described later when we turn to the uses of simulation for theory building, research, and teaching.

The INS is an illustration *par excellence* of the game-as-pre-simulation—the technique of starting with the best theory available, building a game, and then using the game itself as a means to improve theory on which to construct a simulation. Though the INS is still frequently used in more or less its original state, it has continually been improved. Its latest form, the International Processes Simulation, combines an elaborate computer routine with human players who engage in a wide variety of political activities ranging from propaganda manipulation of dissident internal minorities to international business competition. Another elaboration of the INS, which places much more emphasis on the use of the computer, is underway at Systems Development Corporation in Santa Monica, California. These games seem more flexible and promising than such "rigid" games as the TEMPER simulation mentioned earlier, which is an ambitious attempt to simulate the entire nation-state system of the world, incorporating some 130 nations and 4,000 variables in an elaborate program.

Simulation also has been used in areas of political science other than international relations, though with somewhat less frequency. One interesting study is the Simulmatics project, an analysis of voter behavior.[23] The Simulmatics project was undertaken by Ithiel de Sola Pool for the Democratic party during the 1960 presidential campaign. It used poll data to predict voter behavior. (Eugene Burdick has since described this research for popular consumption in his novel *The 480.*[24]) The research technique used in the Simulmatics project is too complex to describe here; suffice it to say that delineations of 480 types of voters were fed into a computer. Each type was analyzed for probable response to several salient campaign issues, with the result that the *computer simulation predicted actual election outcomes far more accurately than any other method to which it was compared.* Pool and his colleagues, perhaps encouraged by the predictive and financial success of this venture, have recently moved into new areas with attempts to simulate community referendum controversies over such issues as fluoridation and, even more adventurously, the cognitive structure and information processing styles of historical political decison-makers.[25]

Two further examples of political games illustrate the range of possibilities open to this technique. The first, the PLANS game developed by Boguslaw, Davis, and Glick, is an INS-like game designed specifically to study the impact of disarmament on the American economy and society.[26] It includes a relatively sophisticated model of the economy, building in long-term natural trends that may be affected by pressure groups and legislative behavior. Players act as members of interest groups and try to affect legislation.

The second example, used primarily for teaching Peace Corps volunteers, is the "Simuland" game devised by Andrew Scott and his colleagues at the Univeristy of North Carolina.[27] The "Simuland" game represents the political, social, and economic processes in a developing country that is patterned after a Latin American model.

These few examples, selected almost at random, merely typify the many games that could be listed to indicate the extensive activity in political simulation since 1958.

## GAMES IN SOCIOLOGY

The first and perhaps best known use of simulation or gaming in sociology is the "Robbers' Cave" experiment, conducted by Muzafer Sherif and his colleagues at the University of Oklahoma. The "Robbers' Cave" experiment combined observation in a natural setting with manipulation of variables. The subjects were eleven-year-olds in a boy's camp called Robbers' Cave. The boys were divided into two groups; tension was induced between the groups by giving them conflicting goals and by using propaganda techniques to exacerbate the conflict until overt hostilities broke out. The experimenters then introduced compelling superordinate goals which the boys could achieve only if the two groups could resolve their conflict and cooperate. The net result, as predicted, was that tension between the two groups was reduced and finally eliminated.[28]

This was a true game rather than a field study in that the experimenters structured the boys' environment in considerable detail, even though the environment was a summer camp rather than a research laboratory. The many ways that the "Robbers' Cave" findings have been applied to politics and international relations demonstrate a point worth stressing: *in dealing with simulations, it often is a mistake to create artificial distinctions by drawing sharp disciplinary lines.* The "sociology" games described below further illustrate this point.

One of the more elaborate games in sociology is SIMSOC, or Simulation of Society, developed by William Gamson at the University of Michigan.[29] This game, designed primarily for undergraduate teaching, is loosely based on the Parsonian AGIL concept in sociology—a general theory of social action. Only a minimum of structure is introduced into the game, and the focus of interest is on the emergent social structure and process as they evolve from the interactions of the players with the developing structure and with each other. Players try to achieve their individual social objectives, private objectives, and formal political objectives. The game incorporates resources, private interests, public programs, private consumption, franchises, police forces, political affiliation, a council of law makers, several geographic regions, and four national indicators—food and energy supply, standard of living, social cohesion, and public commitment.

HOMUNCULUS is a computer simulation of interpersonal relations designed by John T. and Jeanne E. Gullahorn.[30] Incorporating the basic theoretical orientation of George C. Homans regarding group interaction, and translating several verbal theories into programmed terms, HOMUNCULUS not only reveals contradictions among the theories and areas where they overlap, but also allows the researcher to see possibilities for integrating larger bodies of theory.

Erling Schild has developed two games specifically concerned with sociological phenomena. One game explores parent-child relations; the other, called SNOB, deals with social stratification. Abt Associates of Cambridge, Massachusetts, have developed several games to be used as teaching aids in illuminating issues such as the industrial revolution, slavery, mercantilism, and the transition from nomadic hunting to agrarian society.[31]

Sociologists are primarily interested in building and validating simulations based on existing sociological theories, not in testing whether those theories are themselves valid representations of some social reality. They do not ask whether the theory correctly reflects reality; they ask "Does the simulation correctly reflect the theory?" Most notable among these efforts is that of James S. Coleman, who explores the extent to which verbal sociological theory may be transmuted into mathematical models and thence into simulations for use in the analysis of social organization.[32] Some research, however, is focussed on game-playing *per se* to find out, for example, whether the players develop social skills or social attitudes through being involved in such games that they later generalize to real life behaviors and attitudes.

## GAMES IN EDUCATION

Games are used in education for two purposes. Games are now widely used in *teaching* either to enrich the students' understanding of a particular subject, such as the industrial revolution, or to prepare prospective church pastors, through a seminary game, better to understand the communities they are going to serve. Games of this sort, in which students act as players and sometimes as game builders, are widely used as educational tools. The "Occasional Newsletter," cited earlier, and its subsequent issues list hundreds of games currently used for these educational purposes in the United States and abroad. By about 1964, when national attention was focussed on educational gaming and a communication network emerged among its practitioners, it became evident that many teachers had been using similar games as instructional tools for years.

Educators also are employing games as a *research* aid and for self-teaching. Games such as "school board," or "student-teacher," or "school budget," are designed to represent actual parts of the educational system itself. This approach is new. So far, projects of this sort have been carried out chiefly in Fort Lauderdale, Florida; at the Office of Institutional Studies and Development at New Mexico State University; and at Western Behavioral Sciences Institute in La Jolla, California.[33] Since these efforts began only in 1965,[34] it is, at the time of this writing, too early to predict whether the use of gaming to study problems of the educational system will become widespread. We can predict, however, that if current trends continue, the use of games for teaching will be a major educational occupation in the future.

## PSYCHOLOGY

Gaming has not been a vital part of research or teaching in psychology, probably due to the strongly entrenched tradition that sanctions only highly controlled experiments and punctiform data gathering (See Chapter 2) or a clinical orientation. The physiological and mathematical psychologists, however, are now attempting to computerize such processes as cognition, visual perception, and language behavior.[35] Some social psychologists have become interested in using game situations to study interaction among a few (usually two) persons in highly structured conflict situations. Best known are the researches of Anatol Rapoport and his colleagues with Prisoner's Dilemma and other games at the Mental Health Research Institute, University of Michigan, and the work of Morton Deutsch, who uses a variety of two-person games to study the conditions under which trust and suspicion are generated and modified.[36]

However, these are not games in the special sense in which I use the term in this volume, because they are not used to obtain information for the further elaboration of the research game itself, but rather to add to the store of information about human behavior. These studies, of course, contribute to other game-building and simulation efforts, and are thus usually included in the field of specialization of people interested in gaming methodology. In sum, the discipline of psychology has made and continues to make invaluable contributions of theory and data to the field of gaming, but has not itself made much use of this technique.

## ANTHROPOLOGY, LAW, AND THE OTHER SOCIAL SCIENCE DISCIPLINES

We have restricted this brief review to those disciplines in which gaming has contributed most importantly as a research technique. We have ignored areas in which gaming may be widely used, but that are not subsumed under the rubric of social science (e.g., industrial engineering, logistics studies). Gaming has not yet invaded other social disciplines (sometimes called "social" or "human behavior" studies) such as anthropology, law, theology, and philosophy. To be sure, there is the Seminary Game being used by a theological seminary for teaching purposes, and law schools have used "Moot Court" techniques for years. But the latter is primarily a role playing device, not an attempt to build a comprehensive simulation; and the Seminary Game, originally developed for sociological purposes, has simply been adapted for the purposes of organized religion. A conference in 1966 dealt with the applicability of game theory and simulation techniques to anthropology,[37] but the burden of the conference report leaves no doubt that the use of gaming in anthropology was, in 1966, as yet only a gleam in the eyes of a few anthropological innovators.

With the exception of war gaming, most developments in social science simulation and gaming have taken place since 1956. As the report of Abt Associates indicates, simulation research has burgeoned: during 1965, between $3,000,000 and $6,000,000 was spent for economic, political, and social simulation work alone. Even though this methodology is scarcely more than ten years old, there is little question that by 1967, it had reached adolescence. Each month's crop of professional journals can be counted on to include a dozen or more articles on gaming and simulation; comprehensive bibliographies run to several hundred citations.[38] But is such rapid growth, the expenditure of so much time, talent, and money in so young a field, justified in terms of its actual contribution to scientific progress and increased knowledge? This is the question I shall consider in Part II.

## SUMMARY

We have looked at the nature of simulations and games in general, examined the philosophical and epistemological foundations of social science games, and traced their intellectual and historical roots. It was emphasized that whereas several intellectual streams, including small group experimentation, decision theory, and systems analysis, all have fed into the mainstream of simulation work, the use of games and simulations has grown from its genesis in war-gaming in parallel but unrelated ways in several fields, including management training, economic modeling, political and international relations studies, sociology, psychology, and education.

Having seen *who* uses games—economists, political scientists, and others—we will take a look, in Part II, at *why* they are used. We will consider their utility as *theory building devices*, explore their role in *research*, and examine their contribution to *training and education*. Finally, we will probe the thorny question of their *validity*—that is, their dependability in accomplishing their objectives.

## FOOTNOTES

1. KAPLAN, *op. cit.*, p. 4.

2. (Springfield, Massachusetts: Press of Springfield Printing and Binding Company).

3. Most of this discussion on war games is drawn from Sayre, *op. cit.*; from M. G. WEINER, "An Introduction to War Games," P-1773 (Santa Monica, California: RAND Corporation, August 17, 1959); and from CLAYTON J. THOMAS, *The Genesis and Practice of Operational Gaming*,

Proceedings of the First International Conference on Operations Research (Baltimore: Operations Research Society of America, 1957).

4. ROBERT D. SPECHT, "War Games," P-1041 (Santa Monica, California: RAND Corporation, March 1957), pp. 7–10.

5. HERBERT GOLDHAMER and HANS SPEIER, "Some Observations on Political Gaming," *World Politics*, XII, No. 1 (1959), 71–73.

6. RICHARD E. BARRINGER with BARTON WHALEY, "The M.I.T. Political-Military Gaming Experience," *Orbis*, IX, No. 2 (1965), 437–58.

7. cf. *Technological, Economic, Military, and Political Evaluation Routine (TEMPER): An Evaluation*, National Military Command System Support Center Technical Memorandum, Number TM-11-66, July 27, 1966. I use the term "game" rather than "simulation" to describe TEMPER, because it is conceived only as a preliminary and tentative attempt, a "first iteration" to replicate the international political military system, even though TEMPER is an all-computer routine. This is consistent with our earlier distinction between games and simulations.

8. WEINER, *op. cit.*, p. 3.

9. cf. CARTWRIGHT and ZANDER, *Group Dynamics Research and Theory* (Evanston, Illinois: Row, Peterson and Co., 1953); HERBERT KELMAN, *International Behavior: A Social Psychological Analysis* (New York: Holt, Rinehart, and Winston, 1965), especially KELMAN's Introduction and the chapter by GUETZKOW and SAWYER; or A. PAUL HARE, E. F. BORGATTA, and R. F. BALES, eds., *Small Groups: Studies in Social Interaction* (New York: Alfred A. Knopf, 1966).

10. "Isolation and Collaboration: A Partial Theory of Inter-nation Relations," *Journal of Conflict Resolution*, I, No. 1 (1957), 48–68.

11. HERBERT A. SIMON, D. W. SMITHBURG, and V. A. THOMPSON, *Public Administration* (New York: Alfred A. Knopf, 1950); and JAMES G. MARCH and HERBERT A. SIMON with HAROLD GUETZKOW, *Organizations* (New York: John Wiley & Sons, Inc., 1958).

12. The most recent comprehensive statement of their thinking is found in KELMAN, *op. cit.*, the chapter by JAMES ROBINSON and RICHARD SNYDER, and his early work is exemplified by R. C. SNYDER, H. W. BRUCK, and BURTON SAPIN, eds., *Foreign Policy Decision-Making: An Approach to the Study of International Politics* (Glencoe, Illinois: The Free Press of Glencoe, 1962).

13. The description of this game and much of the material in this section is drawn from KALMAN J. COHEN and ERIC RHENMAN, "The Role of Management Games in Education and Research," *Management Science*, VII, No. 2 (1961), 131–66.

14. A. TUSTIN, *The Mechanism of Economic Systems* (Cambridge: Harvard University Press, 1953).

15. ORCUTT, *et al.*, *op. cit.*

16. cf. G. FROMM and L. R. KLEIN, *The Brookings—S.S.R.C. Quarterly Econometric Model of the United States: Model Properties* (Washington, D.C.: The Brookings Institute, Reprint 100, 1965).

17. cf. WALTER ISARD and STANISLAW CZAMANSKI, "A Model for the Projection of Regional Industrial Structure, Land Use Patterns and Conversion Potentialities," *Peace Research Society (International) Papers*, v (1966), 1–13.

18. *Survey of the State of the Art: Social, Political and Economic Models and Simulations* (Cambridge, Massachusetts: Abt Associates, Inc., November 26, 1965).

19. Oliver Benson, "A simple Diplomatic Game," in *International Politics and Foreign Policy: A Reader in Research and Theory*, ed. James N. Rosenau (Glencoe, Illinois: The Free Press of Glencoe, 1961).

20. Richard A. Brody, "Some Systemic Effects of Nuclear Weapons Technology: A Study Through Simulation of a Multi-Nuclear Future," *Journal of Conflict Resolution*, VII, No. 4 (1963), 663–753.

21. James A. Robinson, Lee F. Anderson, Margaret G. Hermann, and Richard C. Snyder, "Teaching with Inter-Nation Simulation and Case Studies," *American Political Science Review*, LX, No. 1 (1966), 53–65.

22. John R. Raser and Wayman J. Crow, *Winsafe II: An Inter-Nation Simulation Study of Deterrence Postures Embodying Capacity to Delay Response* (La Jolla, California: Western Behavioral Sciences Institute, July 31, 1964).

23. Ithiel de Sola Pool and Robert Abelson, "The Simulmatics Project," *Public Opinion Quarterly*, XXV, No. 2 (1961), 167–83.

24. Eugene Burdick, *The 480* (New York: McGraw-Hill, 1964).

25. Robert P. Abelson and Alex Bernstein, "A Computer Simulation Model of Community Referendum Controversies," *Public Opinion Quarterly*, XXVII, No. 1 (1963), 93–122; and Ithiel de Sola Pool and Allan Kessler, "The Kaiser, The Tsar, and the Computer," *American Behavioral Scientist*, VIII (1965), 31–38.

26. Robert Boguslaw, Robert H. Davis, Edward B. Glick, "A Simulation Vehicle for Studying National Policy Formation in a Less Armed World," *Behavioral Science*, XI, No. 1 (1966), 48–61.

27. Andrew M. Scott, Lucas and Lucas, *op. cit.*

28. Muzafer Sherif, *et al., Intergroup Conflict and Cooperation: The Robbers' Cave Experiment* (Norman: University of Oklahoma, 1961).

29. William A. Gamson, *SIMSOC: A Manual for Participants* (Ann Arbor: Campus Publishers, 1966).

30. John T. Gullahorn and Jeanne E. Gullahorn, "A Computer Model of Elementary Social Behavior," *Behavioral Science*, VIII, No. 4 (1963), 354–62.

31. These games are described in "Occasional Newsletter About Uses of Simulations and Games for Education and Training," Project SIMILE (La Jolla, California: Western Behavioral Sciences Institute, No. 1, September 1, 1965).

32. James S. Coleman, "Mathematical Models and Computer Simulation," in *Handbook of Modern Sociology*, ed. Robert E. Faris (Chicago: Rand McNally, 1964).

33. See "Occasional Newsletter," *op. cit.*

34. An exception was reported in 1960 by Norman Fredericksen, *In-Basket Tests and Factors in Administrative Performance*, Invitational Conference on Testing Problems, Proceedings, October, 1960, which is an attempt to use a fairly simple game to develop evaluation criteria for school administrators.

35. For a survey of such work, see Harold Borko, *Computer Applications in the Behavioral Sciences* (Englewood Cliffs, New Jersey: Prentice-

Hall, 1962); or, more recently, issues of *Behavioral Science*, which report current work in this area being undertaken at the Mental Health Research Institute, University of Michigan, The University of Illinois, and elsewhere.

36. cf. RAPOPORT and ORWANT, *op. cit.*; RAPOPORT, "Games Which Simulate Deterrence and Disarmament," *Peace Research Reviews*, I, No. 4 (1967) (Clarkson, Ontario, Canada); RAPOPORT, *Strategy and Conscience* (New York: Harper and Row, 1964); and MORTON DEUTSCH and ROBERT M. KRAUSS, *op. cit.*

37. IRA RICHARD BUCHLER, ed., *Applications of the Theory of Games in the Behavioral Sciences*, University of Texas, Final Technical Report, ONR Grant Nonr (G)-00042-66, December 1966.

38. The last one I have seen that purports to be comprehensive was published in 1960 and already included 322 items. MARTIN SHUBIK, "Bibliography on Simulation, Gaming, Artificial Intelligence, and Allied Topics," *Journal of American Statistical Association*, LV, No. 292 (1960), 736–51. More recent attempts to cover sub-fields such as international relations or education run into hundreds of items. See, for instance, the issues of the "Occasional Newsletter," *op. cit.*, on educational uses of games or HAROLD GUETZKOW, "Simulations and Gaming of International Military Political Behaviors: Survey of Activities" (Evanston, Illinois: Northwestern University, Simulated International Processes Project, May 1966), which reports 135 projects, some of which have several publications.

# PART II

# The Uses of Simulation-Gaming

"Games, then, are world-building activities."

Erving Goffman
"Fun in Games"
Page 27

# 4

# SIMULATION AND THE DEVELOPMENT OF SOCIAL THEORY

> And how will you investigate, Socrates, that of which you know nothing at all? Where can you find a starting-point in the region of the unknown? And even if you happen to come full upon what you want, how will you ever know that this is the thing which you did not know?
>
> Plato, *Meno*

In Chapter 2, I examined some basic epistemological considerations related to the construction of scientific theory: At the outset, I alluded to the need for an orienting network or "web" of tentative theory as a structure against which to match data and new theoretical developments and concluded that since gaming is one practical technique for fulfilling this need, it is a sound scientific method. In this chapter, I will investigate some of the more *specific* functions that gaming and simulation perform in theory construction.

Theory serves understanding in two ways. First, theory explains data parsimoniously; without theory, we have only masses of observations that cannot be interpreted. This function of theory is illuminated by Herbert Simon, who has concerned himself with organization theory for many years. Reflecting on the huge body of observations on organizational behavior, he asks:

> How can this vast mass of fact be reduced to order as a first step toward interpreting it and generalizing from it? Although it is some centuries since astronomers have thought of the matter in this way, they too were once faced with the same dilemma. They had voluminous data on the locations of the heavenly bodies at many points in time. The first step was to describe these in terms of geometrical paths—the cycles of the Ptolemic system. A little later these paths were simplified to the circles of Copernicus and the ellipses of Kepler. But the great simplification came, of course, with Newton, who showed that the scheme of the heavens could be represented far more parsimoniously by replacing the time paths of planets with the differential equations that generated those paths.[1]

Simon argues that equations also should be generated from data in the behavioral sciences, that computerized simulations, which would incorporate these equations, are more advantageous than data banks containing vast amounts of discrete data. Let me draw an example from mathematics.

Suppose one set out to write down all possible pairs of ten-digit numbers and their products (beginning with 0000000001 x 0000000001 = 0000000001) using a pica typewriter and single-spacing on 8½″ x 11″ paper. The resulting stack of pages would extend out into space about the distance that light travels in half a day (bear in mind that the sun is only about eight light-minutes away). Locating any given product would be impossible, and the data, though recorded, would be useless. However, the principles underlying multiplication can be expressed in a few simple equations—mathematical statements of theory. With a small mechanical calculator that is structured to incorporate these principles of multiplication, the product of any pair of ten-digit numbers instantly can be obtained merely by punching the proper keys.

A second function of theory is to cut through the maze of data to a simple statement that does not lose any information, despite its explicitness and simplicity. Thus, theory enables us to *communicate the meaning of the data*. Explicit theory, then, economically explains data and communicates its meaning.

In general, social scientists have not yet been able to develop any theory as explicit and powerful as the examples I cited from astronomy and mathematics. They have relied, instead, on the detailed description of naturalistic observations, often mistaking such description for progress in theory-building. George Homans criticizes sociologists on this basis, but his criticism could be applied equally well to any of the social sciences:

> Much modern sociological theory seems to me to possess every virtue except that of explaining anything. Part of the trouble is that much of it consists of systems of categories, or pigeonholes, into which the theorist fits different aspects of social behavior. No science can proceed without its system of categories, or conceptual scheme, but this in itself is not enough to give it explanatory power. A conceptual scheme is not a theory. The science also needs a set of general propositions about the relations between the categories, for without such propositions explanation is impossible. No explanation without propositions! But much modern sociological theory seems quite satisfied with itself when it has set up its conceptual scheme. The theorist shoves different aspects of behavior into his pigeonholes, cries, "Ah-ha!" and stops. He has written a dictionary of a language that has no sentences. He would have done better to start with the sentences.[2]

In sum, science cannot move ahead without theory, but theory does not consist of descriptive statements or banks of data. Theory states relationships and embodies underlying principles, and thus gives meaning to the meaningless, orders the chaotic, and reduces the complex to the comprehensible. One might say that from "entropy," theory creates "information."

Two basic steps are associated with the development of scientific theory. First, the theorist generates a statement ("theory") about some aspect of the world; he asserts that an entity or process has certain characteristics, or that such-and-such a relationship holds between entities or processes. Second, he formulates one or more hypotheses from that statement and subjects them to test. The theory can be refined through the process of hypothesizing or as a result of testing. If the theory is ambiguous, trying to formulate or test the hypotheses may disclose the ambiguity and compel refinement of the theory. And the process of formulating or testing hypotheses may in itself generate new theory. In any case, both steps are essential.

In this chapter, I shall be concerned with the gaming approach as a way of accomplishing the first of these steps—generating statements. The use of gaming in the second step, that of testing hypotheses, will be the subject of Chapter 5.

The philosophers of science have paid remarkably little attention to the processes implicated in producing theoretical statements. True, they have discussed and analyzed in detail the general procedures of "induction" and "deduction," but this gives little insight into the intellectual prestidigitations that the theorist performs before he pulls a statement of theory out of his hat. Polanyi[3] suggests that much of the process may take place below the level of logical analysis—just as the bicycle rider cannot give a step-by-step explanation of the complicated process by which he maintains his balance. He just does it. In fact, if he had to analyze the process and consciously follow it, he probably couldn't ride at all.

The same may be true of theory generation. Like the bicycle rider, we just do it. We immerse ourselves in the world of data that interests us, and after a time a theory begins to take shape. But we would be hard put to give a step by step account of *how* the theory formed. Scientists talk of "hunches," "intuitions," and "the creative leap" to describe how scattered observations and bits of data seem to coalesce in some sort of relationship, through the operation of an "associative network" whose processes are not under conscious control. Nevertheless, it is possible to suggest some fairly explicit procedures that can increase the probability that theories will be generated and hypotheses suggested.

In a critique of gaming, David Singer[4] specifies or implies five techniques traditionally used by social scientists to facilitate their theorizing: (1) reading history, (2) studying the research literature in the field and in analogous and related fields, (3) merely imagining, (4) analogizing, and (5) observing the natural world. He goes on to argue that gaming does not really involve any of these activities. He is right. What gaming does involve is a series of processes that both *stimulate* and *enhance* all these activities and make it more likely that the exploration will be followed through to the final product—tested theory. I will therefore devote the rest of this chapter to showing how the process of gaming—building tentative constructs, then refining them—contributes to the generation of theory by furnishing at least six important "stimulants." Some of these "stimulants" are, I believe, unique to gaming;

others are present in many experimental techniques, but perhaps to a lesser degree. The first five stimulants result from attempting to *build* games and simulations; the sixth results from *operating* them at various phases in their evolution. I label the six stimulants *confrontation, explication, expansion, communication, involvement,* and *serendipity.*

## CONFRONTATION

It has been suggested that periodically in his career, every scholar should try to build a comprehensive simulation of the phenomenon in which he is interested. Even though this is an excellent suggestion, there is a good reason why few scholars in the social sciences will follow it. It is too humiliating. He who wishes to build a simulation must formulate his assumptions explicitly, state the parameter values, and specify the relationships among variables in mathematical or other equally precise form. Unfortunately, most social science theories crumble before such a test, a painful consequence for the social scientist who has put his trust in impressive sounding but vague generalizations or in overwhelming piles of data connected by nothing more tangible than his own interest in them. Kaplan says:

> Models have this merit, that they do not allow us to comfort ourselves with the notion that we are following up an "idea" when we are only moving from one observation to the next in the hope that something will turn up. Too often the hypotheses with which we work are at home only in the twilight regions of the mind, where their wavering outlines blend into a shadowy background. There they are safe from sudden exposure, and are free to swoop down for sustenance on whatever datum comes their way. Models are at any rate conscious, explicit, and definite; there is nothing ghostly in their appearance or manner; they look healthy even up to the very moment of their death. . . . The model saves us from a certain self-deception. Forced into the open, our ideas may flutter helplessly; but at least we can see what bloodless creatures they are. As inquiry proceeds, theories must be brought out into the open sooner or later; the model simply makes it sooner.[5]

Thus, the attempt to simulate shatters dramatically the complacency of the theorist who has been seduced by temptingly plausible but ill-defined concepts. Only when his complacency is shattered can the scholar be goaded from his lethargy into disciplined analysis and confrontation with the problem of determining what he does know and what he does not know. Such confrontation may be painful, but if it brings contrition, it may also be the beginning of wisdom. Having discovered what he knows and what he doesn't know, the scholar might select one subject from the multitude of those he is ignorant of and go out into the world to learn more about it.

I do not suggest that gaming is the only technique for prodding the careless or superficial scholar. I can report, however, that nearly everyone who has engaged in gaming confesses that his first contact with it stimulated more honest self-evaluation and more intellectual soul-searching than he had previously undergone.

## EXPLICATION

Explication and confrontation go hand in hand. Trying to build a simulation forces the architect to be *explicit, logical,* and *accurate,* and so confronts him, inescapably and humiliatingly, with the magnitude of his ignorance and the fuzziness of his concepts. All who engage in simulation activities, whether it be simulation of international relations or of cognitive processes, have undergone this painful scientific *rite de passage,* as the following statements demonstrate:

> A feature of attempting to simulate brainlike activity, commented on by all who have undertaken to do so, is the rigorous, but most salutary, discipline that it imposes on the thinking of the would-be designer. First, he must define his aims precisely. Does he wish to demonstrate "coordination between muscles"? Then he must define these concepts in terms of actual behavior. It is of little practical use today to explain "coordination" in terms of "integration," the latter in terms of a "higher level," and "higher level" in terms of "consciousness," etc. It is necessary to keep to one *region of discourse,* and the substitution of one word for another offers no solution. Even if an attempt at simulation achieves nothing in hardware, it is usually a most instructive activity, leaving the worker with a far deeper insight into the nature of the proposed phenomenon than he previously had. [Emphasis in original][6]

Even though the above quotation refers to a computer simulation of a physiological process, similar statements with slightly different emphases have been made by social scientists interested in simulating social phenomena. The intellectual rigor imposed by simulation-building is manifest in this analysis by Wayman Crow:

> . . . before a theory can be transformed into a model, the structural elements must be explicitly defined and the relations among the elements must be specified. The process may reveal vagueness, ambiguities, contradictions, and redundancies, and locate gaps in knowledge. Turning a model into a simulation, of course, brings this process one step further, for functional relations must additionally be specified and

> defined. Simulation-construction thus functions, as does any theory-construction, to systematize and order empirical findings, but in addition it *disciplines theory*, since concepts must be explicitly defined and, more importantly, relations among the elements must be completely specified if the simulation is to "run" or cycle. Unlike the theorist, the simulator cannot permit the relationships to remain implicit, and in specifying and defining them, he is forced to bring coherence into his model. This may require premature closure in parts of the theory where knowledge is slight or non-existent, but in doing so it serves to identify these weak points.
>
> In order to use a simulation for research or training, a further and more stringent requirement is imposed. Merely to state the general form of the relationships is not enough; it is necessery to specify the direction and degree of the function of the relation. For example, to test, in a simulation, the statement that "close ties and great involvement make for more intense conflict when conflict occurs at all" (Coser, 1964, p. 68), it would be necessary to specify some threshold level for the occurrence of conflict, and how the rate of increase in conflict is related to closeness of ties and involvement. This example nicely illustrates the need for explicit specification: (1) Does the theorist, in using the phrase "when conflict occurs at all," intend to imply a threshold? (2) are there other elements in the theory, related either to closeness of ties, to involvement, or to conflict, that could affect the form of the relationship expressed? Is there a functional relationship between "close ties" and "involvement"—indeed, are the terms synonymous or do they refer to identifiably different elements of the theory? (3) what is the nature of the functional relations—are they linear, curvilinear, exponential, or of some other form? Are there, in the literature, empirical propositions as to the nature of these relations and what sorts of data would be needed to specify it?
>
> By such questions is inquiry guided toward reducing ambiguity in definition, toward identifying inconsistencies and lack of coherence among concepts, toward assessing the empirical substantiation for functional relations or data deficiencies. By requiring that such questions be asked, simulation-construction is in itself a useful heuristic technique. And because the questions can be stated specifically, there is greater likelihood that their answers can be found by examining the rest of the theory, by further study, or by querying the theorist himself. [The reference is to L. Coser, *The Functions of Social Conflict*, second edition, New York, Free Press, 1964.][7]

As Thomas Schelling attests in discussing the use of games to study bargaining situations, game building has led to the abandonment of theory when the spotlight of simulation showed the theory to be worthless.

> To build a game of this sort, and especially to build into the game particular features that one wishes to represent, requires that one define his concepts operationally. A game of this sort imposes discipline on theoretical model-building; it can be a test of whether concepts and

propositions are meaningful, and a means of demonstrating so when they are. In the actual construction of the game, and in discussion of the game's features with persons who have played it or observed it played, it has frequently been the case that certain plausible concepts had to be abandoned when an effort to identify them (or to incorporate them) in the game revealed that they were meaningless or innocuous, or that they rested on inessential distinctions.[8]

Finally, because it demands specification and explication, simulation-building has introduced a measure of rigor to the study of international relations, a discipline notoriously plagued by inexact theory, general assertions, and platitudes.

> One of the major contributions of simulation research to the development of theory in international relations . . . is connected with the initial design of such a simulation. The process of designing a simulation forces the designer to explicate his model of international relations. At times this may involve not so much the creation of new perspectives on the subject, as the explication of traditional wisdom. One is forced to make explicit what may have been the implicit assumptions about the subject matter—in order that these assumptions may be placed in the operating model. This explication of traditional wisdom, indeed, may be one of the most useful tasks in contemporary social science. In part such explication is useful because much of traditional wisdom may be wrong or contradictory, and the explication will help us to spot these failings. On the other hand, much of traditional wisdom about international relations may be very good, but since the structure of that knowledge is implicit—the ways in which important factors are sorted out from unimportant ones, the ways in which they are weighed, and so forth, are not explicated—the knowledge may not be too useful. If one is forced to design a replica of what one intuitively understands about international affairs, one may be better able to make that knowledge explicit. Furthermore, the replica is to some extent self-correcting. *Just as one could not describe a familiar landscape fully, but could recognize the fact that an important feature was missing if shown a sketch,* so *might the* observer *of a simulation recognize that* some *significant aspect of the real world was missing,* the importance of which he had not made explicit.
>
> But the explication function is not much different from the same function that would be performed if one tried to write a precise verbal or mathematical model of the same phenomena. Where a simulation differs is that it goes on from there. The explicated model is set to work, and, over time, generates data on subsequent states of the simulation. [Emphasis added][9]

This statement, by a scholar not involved in simulation work, presents his view of the heuristic value of trying to simulate a complex system such as international relations. More explicit and more specifically concerned with the concatenated relationship between reality, theory, and model, is the following evaluation by one who has been deeply involved in inter-nation simulation (INS) and who speaks from his own experience.

> INS as a theory-building exercise is valuable not because it produces new hypotheses but because its eclecticism provides the medium through which the existing verbal theories can be made more explicit and coherent. Both explicit and abstract because of the nature of the simulation technique INS represents a model operationalizing many of the exsisting theoretical positions in concrete and testable terms. Forced to represent an entire universe of international politics, the simulators have interrelated numerous middle range theories so that a coherent international system is simulated. This does not mean that the simulators are not interested in developing "new" middle range theory but that the strength of the Inter-Nation Simulation as a theory-building exercise lies in its eclecticism.
>
> The by-product of this eclecticism is to force a greater degree of rigor on the formulations of verbal theorists. While verbal theorists writing in the "traditionalist style" are able to becloud their theoretical positions with all the techniques employed by skillful polemicists since man began to write, and those writing in the "non-traditionalist medium" can introduce their equivocations by loosely defining the relationship between variables or by attaching so many conditions to their hypotheses that insight is sacrificed for validity, the simulators have been forced to allow a few hypotheses to suffice in describing a very large and complex set of phenomena. This greater explicitness in formulating and applying assumptions is valuable to all theorists because it identifies more clearly theoretical questions, aids in classifying the positions of other theorists on those questions, and, in some cases, poses theoretical questions that have not been explicitly raised by the verbal theorists (e.g., preception of comparative advantage in decision-making). . . .
>
> . . . INS represents an essential supplement to the verbal theorists. It is a process of theory-building operated by a group of scholars and open to investigation from many quarters. Therefore, it is a dynamic undertaking inviting the kind of criticism necessary for its development and at the same time complementing the task of the verbal theorist. While it can never be a substitute for the study of the referent world, INS can serve the theorist by providing a vehicle for making explicit his vaguely articulated assumptions and for creating a general model where the implications of his hypotheses for the entire state system can be evaluated. At the very least, by requiring the verbal theorist to be explicit or by subjecting his imprecise hypotheses to explicit formulation, the Inter-Nation Simulation can force some discipline on what has hitherto been a discouragingly inexplicit field of study.[10]

The import of these two statements is clear: simulation prohibits vague generalizations and implicit assumptions. It demands precision—that concepts be explicitly stated, that analysis be detailed—and thereby kindles a greater "need to know." Moreover, these statements imply that the scholar who uses simulation exercises cannot trust to rhetoric or obscure and pretentious circumlocutions to persuade his fellows, but must call on reason and empirical fact. Of course, the further one goes along the road away from gaming toward true simulation—the less he allows himself to use "black boxes" and other informal means of variable inclusion—the more explicit he must be. It becomes more and more difficult to dodge the tough questions as the modeling activity progresses. But if I correctly interpret the enthusiasm in the above statements, they imply that both simulation and gaming may serve more effectively than most other scholarly activities to discipline the formulation of social science theory.

## EXPANSION

In an era noted for specialization, scientific scholarship has not escaped it. The whimsical characterization of the specialist as one who learns more and more about less and less until he knows everything about nothing, is, unfortunately, often too apt for comfort. To be sure, there may be value in narrowing one's scope in order to explore as deeply as possible within it, but too often the specialist is like a dog endlessly gnawing the same bone. One way that gaming stimulates theory-building is that it does not allow such narrow pre-occupation; gaming forces the scholar to "drop his bone" for the moment and explore many aspects of a problem. A person cannot set about to build, say, a comprehensive model of cognitive processes and continue to restrict his interest to purely physiological processes; similarly, it is almost impossible to remain exclusively absorbed in structural-functional models when trying to simulate basic societal processes. This is not to imply that the researcher will *lose* interest in physiological processes or in structural-functional models; indeed, as the experience of most gamers testifies, he is likely to become more interested in his special field as he sees it in a wider context. Again, "context" is the key. The effort to simulate a phenomenon provides a context within which any single field of interest acquires more meaning—for the field is set in a more realistic perspective relative to the discipline of which it is only a part. Simulation expands one's horizons; a gamer cannot ignore the ramifications of his work that reach beyond its immediate scope.

Among scholars, there is a good deal of emotional and intellectual resistance to the idea of broadening perspectives. The emotional resistance probably stems from the fact that when people's horizons are expanded, when they are forced to consider broader problems and their implications, life becomes more difficult; everything is more complicated and demanding. The intellectual resistance may be based on an uncritical adoption of the physical science model in the social and behavioral sciences. Generally speaking, the physical scientist sees his task as that of digging deeper and deeper into the core of things, looking for a simple unifying interpretation or principle that will explain a variety of phenomena. Behavioral scientists have usually assumed that they should—or could—do the same. They might be well-instructed, however, to eschew the search for simplicity and seek, rather, to order the complex.[11]

This discussion is intended as an aside, however. The point I want to make is that the necessity of confronting all aspects of a problem, which inevitably results from attempting to simulate a phenomenon, usually seems to broaden the scholar's horizon and invite him to reconnoiter previously unexplored areas.

## COMMUNICATION

In fact, this enlargement of interest and of the "need to know" usually spills over the boundaries of one's own discipline. Someone once jestingly remarked that he hadn't found the universe to be divided up into departments along the lines of university graduate schools. Nothing so quickly convinces the scholar of the artificiality of disciplinary boundaries as a serious attempt to simulate any but the most trivial phenomena. The same process that widens his area of interest within his own discipline soon pushes him to explore new territories. All at once the literature, the methods, the data, the concepts, and the analogies from related disciplines become formidably relevant. The physiological psychologist who sets out to simulate brain activity is certain to discover how woeful is his ignorance of physics, optics, computer technology, advanced mathematics, and information theory, and that knowledge of these areas is essential to his task. The sociologist who sets out to simulate basic societal processes is soon stopped by his ignorance of psychology, engineering, economics, political science, anthropology, meteorology, architecture, and industrial design; he sees that without expertise in these areas, he is lost. The result is either defeat and despair—or interdisciplinary teamwork.

I do not mean the "interdisciplinary cooperation" so popular during the 1960's, in which scholars from several departments or disciplines meet once a week to give each other seminars on what they are doing. I am talking about the extinction of disciplinary lines; for almost any social system one tries to simulate turns out to be a multifaceted phenomenon and hence requires a multifaceted approach. Each member of a simulation team is forced to learn the language of the other members and to match his own concepts and methods with those of others to discover congruences and incongruities. Each member learns to see his discipline less like a protective redoubt and more like a special area of expertise. Each scholar thus can make his own distinctive contributions, using a shared vocabulary, to the problem under consideration. Wayman Crow, after arguing that simulation is an effective way of studying social recovery after large-scale disaster, suggests that:

> Our efforts to make a more effective contribution from science to the solution of pressing human problems are thwarted as much by piecemeal efforts as they are by ignorance. It is becoming increasingly apparent that an "interdisciplinary approach" will not suffice. As valuable as it is to have multiple perspectives, it is too often little more than that—like blind men touching the elephant each discipline is right but all are wrong. The conclusion seems inescapable that we will eventually have to move beyond an interdisciplinary orientation to the development of a single science—a unitary set of concepts and basic principles for behavioral science. The difficulties are enormous and the immediate prospects of success are dim, and that perhaps has kept us from acknowledging this ultimate aim and from doing what we can now to move toward it. The very real possibility that a single behavioral science may be impossible to create and if possible, will almost certainly be a long time coming, will hopefully not discourage everyone from the attempt.[12]

Crow is implying that knowledge of human behavior is more than fragmented and erratic; it also is encoded in a variety of specialized languages and therefore can neither be communicated nor used effectively on concrete problems. He is further suggesting that this failure of communication and application is largely the result of the rigid walls between disciplines, which have grown higher and more impenetrable as each discipline defends its own territory and turns its back on the developments in neighboring provinces. Crow then goes on to argue the point being made here: that a problem-oriented, simulation-approach is one way of beginning to overcome this disciplinary parochialism. Simulation teams in universities and other research organizations bear witness to this claim. Most of the teams with which I am familiar are drawn from several departments. But because universities are not set up for inter-disciplinary research, such teams have had to create elaborate fictions in order to pursue their work outside the confines of departmental organization.

I am not suggesting that to eradicate the distinctions among disciplines is *ipso facto* good and necessary. I *am* arguing that too much emphasis has been placed on the encapsulation of knowledge within narrow specialities, and that at least one segment of the scholarly community should concentrate its efforts on integrating and communicating the specialized knowledge that has been generated by the concentrated scrutiny of demarcated areas. Theoretical statements should relate to many different dimensions of reality. Simulation is one effective approach for creating more complex links.

## INVOLVEMENT

Caught up in the project of building a simulation, the researcher is soon possessed by a desire to fill in those "blank spots" to which I referred earlier, those spaces that just remain empty because theory is lacking or data are missing. Those empty spaces become a challenge that must be met; the researcher's desire to fill them is transformed into an intellectual and emotional drive more powerful than pure curiosity; now he is goaded, not only by his scholarly interest in knowledge for its own sake, but also by the lust for knowledge with which to construct his simulation. This happens, as I said in the beginning, because gaming is deeply engaging fun; and it is fun to improve the game and to feel that you are making progress toward completing a simulation. It is like working on a picture puzzle, many pieces of which are hidden in various parts of one's house, or even in neighboring houses. One can become obsessed by the need to complete the picture, fill those spaces whose emptiness is so tantalizing.

I will give two illustrations of how the engagement fostered by simulation-building acts as a goad, though more examples could be offered. Both examples are drawn from the development of the Inter-Nation Simulation.

One of the equations in the INS states that the "validators" in the simulation (those groups of people whose support or non-support determines whether the chief of state will remain in office) will be pleased with increased standards of living and with improved "national security." National security is defined as the position of the nation (and its allies, if any) relative to an enemy nation or alliance, in terms of basic resources and military capability. The equation is more detailed than this, but these are the general outlines. Many INS users questioned whether the "real life" national elites who concern themselves with such issues do, in fact, assess the national security of the nation as the equation assumes. This question led to a more elaborate theoretical refinement of the concept of "national security" as perceived by elites, and finally to a data-gathering project in which State Department and Defense Department personnel, academicians, and newspaper correspondents were interviewed and asked to rate the various determinants of national power.[13] It turned out that the equation was indeed inadequate and misleading. Thus, a worthwhile contribution to our general understanding of political processes accrued from an initial interest in increasing the sophistication of a game.

A second example is drawn from my own experience. In my association with the development of the INS, I found myself increasingly concerned with the question of how one could choose "surrogate" decision-makers who would be representative of national decision-makers, or, alternatively, what, if any, personal characteristics of decision-makers are such important determinants of decision-making behavior that they must be included in computer simulations of decision-making. Is culture important? Personality? Sex? Age? Experience? Cognitive structure? If personality is an important factor, what particular aspects of personality? These questions impelled me to review extensively the literature on the personal characteristics of political decision-makers. I concluded that the literature was grossly stereotyped. This conclusion led me to launch a major project for determining what characteristics *do* typify those who rise to high political position. Again, the stimulus of the simulation-building task led me into psychology, sociology, cross-cultural comparisons, and the necessity of learning a new set of research methods. At this point, my interest in the problem is largely "for its own sake," but the initial stimulus came from my intense involvement in the simulation. Such experiences are the norm rather than the exception. They impel the researcher to gather the data and develop the theory he needs to fill those empty spaces in the game.

## SERENDIPITY

What is serendipity? Serendipity is a "gift from the Gods"—as when Jason sets out to find the Golden Fleece and stumbles upon a beautiful maiden as well; when a boy for the first time kisses a girl just to prove to his peers that he's not a "square," and find that the experience profoundly changes his outlook on life; when a researcher sets out to test a hypothesis and finds something he had never thought to look for.

Gaming is serendipity-prone. The gamer is experimenting in an environment so rich, exploring interactions often so complex and so uncontrolled, that he can almost guarantee the generation of outcomes that were not predicted and that, in many cases, prove to be valuable additions to theory. Schelling finds that the bargaining games with which he works

> . . . can be used to discover, and demonstrate, important *possibilities* that might have been missed without it. The significance and relevance of these possibilities may still depend on reasoning and evidence obtained elsewhere; but the existence of the possibilities, and some notion of how they relate to the structure of the game, can be discovered by the artificial game. This would, for example, be true of the proposition that the advantage may well go not to the player who enjoys the increased knowledge and information but to the other player,

> and that it may even be an absolute disadvantage to one of the players to obtain new information if he cannot conceal the fact that he has it.[14]

Scenarios of contingencies that planners should take into account may first be suggested in games—an instance of serendipity. For example, Herman Kahn, famous for his scenarios of the unlikely ways accidental nuclear war could break out between the United States and the Soviet Union, reveals that many of these possibilities were suggested to him by gaming exercises.[15] More directly pertinent to theory construction, however, are examples from other academic gamers. Using the INS in a study of crisis decision-making, James Robinson tested the hypothesis: "In a crisis, as contrasted with a non-crisis, search for information is more likely." The hypothesis was *not* confirmed, but his analysis of the data revealed *reasons* for the failure to search for information that are of equal theoretical interest as the initial hypothesis.[16]

A second example comes from my own work. In 1963, a group at the Western Behavioral Sciences Institute in La Jolla, California, began a simulation study of a deterrence problem. Our question was: "Given two nations in a deterrence relationship, what would be the impact on the inter-nation system of one nation's possession of an invulnerable nuclear retaliatory force?" We searched the literature, extracted some 200 propositions, and reduced them to nine hypotheses, which we tested in the INS. One hypothesis stated that when the nation gained an invulnerable force, it would be seen as stronger than when it was vulnerable; another hypothesis stated that war would be less likely when at least one nation in the system had an invulnerable force. These hypotheses were based on a study of almost all the literature on the subject. When we analyzed our simulation data, some interesting results emerged.

First of all, as we had hypothesized, the invulnerable nation, "OMNE," *was* perceived as stronger, both by itself and by "UTRO," its major opponent. But we found that each nation's perceptions differed considerably as to content: When OMNE achieved invulnerability, it saw itself as *much* stronger; but when it lost invulnerability, it saw itself as only a *little* weakened. On the other hand, its opponent, UTRO, saw OMNE as only a *little* stronger upon gaining invulnerability, but as *much* weakened by its loss.

This result was totally unexpected, but it has enormous implications. It suggests that a see-saw technological race in weapons-development may result in ever greater perceptual distortions between the competing nations—an outcome that could be catastrophic. A subsequent search of the literature revealed that such perceptual distortion has never been predicted. But because it occurred in the simulation, we looked for evidence of its occurrence in the real world—and found it. For example, the Soviets were jubilant when they launched their first Sputnik in 1957, but showed very little concern when American space achievements erased their lead. Again, America insisted that China's explosion of its first nuclear device in 1964 was of relatively little consequence, while China asserted that the whole power structure of the world had been changed.

Even though the usual explanation for these simultaneously paired boasts-and-denigrations is that they are purely propagandistic, the simulation findings—which tapped into the basic perceptions of the participants—indicate that the verbal statements of "real world" nations may accurately reflect their underlying perceptions. The simulation generated a finding that opens up a whole new area for exploration and hypothesis-testing.

The second hypothesis, relating to the reduced probability of war with the advent of one-nation invulnerability, was not confirmed. In fact, war broke out *much more frequently* when one of the nations was invulnerable. Analysis of the data disclosed that war broke out precisely because the invulnerable nation felt more secure and potent, and therefore engaged in behavior that led to war. The invulnerable nation became more aggressive and belligerent, more willing to take risks, and more arrogant in disregarding the objections of its allies and opponents. Such a possibility had never been suggested in any of the literature on military strategy—probably because the theorists, being Americans, were usually talking about potential American invulnerability, and simply did not think in terms of increased American aggressiveness and belligerency. But in the abstraction of the simulation, the psychological processes underlying the transformation were clear.[17] Here again, the simulation findings suggest a new hypothesis. The reader is invited to frame it for himself, and to judge whether, and in what way the hypothesis applies to the "real world" in which two nations have invulnverable nuclear systems.

In both instances, the rich interaction characteristic of gaming generated unexpected outcomes that may have profound significance. Such serendipitous effects are typical of gaming exercises. This is not to say they are *unique* to gaming; certainly they frequently occur in other research activities as well, but they do occur with such regularity in gaming that they are almost predictable.

Earlier in this chapter, I concurred with J. David Singer's proposition that reading history, studying research literature, imagining, analogizing, and observing the real world are traditional aids to the generation of social science theory. I then suggested that because gaming entails confrontation, explication, expansion, communication, involvement, and serendipity, it stimulates these more traditional activities. Thus, gaming contributes to theory building, not only by virtue of its specific research findings, but equally by virtue of the kinds of activity it fosters. Its findings do, however, provide a useful means of testing hypotheses drawn from already available theory, and this is the subject of the next chapter.

## FOOTNOTES

1. Herbert A. Simon, "New Developments in the Theory of the Firm," *American Economic Review*, LII, No. 1 (1962), 13.
2. George Homans, *Social Behavior: Its Elementary Forms* (New York: Harcourt, Brace and World, 1961), pp. 10–11.
3. Michael Polanyi, *Personal Knowledge: Towards a Post-Critical Philosophy* (Chicago: University of Chicago Press, 1958).
4. J. David Singer, "Data-Making in International Relations," *Behavioral Science*, X, No. 1 (1965), 68–80; see page 76.
5. Kaplan, *op.cit.*, pp. 268–9.
6. W. R. Ashby, "Simulation of a Brain," in Borko, *op. cit.*, p. 456.
7. Wayman J. Crow, "The Role of Simulation-Model Construction in Social Research on Post-Nuclear Attack Events" (La Jolla, California: Western Behavioral Sciences Institute, March 1967), pp. 12–14.
8. Thomas C. Schelling, "Experimental Games and Bargaining Theory," *World Politics*, XIV, No. 1 (1961), 57.
9. Sidney Verba, "Simulation, Reality, and Theory in International Relations," *World Politics*, XVI, No. 3 (1964), 499.
10. William Coplin, "Inter-Nation Simulation and Contemporary Theories of International Relations," *The American Political Science Review*, LX, No. 3 (1966), 577–8.
11. "Whitehead once offered to the natural sciences the maxim: 'Seek simplicity and distrust it'; to the social sciences he might well have offered: 'Seek complexity and order it.' " C. Geertz, "The Impact of the Concept of Culture on the Concept of Man," *Bulletin of the Atomic Scientists*, 1966, 3.
12. Wayman J. Crow, "The Role of Simulation-Model Construction in Social Research on Post-Nuclear Attack Events," *op. cit.*, p. 7 .
13. Lloyd Jensen, "United States Elites and Their Perceptions of the Determinants of Foreign Policy Behavior" (Evanston, Illinois: Northwestern University, paper delivered to the Midwest Conference of Political Scientists, April 29, 1966).
14. Thomas C. Schelling, *op. cit.*, p. 57.
15. Herman Kahn, in a talk at the Hudson Institute, Harmon-on-Hudson, New York, September 27, 1967.
16. James A. Robinson, "Simulating Crisis Decision-Making," text of a talk prepared for a panel on Foreign Policy and Affairs at the Joint Meeting of the Institute of Management Sciences and the Operations Research Society of America, Minneapolis, October 7, 1964, pp. 13–14.
17. A full description of this study is contained in John R. Raser and Wayman J. Crow, *Winsafe II*, *op. cit.*

# 5

# THEORY EXPLORATION: RESEARCH WITH GAMES

> The importance of a knowledge of process or change must not be underestimated. Explanations attempt to describe causal relationships by filling the interstices between events or surrounding them within a more inclusive framework. A knowledge of process makes it possible to fill these interstices and provide the more inclusive framework and thus increase our understanding of what is going on. It is one thing to know that if an experimenter introduces a certain change, a given effect will follow; it is quite another thing to be able to learn about the various mechanisms that lie between the given change and the given effect and convert the change into the effect. The experiment can, of course, focus on some of these interstices, and this technique is quite valuable for arriving at an explanation. Simulation techniques, however, are especially well adapted to producing data of a more continuous nature so that long sequences of phenomena can be analyzed.[1]

The acid test for any theory is: Does it predict? If a theory tells us what will happen under certain conditions, then it is good theory. If the theory predicts incorrectly and leads our expectations astray, then it is not good theory. In one sense, then, every good theory is a prediction. In the social sciences,however, most theory does not pretend that it can predict single (discrete) events; as we saw earlier, it is "probabilistic"—it merely predicts processes or trends. Thus, we would suspect the scientific integrity of a scholar who says, "War will break out between Argentina and Brazil in 1983." On the basis of his theories, which indicate certain strong trends, he might predict that many of the conditions for war will exist, or that there is likely to be more warfare in Latin America during the 1980's. But if he makes a flat statement about a discrete event, then we usually assume (a) that he does not believe in chance occurrences; (b) that he is ignoring the fact that there always seem to be more influences on events than we can take into account; (c) that he is transforming tentative theories into certainties; and (d) that he is going beyond the level of prediction justified by the current achievements of social science and entering the twilight realm of Winchellian soothsaying.

Similarly, in using games and simulations as experimental vehicles for testing theory, we do not judge a hypothesis according to whether or not certain *specific events* take place in the game, but according to whether certain *processes* occur. Even though we do pay attention to discrete events, we do so only when they occur frequently enough to indicate some underlying process. In the previous chapter, for example, in describing the use of the INS to test certain hypotheses about the effects of nuclear invulnerability, I referred to the frequent outbreak of war as being an important finding. The event itself was not significant, but the frequency of its occurrence under a specific condition—"invulnerability." This frequency indicated that some process was set in motion by the interaction between invulnerability and other elements in the simulated situation.

A simulator might indulge in the frightening but ego-building fantasy of imagining an aide rushing to his chief from the underground computer simulation room and shouting, "Call the President! The computer says the Chinese are going to attack next Thursday!" but it would be just that—fantasy. It is possible, however, that an aide might report, "The computer shows that the probability of Chinese attack is high." (In the minds of decision-makers, this probability might be transmuted into certainty, and they might then act in such a way as to guarantee the very thing predicted—but this is another problem.[2]) Simulations do not now and will not in the foreseeable future predict single events or "outcomes" of processes. What they can do though, is give us information about the processes themselves. Simulations can tell us about how the relationships among various states of a system might change under given conditions. For example, simulations can yield information about the relationship between frequency-of-communication and level-of-trust; about the interaction between personality and political behavior; or about the impact of power on coalition formation. These findings then can serve as the basis for new sets of assumptions. Incorporated into a new version of the simulation, the findings can in turn be tested and perhaps be combined as part-theories. Simulations can, in other words, help us test social science theory at the level where most of that theory has been postulated—at the level of group process and systems behavior.

The experimenter can test hypotheses to gain information about the changes in a system under "given conditions" in two ways. He can establish his starting conditions, specifying the parameters of the independent variable(s) in which he is interested—for instance, "personality traits"—and let the system "run." Or, he can establish his starting conditions, let the system run for a while, and then introduce the independent variable—a new condition—by intervening either through an accomplice or in a way appropriate to the scenario of the game. After the system has run for a time under the particular condition of interest, that condition can be removed in the same way it was introduced. Since the state of the system can be periodically assessed, it is possible to tap into the processes set in motion by a given condition, and learn something about its impact on other system variables.

Three basic types of games or simulations have been used for such research purposes: simple two-person games; all-computer simulations;

and man-machine, or "complex environment" games. Each typ game has particular advantages as a research tool, and selection of the type to be used in any given study is based on its appropriateness for the research goal. In this chapter, I shall describe each type of game, give examples of its use in theory testing, and indicate why it is considered appropriate. These examples are merely an illustrative sampling of the more interesting and relevant studies among the hundreds that have been carried out in the short history of social science gaming.

## SIMPLE TWO-PERSON GAMES

These games are not simulations, since they are not designed to replicate some entity. They are designed as "settings" that will elicit the particular kinds of behavior the researcher wishes to study. They might, however, be said to replicate certain specific *situations*, thereby making it possible to study human behavioral phenomena in microcosm. The findings may suggest hypotheses about similar behavior in macrocosmic systems, such as international politics, or bureaucratic organizations, which could then be tested in simulations.

The appellation "simple two-person games" is misleading, since the games I shall describe are not necessarily played by two persons only, nor are they necessarily very simple. But the name accurately describes the basic paradigm: two people, in a laboratory setting, play against one another for some sort of pay-off, the amount of which will depend on the choices they make in successive plays of the game. The game may be either "zero-sum" (what one player wins, the other loses), or "non zero-sum" (both players may win or both may lose). The experimenter can control the game in any number of ways. The sexes, ages, or personalities of the players may be varied, as may the initial instructions, amount of communication allowed, length of play, amount of pay-off, and symmetry or asymmetry of pay-off.

Typical of these games is the widely used "Prisoner's Dilemma," the conflict situation of which is discussed below.

Two suspects are taken into custody and separated. The disctrict attorney is certain that they have been partners in committing a specific crime, but he does not have adequate evidence to convict them. He points out to each prisoner that he has two alternatives: to confess to the crime the police know he and his partner are guilty of, or to deny it. If neither confesses, then the district attorney states he will book them on some minor charge, such as petty larceny and illegal possession of a weapon, and they will both receive minor punishment; if they both confess, they will be prosecuted, but he will recommend less than the most severe sentence; if, however, one confesses and the other does not, then the confessor will be treated very leniently for turning state's evidence, whereas the other will have "the book" thrown at him.

Thus, each prisoner can gain most by "double-crossing" the other, but *only* if the other does not also double-cross. If both double-cross, both lose; if both co-operate, both win something, but less than either would have won had he double-crossed the other and "got away with it." The "payoff matrix" may be represented as follows:

| | | B: Not Confess | | B: Confess | |
|---|---|---|---|---|---|
| A | Not Confess | 2 | 2 | 10 | 0 |
| A | Confess | 0 | 10 | 5 | 5 |

The first number in each box represents the payoff to Prisoner A. This game is obviously very rich in possibilities for testing hypotheses about competition and cooperation, the effects of communication, and a great variety of other theoretically interesting phenomena. For example, note that if each prisoner wants to minimize his possible losses, then he will confess, since by doing so he can not possibly spend more than five years in prison and may get off "scott free." But since both prisoners follow this logic, each will in fact receive a five-year sentence; whereas if both prisoners had refused to confess, each would have received only two years. The research is too voluminous to be reported or even surveyed here,[3] but an example or two may show how the games can be used as research tools. (This type of gaming is closely allied to formal game theory. The experimentor who uses simple two-person games knows precisely the optimum choice to be made by the subjects. Such knowledge is gained from the appropriate mathematical formulae in formal game theory. Knowing the theoretical optimum choice, the experimenter is better able to evaluate the actual response of an actor in the game situations and how changes in the gaming structure affect the subject's responses.)

In one experiment by Sisson and Ackoff, two players competing for resources had the power to punish one another for non-cooperative behavior. The experimenters manipulated three variables—the amount of communication allowed, the amount of punishment it was possible to inflict, and the power differences between the players—to ascertain how these variables are related to conflict escalation. They found that increased ability to communicate tends to dampen conflict escalation; that if the ability to punish is high, there is apt to be less communication; and that players escalate to increase their own advantage.[4] This example illustrates how these games can be used to study phenomena that seem relevant to solving problems of international politics and other social systems.

A similar game involving more than two players and thus allowing for the formation of coalitions has been used by Kaplan, Burns, and Quandt to study "balance of power" and the conditions under which it can be maintained.[5]

In a recent study, Deutsch, Epstein, Canavan, and Gumpert used a two-person game to study strategies for inducing cooperation. One player is an experimenter-accomplice; thus, the experimenters can test a variety of strategies, such as "Turn the Other Cheek," whereby the accomplice rewards his opponent for attacks or threats; a "Non-punitive" strategy, in which the accomplice simply protects himself without counter-attack; and the "Deterrent" strategy, in which he makes counter-threats. In the "Reformed Sinner" variation, the accomplice uses a "Deterrent" strategy for the first periods of the game, then changes either to a "Turn the Other Cheek" or a "Non-punitive" strategy. The reader may decide for himself which of these strategies is the more effective; and then risk shattering his opinions by checking the reference.[6]

A researcher might go on to test the most effective strategy under a variety of conditions, and thus contribute to theory-building.

Simple two-person games have become popular in the past seven or eight years. Why? For one thing, even though these games employ the traditional laboratory setting with which most social scientists feel comfortable, they are so gripping that the participants become intensely involved; this fact gives the experimenter greater assurance that the behavior he is observing is "real" rather than contrived by the subject to fulfill what he thinks are the investigator's expectations. Moreover, these games usually require only two or three subjects at a time, and the introduction of an experimenter-accomplice is not difficult. It is possible, also, to select these two or three subjects on the basis of their personal characteristics and to keep the interaction to a minimum—to the diad of interest. At the same time, the processes in which the subjects engage can be made very explicit by keeping the tasks restricted and clearly defined. Thus, the "two-person" game offers certain advantages over more complex games such as the INS, which usually engage up to 20 or 30 people for a single "run"; moreover, both data-gathering and its interpretation are comparatively simple.

The weaknesses of such games are that they may be too simple to elicit the rich behaviors that are relevant for the study of complex social systems, and that they do not allow for very complicated interactions between subject and environment or with other subjects. Nor can they handle more than one or two propositions at once.

The second type of game, the "all-machine," or computer simulation, is in some ways at the opposite end of the gaming spectrum.

Rather than testing hypotheses about specific human behavior, the computer simulation tests hypotheses about the operation of a complex system in which human behaviors, or even specific human personality characteristics, are programmed as system-variables.

## COMPUTER SIMULATIONS

In what follows, I will use the term "simulations" rather than "games" because it is the more conventional term. According to the definitions I suggested earlier, however, I would argue that most computer models are games rather than simulations because few of them pretend to be complete and accurate replicates of the reference systems.

In discussing the problems of simulating social systems, Pool points out that computer simulation offers a way of handling many propositions simultaneously, no one of which, taken singly, accounts for much of the total variance.[7] Add to this advantage the ability of a computer simulation to "compress" time and to allow multiple replications, as well as its controllability and safety, and it is evident why this type of game is now widely employed as a research technique and why it represents a methodological breakthrough, especially in the social sciences.

The advantages of computer simulation are well illustrated in the operations research study by Jennings and Dickens of the Port of New York Authority Bus Terminal, which annually serves more than 25 million passengers.[8] In describing their approach, the authors point out that by using a computer, several weeks of bus terminal operation can be simulated in a few hours, and Monte Carlo techniques* can be included to determine typical arrival times for busses:

> It is impractical for economic and technical reasons to make a definitive study of the problem by empirical observations at the terminal. Adequate analysis of day-to-day probabilistic variations in waiting lines would require many weeks of costly sampling. On each platform bus arrival and departure schedules are fixed by bus operating policy. They are found to differ among loading berths on the same platform as well as between any two platforms. Neither the individual bus schedules nor the random arrival variations are subject to control for observational purposes. Hence, observed data would fail to provide a uniform basis for direct comparison of waiting lines on different platforms. . . .
>
> A limited number of days of peak-hour suburban bus operation were observed at the terminal to obtain frequency distributions of commuter passenger and bus arrivals. With these as inputs to a logic which controls bus access to berths, the simulation method using Monte

* Monte Carlo is a technique for calculating the average and cumulative effects of chance over time.

> Carlo techniques was contrived. For any given bus departure schedule, the method generates a minute-by-minute sequence of commuter bus and passenger waiting line lengths throughout the peak hour.[9]

As we saw in the previous chapter, the use of computer simulations in economics, sociology, and political science was an outgrowth of their use in operations research of the kind just described. In 1957, Guy Orcutt and his colleagues at M.I.T. and Harvard began one of the first attempts to build a large computer simulation of the American economy.[10] The model incorporated demographic projections, trends in the changing composition of the labor force, and assumptions about household economic behavior, to all of which Monte Carlo was applied. The goal of the simulation was the prediction of long-term trends in the American economy. Describing their research strategy, Orcutt says:

> A given experiment involves operating a model after first completely specifying a set of initial conditions appropriate to the model, a set of values of the parameters used in specifying relations contained in the model, and the time paths of those variables used in the model and treated as exogenous. Additional experiments would involve operating the model after respecifying the initial conditions, the parameters, and/or the exogenous variables.[11]

The model is repeatedly cycled under any given set of conditions to produce a range of outcomes. From these sets of conditions and outcomes, a map of probable general trends is extrapolated. Methodologically speaking, this approach is identical to the approach that repeatedly measures the time it takes rats to run a maze and expresses the results as the *mean* or *average* time, rather than as any single measurement of the running time. Most of the experiments I shall describe are based on this sort of approach.

An experimental computer simulation of interest to sociologists is the HOMUNCULUS designed by John T. and Jeanne E. Gullahorn.[12] The name is a double-entendre, for the model incorporates the theoretical orientation of George C. Homans. Several of his micro-theories regarding behavior in small social groups were translated into computer language and juxtaposed in the simulation. It was thus possible to explore the extent to which the theories overlap, contradict one another, and could be integrated. Note that this model did not actually test the *validity* of Homans' theories—how accurately they describe the world; rather, it tested their internal *reliability*—the extent to which they are logically consistent with one another. This focus on reliability, as indicated earlier, is typical of simulation efforts in sociology. It amounts to reshaping, refining, and fitting together pieces that are hypothesized to be part of a larger dynamic pattern.

I have already mentioned three all-computer simulations in political science: Oliver Benson's "Simple Diplomatic Game"; I. de Sola Pool's "Simulmatics" study of voter behavior; and the "Crisiscom" model of Pool and Allan Kessler, a simulation of decision-maker information processing. The initial parameters in each model can be varied according to the interest of the researcher to produce a variety of system-states. Among the findings from the "Diplomatic" simulation are these: (1) under most conditions, the international system tends to shift towards increased polarity, (2) there is a steady shifting in alliances, (3) a balance of power principle apparently functions even in a tight bi-polar world, and (4) the presumed advantage of initiating action, rather than merely responding, is by no means certain.

The "Simulmatics" findings are too complex to report here. But suffice it to say, as I noted earlier, that in the 1960 Kennedy-Nixon presidential election, Pool's simulation more accurately predicted voting outcomes in electoral districts covering the entire United States than did the pollsters. Pool achieved this accuracy by analyzing the differential impact of salient issues on various types of voters. His results indicate that he could have predicted alternative outcomes equally accurately if other issues had been substituted for those actually in the campaigns. If this is true, it raises the disconcerting idea that issues could be so adroitly selected and presented as to achieve mass persuasion more discriminating and potent than anything Goebbels ever imagined.

Using a similar approach, Shapiro and Cherryholmes succeeded in constructing a computer simulation of roll-call voting in the United States House of Representatives. By combining a representative's "cognitive processes" (past voting record, perceived benefits of the bill to his constituency) with a "communication process" (those with strong feelings on the bill try to influence those with weak pre-dispositions), this simulation successfully accounted for approximately 90% of the variance in actual voting on both domestic and international issues.[13] Thus, it is not only the voting behavior of the public that the simulator can reduce to sets of equations, but also the behavior of policy-makers themselves!

"Crisiscom" simulates the way decision-makers process information during international crises. In "Crisiscom," two simulated decision-makers are programmed with different personality characteristics related to attention span and selective perception. Each decision-maker receives messages, analyzes them in accordance with his programmed personality constructs, and then responds. The decision-makers simulated in this particular program were the German Kaiser and the Russian Tsar, and the messages used represented the known exchanges between the two during July 25–31, 1914. But the personality characteristics were varied systematically to determine the effect of different personality configurations on decision-making.

Another example of a computer simulation in international relations is the study by Singer and Hinomoto[14] of the detection of illegal weapons-production. Three different inspection schemes defined on the basis of their ability to detect evasion and to avoid false alarms are represented in the study. The effects of chance are determined by Monte Carlo. Procedures are outlined for comparing the relative costs of installing and operating the alternative inspection schemes and for comparing the costs of successful evasion and false detection. By running 18 experiments, each covering a simulated time-span of 400 days, results for 7200 inspections were obtained.

In discussing why he used a computer model, or simulation, to study the operation of the national economy, Orcutt makes several observations that apply to the use of modeling and simulating or gaming to study any complex social system:

> From a research point of view models are of great importance because they increase the range of feasible predictions, and thus suggest and make possible more extensive testing of the hypotheses and theories which they embody.
>
> From a policy point of view models are essential because the policy maker usually requires predictions about the combined effect of many factors acting on many interacting units. For this purpose a single hypothesis or theory taken by itself is rarely sufficient. It is only by linking several hypotheses or theories together in a meaningful way that it becomes possible to link the things to be predicted with those things which may be regarded as given.[15]

Pool argues that computer simulations are valuable because of the nature of social science theory. To predict human behavior accurately, the researcher must take account of extremely complex idiosyncrasies. Social scientists are thus more like systems engineers who attempt to relate the variables in a complex system than they are like physicists who search for broad underlying principles and elegant simplicity in a highly interdependent system.

As we saw, two-person games enable the researcher to study certain specific behaviors in situations more nearly analogous to "real life" than that of the usual laboratory setting, and hence more likely to evoke "real" responses. They cannot, however, handle complicated interactions between variables or between the human subjects and a complex environment. On the other hand, computer simulations can handle a large number of interacting variables simultaneously, but must use programmed assumptions about human behavior. The third major type of game, conventionally known as "man machine" games but which I call "complex environment" games, is an attempt to combine the advantages and overcome the difficulties of the two other types of games.

## MAN-MACHINE OR COMPLEX ENVIRONMENT GAMES

These games are prototypical of the method of using a game—a pre-simulation—to generate the theory or data needed for a complete representation of a large-scale, complex system. Hence, the primary purpose of this type of game is to improve the game itself, testing hypotheses either about the characteristics of the system the researcher wishes eventually to simulate or about basic human behaviors in interaction with the system or, occasionally, both. The "machine" consists of the major aspects of a system that interest the experimenter. These aspects may be represented physically (as in the use of messengers to simulate aspects of a communication system), programmed on a computer, or expressed mathematically and hand-calculated. They constitute the "environment" with which the human players must cope.

The man-machine game used in operations research is different from the game used in social science research. In operations research, the goal is practical—to make the entire system, including its human components, function better as a unit; the term "better" applies to speed, efficiency, and reliability in the performance of a particular task. Secondly, the machine aspect of the game—the programmed environment—is a complete and accurate simulation of the reference system. The machine can consist of the hardware components of a complex weapons system, the production schedule of a factory, or a rigidly determined set of logistic requirements for a large organization. The human "components" play against the machine; that is, they fill the spot normally occupied in the reference system by human beings. The aim of the man-machine game is to discover what changes in system components or system processes will improve system performance. Thus, these games are used as the flight simulator is used. The experimenter can vary the characteristics of the humans who are "plugged in," the procedures or routines they follow in performing their tasks, or the interface between them and the machine—as when levers shaped like landing gear are tested in the flight simulator to see if recognition-by-feel will improve pilot speed in identifying them during take-off while watching other instruments.

The following examples show how man-machine games have been used to solve real-world problems by illuminating the interactions between human beings and a complex system of one kind or another.

In designing or improving an air defense system, it is important to know what kind of team organization, what configuration of task specialization, and what levels of training will enable the system to identify and intercept enemy planes in the shortest time. To examine these aspects, a research group[16] simulated an air defense system that incorporated the entire hardware complex—radar, a control center, interceptors, the whole paraphernalia of communications equipment—and a team of men, the players, whose task was to evaluate incoming signals and decide whether to launch interceptors. The players were subjected to a variety of conditions to discover which factors contributed to effective task-accomplishment and which detracted from it. The study also provided information about desirable modifications in the hardware complex itself.

In a related study, Sinaiko and Cartwright[17] used a similar air defense system to compare the abilities of a computer and of human operators in handling a heavy target load without performance degradation. It presumably is comforting to know that under heavy load, the human performance was better than that of the computer, apparently because humans learn anticipatory behavior. HAL 9000 has not yet arrived!

In an interesting study to improve the efficiency of an intricate system, RAND[18] used a man-computer simulation to test a real world man-computer operation; as in the Sinaiko and Cartwright study, a computer was used to study the efficacy of using computers! This study was intended to bridge the gap between pure mathematical research on logistics and supply problems on the one hand and knowledge gained from observing the actual operation of such systems by human decision-makers on the other. RAND replicated the entire Air Force organization, accurately reproducing the operating environment. An hour represented a day, decision-forms were used, and management review conferences were held periodically. The four months' simulated time-span included two war situations.

To test the accuracy of the simulation, the researchers compared parts-procurement, distribution, repair, and record-keeping in the simulation with the actual operation of these activities in the Air Force. The simulation proved valid, but analysis of the runs suggested ways to improve the system. Changes were therefore made in the simulation: procurement procedures were altered; buffer supplies of key parts were established; a mathematical formula for determining needs was derived; and the use of a high speed, high capacity, data-processing center was inaugurated. The experimenters found that the new system, constructed as a result of experience with the first set of simulation runs, would provide the same service at about half the cost of the Air Force system then in use. Again, research that started as an effort to improve human performance produced radical changes in system hardware and procedural charateristics as well. In theoretical terms, the hypotheses on which the system was constructed were tested in the first simulation runs, and the outcomes suggested new hypotheses that were in turn tested, found to be correct, and suggested improvements in the reference system itself.

Such simulation activities are common in operations research. These activities test and improve practice, as opposed to the social scientists, who test and improve theory. Despite their pragmatic concern, these exercises paved the way for the development of social and political games, such as the INS and PLANS, to which I shall now turn.

The fundamental concept of theory-testing and practice-testing games is the same: An elaborate physical, symbolic, and temporal environment is created to represent major aspects of the system in which one is interested, and a human player is placed in that environment. He then enacts the role of the human being, or group of human beings, who normally interact with the real environment being simulated. In PLANS, a pressure group game, the national economy and the legislature are expressed mathematically as quantified "values" that rise or fall, and bills, constituencies, resources, communications systems, and meetings are expressed in other symbolic or semi-symbolic ways. The players represent "special interests" and must interact with each other and with the "machine" to achieve their goals.

PLANS was used once for research purposes in two pilot runs; one run used professional administrators and the other used graduate students. The administrators focused their attention on fewer issues than did the students and succeeded in having more policies adopted. In both groups, crystallization of issues accompanied a rise in socio-economic levels in the model.[19]

In the INS, the model, or the "machine," contains many of the features of national and international politics—three or more "nations," each with its voters, national resources, military capability, polls, channels of communication, meetings, advisors, trade, and elections. The players act as chiefs-of-state, diplomats, and cabinet members. The model is a machine in the sense that the components (basic resources, voter satisfaction, and research-and-development) and some of the relationships among the components are expressed mathematically for programming on a computer or desk calculator. As the model "operates," changes in one component produce changes in the others according to previously established mathematical formulae. The players' primary task is to decide how to allocate their resources in order to accomplish the goals they bring to the game or develop during its course. Note that the goals are not pre-set; the players are given a few "rules of the game" and then are on their own. They may negotiate, form coalitions, bargain, threaten, trade, wage war, and try to carry out elaborate plans, most of which involve resource allocations. The consequences of these behaviors and decisions are periodically fed back to the players, and their new decision possibilities are partially based on the outcomes of earlier activities. In most INS studies, the experimenter introduces the condition he wishes to study, such as the spread of nuclear weapons, one nation's nuclear invulnerability, or a particular strategy, after the game has run for several periods.

The INS has been the vehicle for most of the man-machine gaming in social science research. In the first large scale INS experiment, Richard Brody studied the "Nth country problem" in sixteen replications of a seven nation "world," using high school students as players. In each replication, the starting condition was a bi-polar world in which each bloc was led by a large power possessing nuclear weapons. In the early stages of the game, the system was examined for patterns of intra-bloc cohesion and inter-bloc hostility. As the game progressed, nuclear capability spread to all other nations through research-and-development payoffs. As hypothesized, it was found that after the diffusion of nuclear weapons, intra-bloc perceptions of hostility increased, and the bi-polar nature of the world broke down; that is, all nations communicated freely with one another rather than primarily with their own bloc leader.[20] Later, utilizing the data from the first study, Brody and his colleagues analyzed the hostile behavior of each individual in the simulation. They found it related in quite complex ways to national levels of capability, to the hostile behavior of others, and to specific issues of salience to the participants.[21]

In another INS study, my colleagues and I used a similar model to study the impact of nuclear weapons invulnerability on the international system. We conducted 12 replications using U.S. Navy recruits as players. In general, we found that when one nation in the system achieved nuclear invulnerability, it was seen as stronger and more threatening, it was less apt to precipitate accidental war, and it lost interest in reaching formal arms control agreements, even though the interest in arms control of other nations increased. Alliances tended to shift and opponents of the invulnerable nation were more deterred, but wars occurred with greater frequency than when no nation was invulnerable.[22] Certain findings of this study are discussed in more detail in Chapter 4.

Another study was replicated with students at the National University of Mexico to ascertain the effect of cultural differences on the simulation. In general, the results were similar, although as compared to their American counterparts, the Mexican students tended to spend more time on international issues and less on domestic issues.[23]

In an earlier study, Charles E. Osgood's Graduated Reciprocation in Tension Reduction (GRIT) strategy for de-escalating the Cold War was tested in the INS and found to work.[24] The INS also has been used to explore the changes occurring in decision-maker behavior under crisis conditions,[25] and to determine which factors increase and which decrease the cohesion of alliances.[26]

In these INS studies, research was focussed on *system* characteristics—that is, on how the reaction of human decision-makers to different environmental conditions produced changes in the system, such as increased or decreased cohesion, probability of war, level of tension, or changed relationships. The players were selected on the basis of their availability rather than according to particular personal characteristics; for research purposes, they were regarded as "black boxes" that were simply part of the system. Such research designs are attempts to compensate for the lack of information about the personality traits of national decision-makers. Thus we cannot select simulation-surrogates who will replicate the decision-makers. We can, however, increase our understanding of national and international politics by concentrating on *system* processes and at the same time we can study the impact of cultural characteristics on decision-making behavior, as illustrated by the INS experiments comparing U.S. Navy recruits with Mexican university students.

The study of system processes through the use of man-machine games has not, however, been limited to political science and international relations. It also has been applied to organization behavior, as two related studies illustrate. The first study, "Leviathan," by Beatrice and Sydney Rome, was a simulation of an Intelligence Communication Control Center.[27] This study used the interactions of human subjects with a computer to study different methods of receiving and processing information. The Romes found that information was most efficiently processed when there was extensive interaction at lower management levels, and that performance improved during crisis conditions—despite heavier information loads—seemingly due to increased commitment to common values and objectives. A similar study conducted by Ward Edwards at the University of Michigan compares different information-processing techniques for their effectiveness in estimating the probabilities of various occurrences. At the time of this writing, it is too early to report definitive results.

The studies so far discussed in this chapter utilize the man-machine model for studying social system processes and not, as described in Chapter 2, as a complex-environment laboratory for studying human individual behavior. When the man-machine model is so used, the research is focussed on the subject—on how he responds to various stimuli, how his personal characteristics affect his behavior, and how he interacts with his fellows as a function of these variables. Changes in the state of the "machine"—that is, in the state of the system—are interesting to the experimenter only to the degree that they reflect the subject's choices—that is, only insofar as changes in the system constitute data regarding subject behavior—for in this sort of research, the participants are *subjects* as well as game-players.

Some experimenters believe that even if games do not prove to be dependable replicates of social systems, they at least will have fulfilled an important role by serving as complex laboratories in which a wide range of behavioral responses are available to the research subjects. If the philosophy of sciences espoused by Brunswik, Campbell, Crow, and others and briefly set forth in this volume is correct, then such "representative laboratories" make possible more appropriate methods for psychological experimentation and the study of decision-making behavior than does the more traditional, "antiseptic" laboratory setting. As compared to the highly controlled laboratory, the "complex environment" is less likely to elicit stilted behaviors. And likewise, since it more nearly resembles the governmental, business, or other setting to be studied, results can be extrapolated with more confidence.

On the basis of such reasoning, several experiments have been conducted with man-machine games in which the "machine," or simulated system, constitutes the laboratory, and it is the "man" who is studied. I will report a few of these studies to illustrate the kinds of problems that may be addressed. However, because it is my personal opinion that, given its present state of development, the man-machine game is most legitimately and valuably used in this manner, I will devote more space to these experiments than I did to the studies of system processes.

The first studies of this type employed the INS as the laboratory. Michael Driver used ten of Brody's sixteen INS "runs" to study the relation between behavior and a particular aspect of cognitive structure. Using the *Situational Interpretation Test* to measure cognitive complexity, he staffed five replications with "cognitively simple," and five with "cognitively complex" subjects. Driver hypothesized that according to their cognitive structure, the subjects would differentially perceive the complexity of the situation in which they were involved. He also hypothesized that their perceptions of its complexity would vary as a function of the stress level encountered, postulating a U-shaped curve on which perceptions of complexity would be greatest at medium stress-levels, and least at high or low levels. In general, these hypotheses were confirmed. Subjects who scored high on cognitive complexity interpreted simulation events in a more multidimensional way than did the low-scorers, and their perception of multi-dimensionality was enhanced at medium stress levels and dampened at high and low stress levels.[28] In further analysis of these data, Driver found that subjects were more apt to behave aggressively in the simulation when their cognitive complexity was low, regardless of whether it had been induced by high or low stress or was a personality characteristic.[29] A related finding emerged from the Raser and Crow simulations: In two replications of the simulation conducted with Navy recruits drawn from the bottom of their classes, aggressive behavior occurred more frequently than it did in the 12 replications conducted with the top recruits. The differences in aggressiveness appeared to be related to wide differences in intelligence, verbal ability, and general social skills.

In another study involving cognitive structure, Michael J. Shapiro also utilized data from the Brody runs. Shapiro hypothesized that cognitively rigid persons will (1) interpret conflict in moral rather than instrumental terms, and (2) resist attitude change. These hypotheses are drawn from studies of Woodrow Wilson and John Foster Dulles, both of whom are supposed to fit this construct of cognitive rigidity. Participants in the INS were measured for cognitive rigidity with the California F Scale and with the *Situational Interpretation Test* used by

Driver. Extreme moral positions were examined by applying the semantic differential technique to content-analysis of the messages the participants had sent to one another during the course of the game. The findings showed that a moral interpretation of conflict does correlate significantly with cognitive rigidity, but that resistance to attitude-change occurs only among those who score extremely high on the cognitive rigidity measure.[30]

In an INS with Navy Petty Officers as subjects, Margaret G. Hermann studied a model of stress. She hypothesized that (1) the more motivated an individual is to achieve a specific goal, the more negative will be the affect (emotion) he experiences when he perceives it as being threatened; and (2) the more negative the affect he experiences, the greater will be his attempts to cope with it. The second hypotheses was confirmed, but the first was not. She also found that the type and extent of coping behavior were related to the subjects' scores on measures of self-esteem and defensiveness.[31]

James A. Robinson and Alan J. Wyner used the INS to examine two contradictory theories of decision-making. One theory, based on the model of decision-making called *satisficing*, holds that decision-makers search sequentially for alternatives, applying a set of evaluation criteria to each, and discontinue the search as soon as they find an alternative that minimally satisfies these criteria. The other theory, called *maximizing*, assumes that decision-makers continue the search for alternatives until they find the one that *best* meets all the criteria. To test these hypotheses, Robinson and Wyner created a position within the INS framework called "Information Coordinator," whose role is to store and retrieve information. The player filling this office could not enter into the decision processes of the game but could provide information when it was requested by the other decision-makers. The dependent "search" variable was quantified in terms of number of requests for information and extent of search for alternatives. It was found that the data did not clearly substantiate either theory.[32] This challenges the widespread notion that the satisficing theory is more realistic and predictive than the older maximizing theory. Perhaps neither theory adequately describes what actually happens in organizational decision-making. But white-bearded theory can be challenged only with research vehicles that incorporate rich possibilities of action, such as the one used in the study.

My final illustration of an INS-based research project is a study conducted by Kenneth W. Terhune and Joseph Firestone at the Cornell Aeronautical Laboratory in Buffalo, New York. The objective of this study was to examine the effects of group motives on intergroup conflict and cooperation in the context of simulated international relations. Three experimental "worlds" were constructed, two containing five nations, and one containing six. Each nation was composed of a three-man group, and each group was homogeneously comprised of individuals dominated by the "achievement," "affiliation," or "power" motives, as measured by the McClelland Thematic Apperception Tests. The major hypotheses were: (1) groups composed of "achievement" oriented persons would choose goals of economic prosperity, (2) "affiliators" would seek peace and cooperation, and (3) "power" oriented groups would seek international strength and national sovereignty. In addition to these hypotheses about goals, it was hypothesized that (4) "achievers" would be most cooperative, (5) the "power" oriented would be most conflictive, and (6) "affiliators" would be intermediate. Data consisted of simulation decisions and messages.

The hypotheses regarding goals were moderately supported for the "affiliation" and "power" groups, but not for the "achievement" groups. Partial support was found for the behavioral hypotheses: "achievers" were most likely to initiate cooperation, but they were also high in initiating conflict; "power" groups were moderately cooperative and highly conflictive, whereas "affiliators" were lowest in both cooperation and conflict. Finally, the "power" groups were manipulative and sought military strength, whereas the "affiliators" were generally passive.[33]

For some purposes, the full panoply of an INS is not needed; a game can be constructed almost on the spot, designed to meet the specific purposes at hand. Some elegant research designs have employed such *ad hoc* games. One, a study by Streufert, Suedfeld, and Driver that carries froward Driver's earlier interest in cognitive styles, called for the creation of a game in which teams of subjects had to make decisions regarding the invasion of a mythical island. The decision-making groups, supposedly playing against the island's defenders, were in reality playing against the experimenters. During each period, the players were fed information about the situation and their progress, but the amount of information was varied from period to period. The experimenters hypothesized that differentiation and integration in cognition and behavior would increase with increased information-input until an optimal level of information-processing is reached; then a further increase in information would lead to a decline in information processing. This hypothesis was confirmed; it also was found that subjects who scored high in cognitive complexity were less affected by an increased information load than were the low-scorers.[34]

We will examine one more experiment before turning to the reasons for using man-machine games in research. This study is unique in that it attempts, in one set of three experiments, to define variables and their interaction patterns of interest to the psychologist, to the sociologist, and to the political scientist. In this game, Wayman Crow and Robert Noel investigated whether decision outcomes are affected by (1) the individual psychological characteristics of the subjects (psychological variable), (2) the social context in which the subjects function (organizational variables), and (3) the nature of the situation that confronts the subjects (situational variable). The game was designed to simulate the events leading up to the outbreak of the Mexican-American war, in which Texas finally declared independence and later joined the United States. The decision-makers, members of the government of ALGO (Mexico), faced an insurrection in EAST ALGO (Texas); the situation was such that low-level responses might be inadequate to cope with the insurrection but higher-level responses might lead to outside intervention from UTRO (the United States). The elaborate scenario contained "mother countries" across the oceans, explicit levels of land and navy power, complex maps, a history of irredentism among the militant Utronian minority group in EAST ALGO, and an opening crisis in which troops or volunteers from UTRO were reported to be infiltrating EAST ALGO. The decision-makers, confronted with this situation, were handed bulletins from the "front" and from their advisors, giving periodic accounts of new developments.

To select the participants, Navy enlisted personnel were given psychological tests measuring militarism, nationalism, and propensity for risk taking (the three psychological variables); of those chosen, half had scored in the upper quartile and half in the lower quartile on one of the tests. They were matched in three experiments with three situational variables: (1) the level of Utronian provocation, (2) the probability of winning a war if it occurred, and (3) assessment of the aggressive intentions of UTRO. Those with extremely high or low scores on militarism were matched with the first situational variable, those scoring high or low on nationalism with the second, and those scoring high or low on risk-taking with the third. The participants, grouped in fours, made choices from eleven pre-set response levels representing use of military force, first individually and then collectively (the organization variable).

In the first experiment, only the psychological variable significantly affected response level. In the second experiment, using a different psychological variable, the organizational variable (whether the decision was made alone or as part of a collective group) also affected response-level, and there was interaction between personality and organizational variables. In the third experiment, the individual and situational variables had significant main effects on response level—and there was interaction between "organization" and "situation." High scorers on all the psychological variables chose significantly higher response levels than did low scorers, and in the first two experiments, group-consensus decisions were at lower response levels than were individual decisions. More than half of the subjects, regardless of personality, organization, or situation, chose the response level that the experimenters consider representative of the Mexican government's choice in the historical situation.[35]

This study has two major implications. The first is that decision-making behavior in simulations is more strongly affected by perceptions of the opponent's motives than by his objective actions. The second is that individual personality characteristics play an important part in simulated international decision-making. In fact, this latter finding is characteristic of all the studies just reported. This suggests that as we progress in the development of games, personality characteristics must be taken into consideration in selecting participants.

Man-machine games provide rich laboratories with nearly infinite possibilities for testing hypotheses singly and in combination. As I have indicated, these hypotheses may be germane to system-processes and the relationships among the system's units, or they may be germane to the behavior of the human decision-makers in the system and the relationship between their personal traits and their behavior in such an environment.

A similar kind of *ad hoc* game involving 15 players representing 15 nations has been used by John Baldwin to explore the factors that determine whether a subject will use trade or war to obtain desired goods and attain his ends. Baldwin found that, in general, players tend to operate in terms of their own calculations of self interest, and that "trust" norms develop because players believe that the selflessness and short term losses demanded by "trusting" behavior operate to their long term advantage. As Baldwin points out, this is an empirical demonstration of why Hobbes' hypothetical "war of all against all" gives way to the development of cooperative norms.[36]

It should be evident how the outcomes of complex-environment games can give rise to new hypotheses, how detailed analysis of results can suggest new sets of assumptions, and how these assumptions can be incorporated in new, "improved" versions of the game from which they were derived, or introduced in other games. Gradually, small portions of the enormously complex social-behavioral pattern come into clearer focus; bits and pieces are tested for fit. Even though we cannot freely generalize our simulation findings to the real world, they give us clues about processes that may be operating in the real world, about phenomena whose existence may be obscured by the multidimensional complexity of the macrocosm. In essence, this is why the use of these games as research instruments is increasingly widespread. The best way to illuminate the usefulness of man-machine simulations is to use the words of their practitioners.

I have suggested:

> Simulation studies are an attempt to fill a gap in social science research methods. One method is the simple laboratory study, in which all variables but one are held constant, some manipulation is made, and outcome behaviors are studied. A familiar current example of such research, which scholars hope will have relevance to international relations, is the experimentation with "Prisoner's Dilemma" and other two person games played with a simple pay-off matrix. While the simplicity of design yields precision and control, findings do not usually hold up in the complex social situations in which one is interested. Another

> kind of research is carried out in the field; surveys are taken, groups observed, or historical cases analyzed. But here the problems of data control and nonreproducibility become crucial. The experimenter cannot keep track of the possibly relevant variables; they are lost in the complex setting. Simulations provide a way of meeting some of these deficiencies: subjects can be placed in a complex but controlled environment in which the impact of the variables can be traced; several variables can be manipulated and the rich data can be preserved; moreover such studies can be replicated as often as desired. Scientific progress has usually been purchased by narrow encapsulation, at the expense of scope. Simulations are an effort to escape this traditional dilemma.[37]

Several contributors to Harold Guetzkow's early book of readings on social science simulation give their individual versions of why simulations are useful in research. Richard E. Dawson argues:

> One of the most significant advantages of simulation is that it permits the experimenter to study process in ways that nature prohibits. The simulation can be run many times with the values of the parameters being modified between runs and the changes in outputs observed. This makes possible the effective study of operating models containing many different components, variables and interrelationships. The experimenter, in short, exercises a great amount of control through which he can study and evaluate outcomes resulting from a variety of alternative conditions and relationships. Conway, Johnson and Maxwell sum up this advantage: "Simulation is often described as a means of incorporating a fourth dimension—time—in what have previously of necessity been static methods of analysis." (R. W. Conway, B. M. Johnson and W. L. Maxwell, "Some Problems of Digital Systems Simulation," *Management Science* VI, No. 1, 1959, p. 95.)
>
> Simulation also permits the researcher, teacher or trainer to compress or expand real time. He can simulate the operations of a system over a period of years in a matter of minutes, or he can slow down the process so that he can more carefully analyze or demonstrate what is going on in specific areas. In other situations the simulation can be used to reproduce real time.
>
> Experimenting with a simulated system, instead of the real system, permits the social scientist to study problems that would be impractical or altogether impossible to study in real life. It is impossible for a political scientist studying international relations to experiment with the real-nation system of decision-makers, capabilities and organizations, manipulating variables like nuclear weapons to see what results such changes might have on international tensions. However, when significant aspects of the inter-nation system are simulated by physical analogs, mathematical formulas and/or human decision-makers the variables in the model can be manipulated and properties concerning the real system may be useful in the social sciences because moral and physical factors often prohibit experimenting with real people and real social systems. . . .
>
> Many simulation processes are relatively free from complex mathematics, making them more widely comprehensible than other more

> complex systems of formal mathematical analysis. The lack of dependency upon complex mathematical analysis not only has the advantage of making simulation comprehensible to the mathematically unsophisticated, but it can also be used in studying situations where mathematical methods capable of considering all of the desired factors are not available.[38]

Morris Zelditch, Jr., and William Evan use simulation to study bureaucracy. Their comments, however, apply not only to bureaucratic studies, but also to the whole range of social phenomena.

> The natural world has certain disadvantages from the point of view of observation and theory construction. Certain states of great theoretical interest occur quite rarely, while other states, of little theoretical interest, occur profusely. Certain effects of great theoretical interest are obscured by other effects which are, although powerful, of little interest. And there are always more relevant variables than any observer of any theory could conceivably take into account at one time. Through simulation, such processes may be simplified, measured, and manipulated, so that rare states may be created, reasonably exact replicates ensured, necessary contrasts obtained, confounding factors randomized, extraneous disturbances eliminated, and the process observed comprehensively, precisely, and more or less at the will of the investigator.
>
> **RARE STATES**
>
> Where a variable's natural range of variation is narrow it is difficult to investigate its effects. It will appear uncorrelated with other variables and may even seem irrelevant to a system of variables in which, in fact, it plays an important part. The same thing can be said for states that are not so much rare as costly or destructive, such as war. . . . A very important example of a rare state arises when the effect of *a* on *b* is lagged, but the process is, in natural settings, usually found in an advanced stage of progress so that it is difficult to investigate how *a*'s effect on *b* comes about. This is often true of the process by which social structures are built up. To study such states simulation seems a necessary strategy.
>
> **REPLICATES**
>
> Where relatively unique structures are investigated, or where very few of them exist, it is useful to simulate them so that many and exact replicates are provided for investigation. For example, there is only one system of international relations, and even its components are relatively few in number, complex, large, freely varying. . . .
>
> **CONTRASTS**
>
> The classic *ex post facto* method of dealing with contamination is to hold constant the contaminating factor, c. But where a and c, or *b* and c, are highly correlated in natural settings, obtaining a sufficient number of the necessary contrasts may be costly or even impossible. In such a case it may be useful or necessary to create the required contrasts

artificially. The contaminant may be a *cancelling* factor, the effects of which run counter to the effect of *a*; an additive factor, independent of *a* but obscuring the relative importance of *a*; an irrelevant factor, unrelated to *b* but highly correlated with *a* so that the package *ac* requires purification; or a *confounding* factor, spuriously generating the correlation between *a* and *b*. The first three effects may be investigated by the usual methods of field studies and surveys if appropriate contrasts are available; but sometimes, perhaps often, they are not. The effects of confounding are never entirely controlled by investigations in natural settings, since randomization is the only (relative) safeguard against the indefinitely large number of relevant factors of which we are, at any moment, quite ignorant.

**DISTURBANCE AND COMPLEXITY**

The real world is intricate, entangled, continuously varying. It is virtually impossible to study all variables at once; it is equally impossible to study a small subset of them while these are continuously altered by the effects of some larger set. The subset may in fact appear to be entirely without regularity if the variables in the "external" set are not held constant. *Simplification* reduces the number of variables, and often their permissible values; *isolation* removes the investigated system from the effects of a varying environment. Isolation may be accomplished *ex post facto*, just as the control of other factors that can be so controlled and, like confounding factors, their number if indefinitely large and our own knowledge of them is limited.

**OBSERVATION**

A simulate is usually small by comparison with the real system it represents; it can be instrumented at will; and its processes can be started, and often even stopped, at will. These properties make it readily observable. Because of them simulation is often convenient and useful even where none of the previous functions is served. Of these properties, optional starting is perhaps the most useful. Complete investigation of a response curve is facilitated if one is able to vary the initial states at will; and complete investigation of a correlation is facilitated if one is able to reverse the relations of variables at will. It is particularly an advantage where the effect in which we are interested occurs in a very brief period of time or in minute magnitudes, and repetition is consequently a great help.[39]

Zelditch and Evan are primarily interested in researching the characteristics of formal organizations, whereas Richard Snyder is concerned with international relations and explores the usefulness of simulation in this field:

In addition to its values in permitting direct observation, thereby decreasing the rigidity with which social systems are perceived, simulation allows penetration of systems which seem hopelessly complex. It perhaps will permit analysis of change, specification of the interrelations of quantifiable and qualitative variables, and the exploration of linkages between levels of analysis. Consider an example of each of these potential utilizations from the field of international relations, with all its complexity in this order:

First, both as a matter of policy and as a matter of explanation and prediction, the impact of technological developments on foreign policy and on the stability of strategic deterrence is not completely understood. No adequate definition of the problem is commonly accepted. What are the consequences of the rate and direction of growth of the science and technology of weapons and industrial productivity? What are the consequences of different rates of growth among national antagonists? What are the effects of estimated projections of technological change on current decisions and planning? As a supplement to other kinds of study, the simulation technique appears to offer an immediate and economical way of identifying more precisely a likely range of implications of basic changes in one significant set of variables. . . .

Second, what are the interrelations of political and military factors—of hard and soft variables? More specifically, how (if at all) do weapons systems condition political choices? What is the perceived significance of certain weapons and their deployment in a certain fashion? Is an arms race a vicious circle of hardware production with its own internal logic, or is it a problem of perception, expectation and risk-taking by political elites, or a mixture of these? . . . variation under controlled conditions might illuminate a cycle of changing relationships between hardware and nonhardware factors in which rational decisions at one stage lead to irrational bases of choice at the next stage.

Third, at the nexus of unit (society, nation) characteristics and actions on the one hand, and interunit (intersocietal, international) interactions on the other, lies (we all strongly suspect) a set of crucial empirical and theoretical relationships. Most propositions concern either of these two levels of analysis. Few specify interrelationships. There is perhaps more than an interesting parallel between these two levels in inter-nation relations and the two levels present in group experiments: the objective (observer-oriented) and the subjective (actor-oriented) structures; the internal (perceived) and external (observed) structures. The interlevel problem here is no less complex, as perceptual discrepancies among group members and as hidden but embarrassing discrepancies between observer's construed structure and actors' perceived structure amply demonstrate. As already noted, however, in the experimental situation it is possible to collect data on the ways both levels are perceived by the actors, as well as on observer-actor differences in perception. Furthermore, surface parallels of another sort may be suggestive, namely, the conflict between private (individual) and collective (group) aspirations and between official and secret value systems.[40]

The final quotation is a recent observation by Sidney Verba, who, like Snyder, is chiefly interested in the use of simulations for political research:

. . . of what use are these data gathered from a simulated world? We may have information that particular actors in a contrived model of the international system behaved in a certain way—they went to war, they formed alliances, they were overthrown in a revolution. But why go to all that trouble to collect data about an unimportant world that exists within the confines of a simulation laboratory? In some sense, this is the crucial question about the uses of simulation research.

To answer this question we have to look first at the kinds of data that are generated in simulations. The data thus generated differ from those generated by real political events in several important ways. In the first place, one can generate in a simulation study data about certain kinds of situations that happen rarely in the real world, or perhaps that have not happened yet. One of the problems in carrying on research in the real political world is that some of the situations one wants to explain happen so infrequently that one cannot obtain enough cases to allow the development of generalizations. In a simulation study, one can replicate some of these rare events and run the simulation over and over again as long as the researcher's funds and patience hold out. One can repeatedly simulate particular types of international system of which there are few historical examples, or even the outbreak of a world war. Or one can simulate events that have not yet taken place—such as international conflict in a multinuclear world, or, as Brody has done, the spread of nuclear weapons. Thus, while such techniques as survey research or content analysis have given us relatively precise methods of dealing with political events that occur in great numbers—voting decisions, attitude changes, symbol manipulations—simulation techniques may be most crucial for macro-political phenomena that occur less frequently. Thus, for example, simulation techniques have been used to deal with the macro-phenomenon of electoral outcome. Whereas survey studies provide a wide range of data on individual voting decisions, the study of the electoral system on the macro-level involves different problems; and several attempts to apply simulation techniques to these problems suggest that this may be a fruitful approach. . . .

Another difference between simulation data and real-world data is that the former are clearer and simpler. There is less going on in a simulation than in the real world, and what is going on is under greater control. Suppose one wants to observe the reactions of the decision-makers in one nation to the actions of another nation in the real world. The very identification of the decision-makers is difficult, as is the observation of their behavior. Furthermore, they are involved in so many complex interactions at the same time that one cannot be sure they are reacting to the particular stimulus one has in mind. In the simulation, on the other hand, where the flow of interactions is more limited and under control, one can obtain more unambiguous results. Furthermore, data generated in a simulation can be observed more carefully and precisely. One has almost total access to the history of the simulated world, one can measure attitudes, record conversations, and monitor messages at will. And since the number of actors involved is limited and clearly specifiable, one can record an almost total history.

Most useful of all may be the possibility of compressing time. Single sessions of the simulation may be made to represent periods of time from a few days to a few years. And time is a valuable commodity for the researcher. Studies of attitude formation or political socialization ideally ought to involve the observation of individuals' life his-

> tories; but, as has been said, to study a life history takes a lifetime. In international relations, the researcher may be interested in patterns of alliance formation or disintegration that take quite a long time to develop. In relations to the practical questions of policy, he may want to project swiftly into the future before the future arrives—to analyze, for instance, the implications of nuclear proliferation before that happens. The simulations can allow a condensation of time in this respect—subjects can play out the events of a year in a short period of time. The researcher has the world of his simulation in his grasp in a way not available for the researcher who works on the real political world.
>
> The various studies carried on with the Inter-Nation Simulation exhibit these advantages. The patterns of alliance formation are clear; the motivations for the formation and disintegration of alliances are also clear. The participants are given a variety of tests to tap their attitudes at various points in the simulation; the message flow among the nations is recorded and subjected to content analysis; and the participants are asked to write historical accounts explaining their actions. The simulator has complete access to data on the state of the domestic economy and politics of the various simulated nations—and since these are simplified and stylized economies and politics, such data are manageable. The more policy-oriented studies using the simulation project their international systems well into the future, thus taking advantage of the ability to compress time. And, above all, the various measurements and observations can be taken repeatedly and with careful concern for time sequence. One can gather a complete account of the way in which the system changes over time, and of the sequence in which various aspects change.[41]

It is surely time to try to summarize what these men are saying and to extract the basic arguments. In selecting the examples of research I offered in this chapter, I tried to illustrate the arguments of the scholars quoted above. These arguments in favor of using man-machine games for research in the social sciences can be summarized as follows:

1. Man-machine games provide a laboratory midway in complexity between the traditional setting, in which all variables but one are held constant, and the bewildering and convoluted labyrinth of the real world. Thus, they enable experimenters to use "representative design" in their settings without losing control of the environment.
2. Man-machine games permit repeated replications, and experimenter-controlled manipulations of starting parameters and other variables of interest.
3. They permit time compression or expansion; this enables execution of studies otherwise impossible, either because they would take too long or because the phenomenon under study is too fleeting.
4. They permit reduction in the number of variables that must be considered; this gives the experimenter increased control of the processes as they occur, and renders them more visible.
5. They permit multiple methods of data gathering, which may be employed simultaneously and used as checks against one another. For example, one can compare subject's responses to questionnaires

with content-analysis of the messages they write to determine inter-method reliability. Thus, man-machine games provide a vehicle for methodological innovation and improvement.

6. They permit the study of processes that cannot be investigated in nature, either because they are too rare, too dangerous, inaccessible, or because they have not yet occurred.
7. They are relatively free of complex mathematics, since many of the properties often dealt with mathematically are displayed in other ways that are more easily observed by the mathematically unsophisticated.
8. By permitting the free fluctuation of many variables at once, man-machine games permit interaction effects to be explored in ways impossible in highly controlled experiments.
9. They allow us to study behavior directly instead of merely studying attitudes or second-hand reports of behavior.
10. They provide a vehicle for studying the nexus between the individual and society, and between individuals or groups and the "hardware" aspects of a social system.
11. Finally, games may be started and stopped at will; this enables the experimenter to begin where he wishes, and to alter conditions where appropriate.

Some of the above statements apply, of course, to all-computer simulations, and others apply to two-person games. But the primary advantage of man-machine games over the other two types lies in this: because the structure of the two-person game is highly programmed, it can generally be used *only* to study individual human behavior; because the all-computer game must employ programmed assumptions about behavior, it can be used *only* to study system behavior; but the man-machine game can be used to study both individual and system behavior as well as individual-system interaction.

In this chapter, I have presented the types of games used in social sciences research, given examples of research conducted with each, and shown why each type is considered a useful research technique for certain kinds of problems. In the next chapter, I will turn to games as teaching and training devices, again giving examples of different uses and explanations of why given types of games are used for various purposes.

## FOOTNOTES

1. Bernard S. Phillips, *Social Research: Strategy and Tactics* (New York: The Macmillan Company, 1966), p. 152.

2. For a sobering account of the dynamics involved in such a scenario,

see Louis Ridenour, "Pilot Lights of the Apocalypse: A Playlet in One Act," *Fortune*, XXXIII (1946), 116.

3. Anatol Rapoport and Carol Orwant reviewed what they believed to be *all* the research in the field in 1962 (Rapoport and Orwant, *op. cit.*), covering thirty games. Since that time, *Behavioral Science* has carried reports of further experiments in almost every issue, the *Journal of Conflict Resolution* has included a Gaming section that usually reports three or four studies with such games, and other social science professional journals frequently carry reports of experiments with these games. In Anatol Rapoport and Melvin Guyer, "A Taxonomy of 2 x 2 Games," *Peace Research Society (International) Papers*, VI (1967), 11–26, Rapoport and Guyer list 78 such games falling into 14 different categories of equilibria—a listing that they believe to exhaust all possibilities.

4. Roger L. Sisson and Russell L. Ackoff, "Toward a Theory of the Dynamics of Conflict" (Philadelphia: University of Pennsylvania Management Science Center, n.d., mimeographed).

5. Morton A. Kaplan, A. L. Burns, and Richard E. Quandt, "Theoretical Analysis of Balance of Power," *Behavioral Science*, V, No. 3 (1960), 240–52.

6. Morton Deutsch, Yakov Epstein, Donnah Canavan, and Peter Gumpert, "Strategies of Inducing Cooperation: An Experimental Study," *Journal of Conflict Resolution*, XI, No. 3 (1967), 345–60.

7. Ithiel de Sola Pool, "Simulating Social Systems," *International Science and Technology*, XXVII (1964), 62–71.

8. Norman H. Jennings and Justin H. Dickens, "Computer Simulation of Peak Hour Operations in a Bus Terminal," in Guetzkow, 1962, *op. cit.*, pp. 151–65.

9. *Ibid.*, pp. 153–4.

10. Orcutt, *et al.*, *op. cit.*

11. G. H. Orcutt, "Simulation of Economic Systems," in Guetzkow, 1962, *op. cit.*, p. 95.

12. John T. and Jeanne E. Gullahorn, *op. cit.*

13. Michael J. Shapiro, "The House and the Federal Role: A Computer Simulation of Role Call Voting" (Evanston: Northwestern University, Ph.D. dissertation, 1966); Cleo H. Cherryholmes, "The House of Representatives and Foreign Affairs: A Computer Simulation of Roll Call Voting" (Evanston: Northwestern University, Ph.D. dissertation, 1966).

14. J. David Singer and Hirohide Hinomoto, "Inspecting for Weapons Production: A Modest Computer Simulation," *Journal of Peace Research*, II, No. 1 (1965), 18–38.

15. Orcutt, *et al.*, *op. cit.*, pp. 9–10.

16. Robert L. Chapman, J. L. Kennedy, Allen Newell, and William C. Biel, "The Systems Research Laboratory's Air-Defense Experiments," in Guetzkow, 1962, *op. cit.*, pp. 172–88.

17. H. Wallace Sinaiko and Glen P. Cartwright, *Careful: A Pilot Study of the Effects of Heavy Target Load on Human and Automatic Decision-Makers*, Coordinated Science Lab Report, No. R-115, 1959, p. 35.

18. Murray A. Geisler, "The Simulation of a Large-Scale Military Activity," *Management Science*, V, No. 4 (1959), 359–69.

19. ROBERT BOGUSLAW, ROBERT DAVIS, and EDWARD B. GLICK, *op. cit.*

20. RICHARD A. BRODY, *op. cit.*

21. RICHARD A. BRODY, ALEXANDRA H. BENHAM, and JEFFREY S. MILSTEIN, "Hostile International Communication, Arms Production, and Perception of Threat: A Simulation Study" (Stanford, California: Institute of Political Studies, July 1966).

22. JOHN R. RASER and WAYMAN J. CROW, *Winsafe II, op. cit.*

23. WAYMAN J. CROW and JOHN R. RASER, "A Cross-Cultural Simulation Study" (La Jolla, California: Western Behavioral Sciences Institute, November 1964, mimeographed).

24. CHARLES OSGOOD, *An Alternative to War or Surrender* (Urbana, Illinois: Illini Books, 1962); WAYMAN J. CROW and LAWRENCE SOLOMON, "A Simulation Study of Strategic Doctrines" (La Jolla, California: Western Behavioral Sciences Institute, 1962, mimeographed).

25. JAMES A. ROBINSON, *op. cit.*; and CHARLES HERMANN, "Crises in Foreign Policy Decision-Making: A Simulation of International Politics" (Princeton: Princeton University, April 1965, mimeographed).

26. PHILIP M. BURGESS, "Memorandum re Simulation Project—OSU/INS/03 of JAMES ROBINSON, PHILIP BURGESS, and EDWARD FEDDER" (Columbus: Ohio State University, March 1966, mimeographed).

27. BEATRICE ROME and SIDNEY ROME, "Communication and Large Organization" (Santa Monica, California: Systems Development Corporation, SP 1690/000/000, September 1964).

28. MICHAEL DRIVER, "The Perception of Simulated Nations: A Multi-Dimensional Analysis of Social Perception as Affected by Situational Stress and Characteristic Levels of Cognitive Complexity in Perceivers" (Ph.D. dissertation, Princeton University, 1962).

29. MICHAEL DRIVER, "A Structural Analysis of Aggression, Stress, and Personality in an Inter-Nation Simulation" (Lafayette, Indiana: Purdue University, June 1966, multilith).

30. MICHAEL SHAPIRO, "Cognitive Rigidity and Perceptual Orientation in an Inter-Nation Simulation" (Evanston: Northwestern University, April 1966, mimeographed).

31. MARGARET HERMANN, *Stress, Self-Esteem and Defensiveness in an Inter-Nation Simulation* (China Lake, California: Project Michelson, U.S. Naval Ordnance Test Station, April 1965).

32. JAMES A. ROBINSON and ALAN J. WYNER, "Information Storage and Search in an Inter-Nation Simulation" (Columbus: Ohio State University, May 1965, mimeographed).

33. KENNETH TERHUNE and JOSEPH M. FIRESTONE, *Psychological Studies in Social Interaction and Motives (SIAM) Phase 2: Group Motives in an International Relations Game*, CAL Report No. VX-20 18-G-2 (Buffalo: Cornell Aeronautical Laboratory, Inc., March 1967).

34. SIEGFRIED STREUFERT, PETER SUEDFELD, and MICHAEL J. DRIVER, "Conceptual Structure, Information Search, and Information Utilization," *Journal of Personality and Social Psychology*, II, No. 5 (1965), 736–40.

35. WAYMAN J. CROW and ROBERT NOEL, *op. cit.*

36. JOHN BALDWIN, "The Economics of Peace and War: A Simulation," *Journal of Conflict Resolution*, XI, No. 4 (1967), 383–97.

37. JOHN R. RASER, "Cross Cultural Simulation Research," *Journal Internationale de Psychologie*, II, No. 1 (1967), 59–68.

38. DAWSON, *op. cit.*, pp. 12–13.

39. MORRIS ZELDITCH, JR. and WILLIAM EVAN, "Simulated Bureaucracies: A Methodological Analysis," in GUETZKOW, 1962, *op. cit.*, pp. 48–60.

40. RICHARD SNYDER, "Some Perspectives on the Use of Experimental Techniques in the Study of International Relations," in GUETZKOW, *et al.*, 1963, *op. cit.*, pp. 9–10.

41. SIDNEY VERBA, *op. cit.*, pp. 499–501.

# 6

# GAMES FOR TEACHING

In twenty years as a student of international relations there is just one thing I've learned with absolute certainty. You can't trust the Algonians!

Professor after participating in an Inter-Nation Simulation

In the past decade, there has been widespread disillusionment with traditional teaching methods. Educators are distressed by the apathy and boredom of so many students, and by the increasing numbers who drop out of the educational system, apparently because their school seems irrelevant to the issues they face. Social and political theorists, finding that large portions of the adult population are similarly apathetic and alienated, speculate that their educational experiences have improperly prepared them for the world they live in. On all sides, there is growing realization that the world of tomorrow will be characterized by ever-accelerating change, by an explosion of knowledge, and by a transformation of the technological and social environment, and that much of what students learn in school is likely to be outdated by the time they attempt to apply it. Scholars such as Marshall McLuhan suggest that the nature of consciousness is changing as a function of technology, and that in the future, each generation will be so different from the preceding one that the transmission of concepts between generations will be almost impossible.

These concerns about the future have added new and more serious questions to those already raised about the value of present curricula and the efficacy of instructional techniques. Some educational theorists suggest that our approach to education should be radically changed, and that we should begin to seek new goals for education by asking such questions as: What are people like? How do they learn? What will the world be like in the future? What personal qualities will people need if they are to thrive in such a world? What educational experiences should be provided now to help them develop those qualities?[1] Other theorists, assuming that they know the answers to the first four questions, have focussed on providing more appropriate educational experiences based on new concepts and goals. The three most frequently recommended concepts point directly to gaming as an instructional technique.

According to one concept, the mind should be viewed as an instrument to be honed or tuned, rather than as a bin to be filled. The goal of education should be to develop the learners, not to create "the learned."

A second and related concept suggests that the emphasis in education should be on engagement. If an environment can be created that will open the mind, stimulate inquiry, arouse curiosity, and provide resources for finding answers, the task will have been accomplished. To the maxim "You can lead a horse to water but you can't make him drink," proponents of this concept add that you need only make the horse thirsty; he will then find the water for himself and drink deeply. They also emphasize that because human beings are so complex, no real learning will take place unless all aspects of the personality can be engaged by the educational process. The target of education cannot be merely "the mind"; the whole person must be involved.

The third concept of education is specifically future-oriented. Its proponents argue that in the automated, cybernated world of the future, knowledge of complex systems will be more important and relevant than specialized skills or expertise in a single subject. Students therefore must learn to think in terms of "system," to grasp the interconnections among elements, to understand information flow and developmental constructs; in short, to see the world in terms of dynamic process, not as a series of static "events."

Perhaps you already see how gaming might be appropriate to these educational concepts and might contribute to its goals. For gaming is, in essence, a process of learning to learn, of developing skills that increase one's ability to learn new facts and skills. Nearly everyone who has played or administered games reports that gaming creates intense engagement and unusual excitement about the learning process. To a remarkable degree, gaming focuses on process and system behavior, rather than on the accumulation of detailed bits of knowledge.

These and other benefits are affirmed for the classroom use of games. For example, in a survey of the use of the INS at the college level, Chadwick Alger has summarized the advantages claimed for gaming as a teaching technique:

1. Simulation (or gaming) heightens the interest and motivation of students in several ways. It is stimulating, involving, provides a shared experience as a basis for later discussions, and is a catalytic agent, providing students with objectives for sharing background information.
2. Simulation offers an opportunity for applying and testing knowledge gained from reading and other experiences.
3. Participation (as a decision-maker, for example) gives the student insight, empathy, and a greater understanding of the world as seen and experienced by real decision-makers.
4. Most simulations provide a simplified "world" that is easier for the participant to comprehend as a whole than are the real institutions being represented.[2]

Relevant to the "real life" quality of the gaming experience, William James asserted that learning does not take place until the student translates what he has received into his own action. Snyder goes on to say that gaming, in its several varieties,

> offers an opportunity to play out a strategy over a period of time and to observe concrete consequences of decision. Moreover, the importance of theory is easier to demonstrate when a system is actually in operation. The degree of transferability of experience will depend heavily on the particular domain of social behavior, on the state of research and theory, and on the sophistication with which games are designed. But the explicitness required by calculations, decisions, and actions that characterize business and political gaming is usually missing in reading a case study or listening to a lecture.
>
> . . . Much student apathy concerning politics and national issues may be due to the relatively long postponement of adult roles and to the presentation of abstractions or facts that are outside the student's real life experience. On the basis of trials in a small number of colleges and high schools, reactions of students and teachers suggest that social sciences may be developing in simulation a most effective means of bringing distant policy realism within the individual's personal experience in a manner which cannot be matched by other teaching materials.[3]

Erving Goffman suggests what might seem a contradictory argument for the use of simulations—their simplifications of real life:

> Games seem to display in a simple way the structure of real-life situations. They cut us off from serious life by immersing us in a demonstration of its possibilities. We return to the world as gamesmen, preparing to see what is structural about reality and ready to reduce life to its liveliest elements.[4]

The two views, however, are not contradictory. In effect, Snyder is saying that experience is the best teacher; whereas Goffman is saying that the simplification and abstraction of the game enables the gamer to stand back and discover the underlying structure of every day social activities.

Discussing the use of games in teaching international politics, Thomas Schelling suggests that they not only awaken the student to the complexities of the international system, but also sharpen his analytic skills.

> The game may be organized . . . to give students vicarious experience in the complexities of international politics.
>
> And *complexities* are precisely what the game usually generates. Games organized for the benefit of students are invariably reported as having opened their eyes, in an unprecedented way, to the varieties of choice that can confront nations, to the varieties of interpretation that can be put on a country's behavior, to the great cloak of detail that surrounds even the simplest international crisis, and to the limitations of formal theory as a guide to international conduct in the real world.

These complexities motivate, too, the games organized to examine a problem rather than to raise the sophistication of a student; part of the rationale of game organization is that no straightforward analytical process will generate a "solution" to the problem, predict an outcome, or produce a comprehensive map of the alternative routes, processes, and outcomes that are latent in the problem.[5]

Even though I could cite hundreds of similar plaudits on the value of games as teaching tools, I will end this portion of the chapter with a statement from James C. Coleman's introduction to two special issues of *American Behavioral Scientist* on the use of games in teaching. Note, incidentally, what Coleman implies about the importance of play as a way of simplification and of intensifying one's interactions with an all-too complex environment.

A game—nearly any game, not merely those termed "simulation games"—constitutes a kind of caricature of social life. It is a magnification of some aspect of social interaction, excluding all else, tearing this aspect of social interaction from its social context and giving it a special context of its own. . . . A boxing or wrestling match abstracts from its context the direct physical violence that resides in social life and recreates this violence under a set of explicit rules. When I was a boy in the midwest cornhusking contests abstracted one activity from the life of farmers, established a set of rules, and gave this activity a temporary but central position for the participants.

This unique relation of games to life can be seen even better in other ways. The informal games of young children appear to be crucial means for learning about life and experimenting with life. One of the most perceptive students of the social and intellectual development of young children, Jean Piaget, has observed this development in the simple games children play, such as the game of marbles. It appears that for children, games are more than a caricature of life; they are an introduction to life—an introduction to the idea of rules, which are imposed on all alike, an introduction to the idea of playing under different sets of rules, that is, the idea of different roles, an introduction to the idea of aiding another person and of knowing that one can expect aid from another, an introduction to the idea of working toward a collective goal and investing one's self in a collectivity larger than himself. It appears that games serve, for the young child, all these functions as an introduction to life . . .

But beyond this there are certain special characteristics to the games described in this issue, and to the games that sociologists find of particular interest. Some games involve the interaction of a player with his physical environment, for example a maze or a jig-saw puzzle, or block puzzles, or a cornhusking contest, or a pole vault. These games abstract from life either certain physical skills or certain intellectual skills of inference from physical evidence. Other games such as number puzzles or crossword puzzles involve interaction with a symbolic environment, in these two instances an environment of numbers and an environment of language.

Such abstractions of activities from life hold some interest for the sociologist, but much less interest than another class of games which abstract from life some elements of social relations or social organization. Many games incorporate some aspects of such relations, but a few games incorporate enough such relations that a special term has been used to describe them: social simulation games. Such games pluck out of social life generally (including economic, political and business life) a circumscribed arena, and attempt to reconstruct the principal rules by which behavior in this arena is governed and the principal rewards that it holds for the participants. Such a game both in its construction and in its playing then becomes of extreme interest to the student of social organization. For from it he may learn about those problems of social relations that are his central concern. The game may provide for him that degree of abstraction from life and simplification of life that allows him to understand better certain fundamentals of social organization.

It is this, then, that makes the sociologist fascinated with a certain kind of game—the possibility of learning from this caricature of social relations about those social relations themselves.[6]

In the preceding two chapters, I discussed the enthusiasm engendered by the use of gaming in theory building and research, and concluded that this enthusiasm is largely justified. For many, the use of gaming as a teaching device has generated equal enthusiasm. But is it equally justified? I will deal with this question in the rest of the chapter, first examining in some detail the pedagogical uses of gaming, and then evaluating them. As before, I will select only a few illustrative examples from the hundreds available.

Games are used primarily for one of three educational purposes: to teach specific skills to trainees; to educate students in schools; and to solve practical problems. Simulations and games are used in skill-training if the skill to be acquired is quite explicit and if measures of skill-level are relatively objective. Examples include the flight simulator for training prospective pilots, anatomical simulations for training medical students to identify various bodily functions, and weaponry-target simulations for teaching heavy gunnery skills to military recruits. Such training techniques have proved highly effective; indeed, their usefulness is unquestioned. No one would think of putting a neophyte pilot in a multi-million dollar jet and trusting to luck. A medical student does not have unlimited access to cadavers, no matter how many persons will their bodies to science. Inexperienced gunners cannot learn to hit a target by reading books or listening to lectures. The acquisition of any skill requires *practice*, and if practice is not feasible in the real environment, simulations are the obvious answer. However, because this use of simulations is so well established, because its value is nearly axiomatic, and because it has little relevance to social sciences education, we will not dwell on it further.

The other two uses of simulations are intended to teach students about social processes; the uses differ only as to the kinds of students involved—those in the formal educational system, from kindergarten through graduate school, and adult policy-makers or administrators in business or government who come together to play a game designed to help them gain better understanding of their problems. We will deal with each use in turn.

## GAMES IN SCHOOLS

A fascinating aspect of using games in a school system is that often the same game can be played profitably by students of almost any age—from third graders to graduate students! Many games that operate on a very simple level and are appropriate for ten year olds also incorporate enough richness and diversity to challenge professionals. Almost every game I shall discuss is of this type; in fact, several of them have been used across the entire grade-spectrum.

This quality gives the games greater flexibility in use—that is, they are less sensitive to problems of "grading," as compared to conventional materials, and therefore need not be geared as carefully to a particular grade, age, or intelligence level. The extent of the detail, complexity, and richness that can be mined from a game depends on the student himself, not on the success of a curricular specialist in finding a common denominator for a particular group. Thus, such games are a form of individualized instruction not dissimilar to programmed learning materials or individual computer-assisted instruction. Indeed, the creators of two games, in which a computer provides the environment within which the student plays a role, argue for their efficacy on these grounds.

> Perhaps the greatest potential virtue of combining simulations as a method and computer-based technology as a medium is its ability to provide *individualized instruction*. Unlike the typical classroom situation in which groups of students are training at a fixed rate with no particular attention to differences in abilities and interests, the computer games developed at BOCES* allow in particular for:
>
> 1. *Variation in pace*. Students proceed at their own pace, so that they are neither held back nor forced to keep up with other students.
> 2. *Variation in scope*. The segments presented to the students were of differing length, depending on the student's previous success in the game.[7]

One game teaches elementary students about the transition from nomadic hunting cultures to agricultural communities; the other simulates

* Board of Cooperative Educational Services, located in Westchester County, New York.

the economic problems of an industrializing nation. The following description gives an idea of the approach used.

> The first of the games developed at BOCES was the Sumerian Game, designed to teach sixth graders some basic principles of economics as applied to the time of the Neolithic revolution in Mesopotamia. During an introductory programmed tape and slide presentation the child playing the game sees himself as a ruler's son in the city-state of Lagash about 3500 B.C. At the conclusion of this orientation, the rules and the initial economic conditions are given to the child by means of typewriter terminals controlled by the computer. He then assumes the role of Luduga I, priest-ruler of Lagash, and is presented with his first problematic situation: "We have harvested 5,000 bushels of grain to take care of 500 people. How much of this grain shall be set aside for the next season's planting, and how much will be stored in the warehouse? The remainder will be given to the people to eat."
>
> The child makes decisions and enters his answers at the computer terminal. The computer immediately returns a progress report, including the harvest reaped from the seed grain set aside for planting, a verbal description of the standard of living, and a report on his inventory. This kind of problem is repeated throughout the entire game, each harvest representing six months in the life of a ruler. As the game progresses, it becomes more complicated: the ruler must take into account a changing population, and is also faced with the problem of expansion, which entails the acquisition of new land and irrigation. At intervals the ruler is presented with technological innovations and disasters which alter the outcomes of his decisions.
>
> The rule of the first Luduga is devoted to the solution of problems pertaining to an agricultural economy. In the second phase of the game the child, as Luduga II, is given the opportunity to apply his surplus grain to the development of crafts. In the third and final stage he is introduced to trade and the more complex problems which confront a changing economy. The rate and trend of development are dependent upon the wisdom of the child's decisions.[8]

The classroom use of computer-based (or "man-machine") games has been rare, however, partly due to the technological requirements. More typical have been the "all-man" games employed at M.I.T., the California Institute of Technology, and elsewhere. The M.I.T. games, first used in 1958, often are referred to as "crisis games." In a "crisis game," the students are presented with a short history, assigned roles of real world leaders, then confronted with a crisis. They must try to cope with the crisis by managing their governments, commanding their military forces, and influencing the decision-makers in other countries. There is no formal model; each move is judged for plausibility by a faculty umpire. Crises studied include a succession-crisis in the Polish government, the Berlin crisis, and deterrence issues involving Polaris submarines.[9]

Each winter since 1965, the California Institute of Technology has conducted similar games using the M.I.T. format. Each game embodies a hypothetical crisis in Africa or the Middle East, usually set some months in the future. A faculty team acts as umpires. In the three years since its inception, this game has become a major event on the Cal Tech campus, involving about 100 students and faculty. The game is not played during class periods; instead, an entire weekend is devoted to it, beginning on Friday evening and continuing until Sunday noon; a debriefing period and a discussion session occupies the rest of the final day.

Man-machine games have been widely used in military education. The Strategy and Force Evaluation (SAFE) game developed at RAND as part of their war-gaming activities, and then adapted for training seniors at the Colorado Springs Air Force Academy is illustrative. In the SAFE game, it is assumed that a strategic war will take place either in 1968 or in 1970. The game is played in two stages, "material procurement" beginning in 1961 and "operations." The players have limited funds and resources to prepare for a war, the exact timing and nature of which they don't know. They may invest in research and development and in other risky ventures. Stochastic elements are built into the game. There are no human umpires; the consequences of all decisions are calculated on a computer according to a pre-programmed model.[10] Because the hardware requirements of this game are beyond the resources of most schools and colleges, its use has been limited to the more affluent military establishment.

When man-machine gaming has been used in civilian education, simpler models such as PLANS or INS usually are employed. One of the first major projects was conducted at the Lawrence, Kansas, High School, during 1962–1964, when more than 500 students took part in eight "runs" of an INS-like game.[11] In a later project (Project SIMILE), conducted by the Western Behavioral Sciences Institute under a grant from the Kettering Foundation, a team worked with more than 60 teachers of the San Diego County School system, training them in conducting a variety of social science games appropriate for the classroom—INS, PLANS, a legislative game, a disarmament game, a career-planning game, and several others. The teachers used these games in their courses with varying degrees of success. Some teachers tried them once, then gave them up as too much work and not enough reward; others found the games extremely exciting. In one school, the entire social science curriculum was revamped to center around game building and playing.

An outstanding example of such enthusiastic use of gaming is the Nova Academic Games Project at Nova High School in Fort Lauderdale, Florida. Under a grant from the Ford Foundation, Herbert Karl and Robert Allen have been trying to establish a set of scholastic activities that emphasize academic excellence while maintaining the competitive and status-establishing aspects of sports and other more traditional student activities. The Nova Project also is trying to integrate all subject areas and grade levels in order to develop a single program that meets the educational needs of students classified as "non-motivated," "under-achievers," and "gifted." To accomplish these objectives, a series of games has been inaugurated within a competitive structure comparable to athletics, with intramural and inter-school competition and "Olympic Games." The games include the logic developing game of WFF 'N PROOF, Equations, Allegiance, The Career Game, The Great Game of Legislature, The Presidential Role Game, Propaganda, Eurocard, Structural Linguistics, The Idea Game, The School Budget Game, an Inter-Nation Game, and a Mathematical Golf Game.[12] Venturesome variety indeed!

A less radical but nevertheless audacious project also is underway at the University of Michigan, where William Gamson and Michael Inbar are using games to teach introductory sociology. An entire semester is devoted to gaming, with the students playing the Diplomacy, Legislature and Career games; Schild's Parent-Child and SNOB games; a Disaster game and a basic Interaction game, both designed by Inbar; and Gamson's SIMSOC. Note that several of these games also are being played by elementary and high school students at Nova. However, the University of Michigan students not only play the games, but also are required to criticize the model of social theory embodied in the game, suggest improvements in the model, and, toward the end of the semester, build a game of their own that simulates some social process or sociological theory drawn from such writers as Weber, Pareto, Mosca, Michels, or Parsons.[13]

Such use of gaming is spreading to other countries. I have conducted demonstrations of the Legislature game and the INS with academics from several European countries who are interested in using games for teaching; a teacher at University College, London, England, has been using a simplified international-relations game with students for several years.[14]

Other examples of classroom gaming can be selected at random to give the reader a more complete feeling for their use.

> Mr. Stanley A. Schainker, a teacher at Horton Watkins High School, 1201 S. Warson Road, LaDue, Missouri, is using simulations in American Principles classes dealing with American government, international affairs, and economics. Last spring he used an adaptation of Cleo Cherryholmes' international model, and this year he added James Coleman's Legislature Game and an adaptation of Dale Garvey's Legislative simulation. He has also developed a Political Party Nominating Convention Game and has asked students to build simulations regarding various aspects of consumer spending and investments. He has found that while the students' simulations were "relatively poor," they learned economic concepts and were better able to apply them to

new situations than students learning in the traditional manner. In addition, they appeared to be far more enthusiastic about the subject matter.

Mr. David Yount and Mr. Paul deKock, instructors at El Capitan High School, P.O. Box 698, Lakeside, California 92040, have developed a simulation of the election of 1860 called VOTES, using the format of PLANS, a simulation of pressure group activities. Before the simulation begins, the students study the positions of the opposing political factions on key issues. They then take part in simulated political conventions. The simulation is a major part of an American Studies unit on The Mind of Nineteenth Century Democracy; in another closely related activity in this unit the students write speeches, letters, editorials, diaries, etc., which fit the climate of the times. Pre- and post-tests suggest that the unit is effective in helping students learn historical facts.

Mr. Yount and Mr. deKock are now working on a game involving interactions between special interest groups in suburbia.

An Elementary School Economics Program is being developed by the Industrial Relations Center of the University of Chicago. Programs have already been developed and field tested for the fourth and fifth grades, emphasizing Consumption (4th) and Production (5th). Mr. William D. Rader, Director of Elementary School Social Studies at the Center, plans to incorporate a simulation of a market economy as one of the units of study at the sixth-grade level. The educational objectives of this program emphasize active involvement of students with materials and the inquiry approach to teaching.[15]

For a course in pastoral leadership of a local church, three teaching assistants at San Francisco Theological Seminary, San Anselmo, California—Robert Shukraft, John Moyer, and William Relf—built a model of "Augustine City, New Sylvania," which has eight Presbyterian churches of varying size and kind with ministerial staffs of 2–6 men. Students are given a scenario of the city with its political, social, and economic makeup and sketches of community leaders. As ministers, the participants allocate clergy and lay influence to various areas through "plan sheets" which are then calculated. Crises, such as a flu epidemic or a bus strike, are inserted frequently to emphasize the various interactions and pressures of the professional in a local church.[16]

Mr. Douglas Campbell of the Bloomfield Hills Schools, Bloomfield Hills, Michigan, reports that their new high school will have a political science game room. They are interested particularly in games which illustrate a basic principle, and have developed several during the past few years: World Diplomacy, Civilizations, World Economics and Politics, Explorations and Discovery, Electoral College, and various geography games for use in a geography game book.[17]

With the burgeoning use of games in the classroom, as illustrated by these examples, it is not surprising that public and private curricular-materials centers are turning to game development in anticipation of a potentially enormous future market. For example, The Social Studies Program of Educational Services, Incorporated, of Cambridge, Massachusetts, has commissioned a private firm, Abt. Associates, also of

Cambridge, to build a variety of games keyed to historical processes such as the industrial revolution, the slave trade, and mercantilism.[18] Science Research Associates, Chicago, has prepared a "kit" for the INS and may develop other games in the future, and the Western Behavioral Sciences Institute also is marketing several of the SIMILE games.[19] The Nova project began national marketing efforts in 1968.

Games also have been widely used as teaching devices in management training, in undergraduate and graduate university business curricula, with internal company-training programs, and in executive-development programs offered by a university business school and by groups such as the American Management Association. Since I have described several of these games in a preceding chapter, I will not dwell on them here, though we will return to them when we discuss the evaluation of games for teaching.

## GAMES FOR POLICY-MAKERS

As might be expected, the games used as adjuncts to policy planning in the military, in government, or at high levels in business, differ somewhat from those used in formal education. Advocates argue that gaming sharpens the understanding of already knowledgeable policy-makers; that it stimulates and frees official thinking; that it provides opportunities for interaction among government agencies; that it gives policy-makers the opportunity to experience or "live through" probable crises in advance and thus be more comfortable with them when they actually do occur; that it sometimes unearths contingencies that had not been considered; and that, in general, gaming is a powerful aid to theorizing and planning.[20]

The center for the development of such games has been RAND Corporation, where "experts" and policy-makers have joined to play a large variety of games ranging from simple, two-person exercises conducted with a board, to elaborate, computer-assisted scenario games involving hundreds of people and complex problems of logistics, defense, battlefield tactics, and war strategy.[21]

Whereas the RAND activities have tended to focus primarily on military problems, the games developed at M.I.T. incorporate politics and economics into the military game structure, and rely mainly on the "all-man" or "manual" games used in their undergraduate teaching. Since about 1959, M.I.T. has conducted games for high-ranking government officials, primarily those from the Departments of Defense and State.[22]

Other games for policy-makers include one focused on the analysis of arms control problems;[23] one developed by a joint Canadian-British team designed to give both "average citizens" and high level decision-makers a chance to try out their schemes for solving Vietnam-like conflicts;[24] a simulation of a developing society, originated by Andrew Scott and his colleagues at the University of North Carolina and intended for use in training Peace Corps volunteers and others about to be sent abroad to work in such societies;[25] the TEMPER model (already described), which offers a training environment for top-ranking military personnel; and a recent effort, a simulation of the unfamiliar social situations that a visitor to another country is likely to encounter, intended, as is the Scott game, to train foreign service personnel.[26]

These examples should suggest the many types of games used for education and training. But how effective are they?

In trying to evaluate games as educational tools, two things are soon evident: first, that nearly everyone who uses them or observes their use is highly enthusiastic; and second, that this enthusiasm is based to a great extent on subjective estimates of what the games accomplish rather than on objective measures of learning or on other empirical data. For example, one advocate of simulations says:

> Simulation may be employed to emphasize and clarify some concept. . . . A model that shows a point vividly not only carries conviction, but stimulates the watcher into seeing all sorts of further consequences and developments.[27]

Most enthusiasts stress the experiential value of gaming, as the following reports illustrate:

> Mr. Dale Garvey and Mr. William H. Seiler have completed a final report of their research project comparing the effectiveness of traditional methods and the Inter-Nation Simulation as means to "enhance the ability of high school students to acquire more factual and conceptual knowledge and to think critically." They found little statistical difference on results of a content examination, critical thinking tests, and an attitude survey. However, the subjective evaluations by the experimenters and their cooperating teachers suggested that the students in the simulation enjoyed their classroom experiences more and became more involved in their course of study.[28]

John Burton bases his positive evaluation of classroom gaming at University College, London, on three factors: the absence of rules and the simplicity of arrangements facilitate insights into basic social processes; the involvement generated in the participants extends to students in other classes; and it gives all students, not just a few, the chance to take part in laboratory experiments.[29]

The final report of a conference on business games, sponsored by the Ford Foundation, includes the following detailed assessment of student gaming:

> Most of the conferees reported that to one extent or another they use games to provide students with a form of synthetic experience. It was maintained that gaming experiences can be helpful preparation for "living with uncertainty" and "functioning within the organization" in the business world. More emphasis was placed upon the use of gaming as a type of activity in which students can practice various skills, and presumably sharpen them by doing so. Some of these skills are rather tenuous, and it is perhaps here that the idea of "teaching the unteachable" was most strongly represented. For instance, some felt that skills pertinent to executive work can be developed as a result of undergoing experiences which require decision making under uncertainty and stress in complex situations. It was suggested that gaming can help to condition "good" attitudes toward risk, and to habituate players to make decisions. One conferee advocated gaming as a means for developing realistic, but confident, attitudes toward problem solving. Others felt that playing games provides valuable experience in conceptualizing and logical thinking.
>
> Several of the conferees spoke of the value of gaming for exercising and improving human relations skills. It was proposed that gaming can provide a background superior to traditional classroom procedures for practicing communications skills—oral and written, formal and informal. Several conferees were enthusiastic about using games to give students experience in writing operating reports, and in formulating and articulating operations procedures and policies.
>
> The value of games as exercises in the interpretation and use of accounting data was asserted by several speakers; and others, referring to the more complex games, mentioned the design of reporting and control systems. The use of games as bases for practice with statistical and mathematical techniques was stressed by several conferees, who emphasized operations-research-type problem-solving tools, and who saw the game as a situation in which students could get some experience in model building as well as analysis. Largely in this connection, one speaker suggested that game participants "learn how to learn" about systems and situations from the data which they generate. . . .
>
> Many of the conference participants mentioned motivation of students and orientation toward subject matter as explicit purposes of gaming. In some cases, games were frankly used as means for increasing a course's appeal to its students by making the subject matter more interesting (but something along the line of demonstrating concepts, principles, and facts was also involved in such instances). In other cases, games were expressly designed to pose problems which would virtually force the players to seek pertinent factual knowledge and/or to acquire certain analytic techniques. Intermediately, many applications of gaming were described as having, as one of their purposes, building of interest in subject matter by demonstrating it in concrete form. Motivation of teachers, as well as of students, was mentioned as important by several

speakers. Similarly, some conferees mentioned game runs in executive programs and elsewhere whose special object was to "break the ice" and thus put players into frames of mind which would favor fruitful participation in the rest of the program.

Finally, games were described as useful devices for student evaluation. On the one hand, evaluation by instructors was mentioned, not so much to grade students as to determine whether the educational program which they had undergone had satisfactorily achieved its objectives. Self-evaluation by students was stressed more. It was said that games sometimes reveal areas of ignorance or impracticality to their players. Also, it was proposed that gaming can give students a chance to evaluate attitudes which are relevant to their career objectives, e.g., attitudes toward risk and toward team problem-solving.[30]

This is praise indeed, and it is echoed by those who have used games to train policy-makers and other high-level governmental personnel. For example, in discussing his use of games for training Peace Corps volunteers, Andrew Scott reports:

> The Brazilian exercise was designed primarily as a teaching exercise and in that respect it was an almost unqualified success. To aid in its evaluation, a questionnaire was administered to the Peace Corps trainees at the conclusion of the game. Twenty-three respondents felt that the exercise had added to their knowledge of Brazil, and the other three gave qualified answers that were still affirmative. To the more important question, "Did the game help you gain an understanding of the process of development?" twenty again gave an unqualified "yes," while only one answer was negative. Nineteen of the twenty-three indicated that "the time spent on the game was more useful than an equivalent amount of class time," while only one felt that it had been less useful.[31]

Bloomfield and Whaley at M.I.T. judge that their "political-military" exercises are excellent training devices for policy-makers since they illuminate policy alternatives and constraints, acquire a self-sustaining momentum, and force the participants to live with the consequences of their decisions.[32]

There are, however, a few negative assessments. Robert Davis argues that the emotional overtones characterizing such events as crises in international politics can seldom, if ever, be simulated in the laboratory, and that players don't, in fact, have to live with the consequences of their decisions.[33] Bernard Cohen, who used an international relations game for teaching undergraduates at the University of Wisconsin, reports that even though high interest was generated, there was no real evidence that the students gained any particular insights or that their interest was maintained after the experience was over.[34] At the first national conference on management games, Martin Shubik questioned whether it has ever been shown that participants really learn anything from gaming and asked whether the enthusiasm displayed at the conference might not simply be due to the fact that everyone has "a whale of a time in playing these games?"[35]

Clearly, favorable and unfavorable comments are highly subjective. They are not based on objective evidence that learning of any kind has or has not taken place, but rather reflect the personal reactions of users, observers, and participants. Hence, when the Project SIMILE team at the Western Behavioral Sciences Institute collected and analyzed hundreds of such observations in order to distill a coherent assessment of games and simulations as educational tools, they could not produce a report of evidence, but only an extremely tentative "inventory of hunches."

> 1. Maybe simulations are "motivators." Their main payoff may be that they generate enthusiasm for or commitment to: (a) learning in general, (b) social studies or some other subject area, (c) a specific discipline like history, (d) a specific course, or (e) a specific teacher.
>
> 2. Maybe a simulation experience leads students to more sophisticated and relevant inquiry. That is, perhaps the important thing is what happens after the simulation is over, when students ask about the "model" which determined some of the elements of the simulation, about processes like communication, about ways of dealing with stress and tension. Maybe participation leads naturally into a critique and analysis of the simulation by the students, and maybe this can lead easily into a model-building experience. . . . And maybe the greatest learning occurs when students build their own simulations.
>
> 3. Maybe simulations give participants a more integrated view of some of the ways of men. Maybe they see the interconnectedness of political, social, interpersonal, cultural, economic, historical, etc., factors. Maybe simulations help people understand the idea of a "social system." Maybe the simulation experience helps them integrate ideas and information they already had.
>
> 4. Maybe participants in simulations learn skills: decision-making, resource allocation, communication, persuasion, influence-resisting. Or maybe they learn how important those processes are. Maybe they learn about the rational and emotional components of these skills.
>
> 5. Maybe simulations affect attitudes: (a) maybe participants gain empathy for real-life decision-makers; (b) maybe they get a feeling that life is much more complicated than they ever imagined; (c) maybe they get a feeling that they can do something important about affecting their personal life or the nation or the world.
>
> 6. Maybe simulations provide participants with explicit, experiential, gut-level referents for ideas, concepts, and words used to describe human behavior. Maybe everyone has a personal psychology or sociology . . . maybe a simulation experience brings this personal view closer to reality. Maybe people know many things they don't know they know, and simulations act as an information retrieval device to help bring this knowledge to consciousness.
>
> 7. Maybe participants in simulations learn the form and content

of the model which lies behind the simulation. That is, in a corporation management simulation, maybe they learn about the ways in which certain aspects of the marketplace are related; in an inter-nation simulation, maybe they learn the relationship between the relative satisfaction of political influentials and the probability that leaders will retain office.

8. Maybe the main importance of simulations is their effect on the social setting in which learning takes place. Maybe their physical format alone, which demands a significant departure from the usual setup of a classroom (chair shuffling, grouping, possibly room dividers, etc.), produces a more relaxed, natural exchange between teacher and students later on. Since simulations are student-run exercises, maybe they move "control" of the classroom from the teacher to the structure of the simulation, and thereby allow for better student-teacher relations. Simulations are usually very engaging; maybe one product of such engagement is that students drop their usual interpersonal facades, and maybe this leads to a more open classroom atmosphere in later sessions. Maybe simulations have their main effect on the teacher: perhaps he sees his students as more able than he had thought before, and the result may be that he looks to himself more to explain failures in the classroom. Maybe simulations—like any new technique—cause teachers to look at their normal teaching methods with a more critical eye. Maybe simulations' main payoff is that they create student enthusiasm in one classroom which may spread by informal student channels throughout the school.

9. Maybe simulations lead to personal growth. The high degree of involvement may provide some of the outcomes hoped for from T-groups, sensitivity training, basic encounter groups, etc. . . . that is, a better sense of how one appears to others; discovery of personal skills, abilities, fears, weaknesses, that weren't apparent before; opportunities to express affection, anger, and indifference without permanently crippling consequences.[36]

Now, *if* these hunches are correct, if the "maybes" can be translated into certainties, then it is clear that games and simulations are extremely valuable educational tools that would be appropriate to the concepts of education discussed at the beginning of this chapter. But what little concrete evidence there is—and most of it has been accumulated only since late 1965—does not bear this out. When Cherryholmes tested his Lawrence High School students, he found that they developed more "realistic" attitudes towards international affairs after taking part in his games. But there was no follow-up to determine how long this attitude was maintained.[37] Evidence gathered by the Project SIMILE group from their work with San Diego County high schools shows that even though student involvement and learning-motivation increased during the play of a game, they dropped to pre-game levels a few days later. This casts doubt on the permanence of Cherryholmes' findings as well.[38]

An elegant experimental design was developed at Northwestern University to compare the "case study" method and the INS for effectiveness in evoking student interest and enhancing learning. Students from three upper-division courses were divided into two groups, one of which took part in the simulation while the other used case studies. The groups were controlled for intelligence and such personality traits as cognitive style, and needs for achievement, affiliation, and power. Class attendance, visits to a professor's office, and library use were some of the factors used as indicators of student interest. Interestingly, when the students were asked in advance which method they thought they would prefer, most said that the case study method would be more interesting; but their subsequent behavior as measured by the indicators showed that more interest was evoked by the simulation method. With respect to learning, there was no significant difference between the two methods, though those who had expressed a preference for case studies did better on mastery of facts, whereas those who had preferred simulations did better on understanding principles—regardless of the method to which they had actually been exposed![39]

In his analysis of the learning effect of the two BOCES computer games mentioned earlier, Richard Wing found that on the basis of tests for retention, "no claim to superiority can be made either by the computer game technique or by the conventional classroom method of instruction."[40] Finally, in an attempt to assess the efficacy of educational games in general, Cherryholmes set up five hypotheses as to their effects.

> Hypothesis 1: Students participating in a simulation will reveal more interest in a simulation exercise than in more conventional classroom activities.
>
> Hypothesis 2: Students participating in a simulation will learn more facts and principles of information than by studying in a more conventional manner.
>
> Hypothesis 3: Students participating in a simulation will retain information learned longer than if they had learned it in a more conventional manner.
>
> Hypothesis 4: Students participating in a simulation will acquire more critical-thinking and decision-making skills than will students in more conventional classroom activities.
>
> Hypothesis 5: Students participating in a simulation will have their attitudes significantly altered relative to attitude-change produced by more conventional classroom methods.[41]

In reviewing the findings of six major educational simulation studies, involving five different games, he found support only for the first hypothesis.

Thus, although there were some differences among studies, cited above, so far *there is no justification for concluding that simulations are either more or less effective than traditional teaching techniques.*[42]

But from the preceding review of attempts to evaluate simulations as teaching tools, one conclusion does emerge: There is almost universal enthusiasm for them, even though there is practically no hard evidence to justify that enthusiasm! Why is this? Why should there be such great enthusiasm when there is apparently so little to be excited about? I would like to suggest an explanation; it involves two issues, each related to earlier discussions in this volume.

The first issue has to do with the "discovery" aspect of learning. All the research on student learning, as far as I have been able to discover, was carried out in situations where students were merely required to play an already-constructed game—and usually for only a few sessions. I have argued that the power of simulations, as a tool for developing and testing theory, derives less from their operation *per se*, than from the attempts to *construct* and *refine* them. If this argument is valid, then it should hold true for students. I suggest that there is a greater likelihood of student learning if the students first study games in general, then actually design, play, re-design, re-play, and again re-design their own simulations, rather than simply play an already-completed game.

My own observations of the few cases in which this approach has been tried indicate that, as compared with "play only" use of games, student involvement was more intense, students were pushed harder, and their interest was sustained to such a degree that they spontaneously sought, through reading and other research, the knowledge they found they lacked. Students who have either engaged in the *game building* process or have observed others doing so are usually more enthusiastic than those who have merely played a game or watched one being played.

In sum, I believe there is evidence to suggest that *building* games and simulations is a more powerful learning experience for students than merely *playing* them, and that this aspect of gaming has largely been ignored by the early research on their educational effectiveness. After examining the evidence for his five hypotheses, Cherryholmes comes to a similar conclusion:

> In addition to using existing simulation as a way to revive flagging student interest and/or to introduce them to social and political processes that may not be covered well by conventional methods and materials, one may give students the task of designing a simulation before playing it, either re-designing an existing game or constructing a simple game of their own . . . a major benefit of participating in a simulation may come from constructing it prior to operating it. Designing a simulation raises the problems of building explicit theory about a referent system. Selecting variables, relating variables and weighting parameters is the work of a scientist in building theory . . . the learner should take the place of the scientist in discovering a subject much as a scientist *discovers* new information and creates theory in a field of study.
>
> Another strategy is to have students attempt to validate the theory embedded in a simulation by a variety of comparisons with the real-life

> referent system. This may prove a valuable exercise whether or not the theory being validated was created by the students; though ideally, combining a student-designed simulation with a student validation assignment puts students in the position of *testing their beliefs* about the referent system rather than testing theories presented to them. Whether significant learning will be produced by such a plan is of course subject to experimental evaluation.
>
> A last strategy would have students re-design a simulation on the basis of their validation efforts. This alternative is related to the earlier suggestion of a student-designed simulation. By revising a simulation students would have to look critically at their simulation behavior.[43]

If his analysis and mine are correct, then there can be no real evidence of the instructional value of gaming until such "build-and-play" programs are instituted in more educational systems, in the same way they are now being used at Nova High School in Florida, the University of Michigan, and Poway High School in San Diego County, California. Unfortunately, most educators are not likely to permit such a radical departure from usual classroom methods until there is hard evidence that games do enhance learning, and so the self-defeating circle can be broken only by the few willing to make major innovations on the basis of impressions and subjective observations.

The second issue, and another reason for the remarkable marriage of large enthusiasm and small evidence, has to do with the problem of evaluating pedagogical methods. In the first place, most of the reported research on teaching offers results that are ambiguous or that show no significant correlation between learning and instructional method. This is due to the extreme difficulty both of determining the exact educational goals of any given set of materials, and of designing reliable measures of learning.[44] Moreover, the problem of data-based evaluation is even more complicated if what one wants to test is a hunch that what is learned by gaming is not so much factual information as a new way of integrating information, enhanced appreciation of the complexities of social relations, and greater insight into strategies of bargaining, communications, and decision-making. No tests have yet been devised to measure such abstract qualities, and tests that measure factual learning and specific attitude changes miss the point. So again, I suggest that the educational effectiveness of gaming cannot be appraised until there is more awareness of the purposes and potentials of the games, and a concomitant development of tests for measuring changes along the dimensions referred to above.

In this chapter, I have indicated that all kinds of games are used to teach students ranging from elementary school pupils to top-level governmental elites. There is wide-spread enthusiasm for games as an educational device, but to date, this enthusiasm is not supported by hard evidence. This lack of evidence may, however, be due to the fact that the games have not been put to their best use, and that we really have no adequate tests for measuring what gaming does teach. If, as I have suggested, the main value of gaming is in enabling students to grasp more or less abstract concepts and to gain insights into complex relationships, then no wonder we have not been able to measure what gaming teaches. The tools do not exist! In most research on the measurement of learning, the emphasis has been on developing measures to tap the acquisition of punctiform data—the retention of factual material. Only a few isolated efforts have been made to measure learning of concepts and relationships, or even to discover how such learning is facilitated, and none have been directly applied to gaming.

One of these efforts, however, is exceedingly interesting and revealing. Alex Bavelas, at Stanford University, has been conducting research to discover to what extent verbal transmission of an abstract concept—of the "principle of the thing"—enables its recipients to apply it in a concrete situation. His subjects watch short films of formations produced by smoke as it billows up under a variety of conditions. After watching about fifty such films, most subjects are able to predict quite accurately the shape that a cloud of smoke will take in future frames. Bavelas then has the subjects write instructions for making such predictions. A second group of subjects is asked to read the instructions, then watch the films, and start making predictions. The instructions have no effect—it takes the new group as long to arrive at a high level of predictive ability as it did the original subjects. A third group of subjects is allowed to watch one film; *then* they are given the instructions to read and are shown more films. This group needs only 10% as long as the other two groups to make equally accurate predictions. Watching one film makes the language—the concepts—used in the instructions meaningful.[45]

It may be that the same is true of students of social processes. Reading or hearing material about such abstractions as coalition formation, negotiations, roles, and status may have greater impact—make much more sense—once the student has been involved in forming a coalition, engaged in negotiations, or experienced role constraints. Most people do engage in these activities daily but often are unaware of the processes in which they are involved. The chiaroscuro of the game situation may give these processes greater clarity and immediacy, but, as I have indicated, we don't really know because we don't yet have adequate tools for finding out. Like the architect who, before he arrives at a final design, tries to imagine himself *moving around* in his building, who tries to *experience* it rather than simply peering at it from the outside, it may be that the student of social processes gains a more meaningful comprehension of those processes by getting inside them, by experiencing their dynamics in the microcosm of the game, instead of by looking at them from the distance of a book or a lecture.

So we can argue by analogy, by logic, and by subjective experience, that gaming is a powerful teaching tool. But until we develop and apply adequate measurement techniques, we can neither prove it, demonstrate it to be false, nor compare gaming to more conventional instructional methods. Meanwhile, this discussion of the validity of games as a teaching technique leads us into the final chapter, a discussion of research and thinking about the validity question as it applies to other uses of games and simulations.

## FOOTNOTES

1. Hall, T. Sprague, "Changing Education in America" (La Jolla, California: Western Behavioral Sciences Institute, September 1966, mimeographed).
2. Chadwick Alger, "Use of the Inter-Nation Simulation in Undergraduate Teaching," in Guetzkow, 1963, *op. cit.*, pp. 152–4.
3. Richard Snyder, *op. cit.*, p. 12.
4. Erving Goffman, *op. cit.*, p. 34.
5. Thomas C. Schelling, *op. cit.*, p. 47.
6. James C. Coleman, "In Defense of Games," *American Behavioral Scientist*, X, No. 2 (1966), 3–4.
7. Richard L. Wing, "Two Computer-Based Economics Games for Sixth Graders," *American Behavioral Scientist*, X, No. 3 (1966), 31.
8. *loc. cit.*
9. Lincoln P. Bloomfield and Norman J. Padelford, "Three Experiments in Political Gaming," *American Political Science Review*, LIII, No. 4 (1959), 1105–1115; and Barton Whaley, Peter C. Ordeshook, and Robert H. Scott, *INDEX III*, C/64-33 (Cambridge, Massachusetts: Center for International Studies, Massachusetts Institute of Technology, October 1964).
10. Olaf Helmer and R. E. Bickner, *How to Play SAFE—Book of Rules of the Strategy and Force Evaluation Game*, RM-2865-PR (Santa Monica, California: RAND Corporation, November 1961).
11. Cleo H. Cherryholmes, "Developments in Simulation of International Relations in High School Teaching," *Phi Delta Kappan* (Jan. 1965), 227–31.
12. Described in "Occasional Newsletter," *op. cit.*, No. 1, p. 4, and No. 2, p. 2.
13. Conversation with Michael Inbar and William Gamson, September 18, 1967.
14. John Burton, "International Relations Simulation on the Cheap" (Evanston: Northwestern University, 1966, multilith).
15. These examples are all selected from the "Occasional Newsletter," *op. cit.*, No. 2, pp. 5–6.
16. From "Occasional Newsletter," *op. cit.*, No. 3, p. 5.
17. From "Occasional Newsletter," *op. cit.*, No. 5, p. 7.

18. From "Occasional Newsletter," *op. cit.*, No. 1, p. 3.

19. *Ibid.*, p. 4.

20. cf. SIDNEY F. GIFFIN, *The Crisis Game: Simulating International Conflict* (Garden City, New York: Doubleday and Company, 1965); or MAURICE T. PRICE, "Applying Wargaming to the Cold War," *PROD*, III (1959), 3–6; or GOLDHAMER and SPEIER, *op. cit.*

21. cf. GOLDHAMER and SPEIER, *op. cit.*; M. G. WEINER, *War Gaming Methodology*, RM-2413 (Santa Monica, California: RAND Corporation, July 10, 1959); OLAF HELMER, *Strategic Gaming*, P-1902 (Santa Monica, California: RAND Corporation, February 10, 1960); E. W. PAXON, *War Gaming*, RM-3489-PR (Santa Monica, California: RAND Corporation, February 1963); or H. AVERCH and M. M. LAVIN, *Simulation of Decision-Making in Crisis: Three Manual Gaming Experiments*, RM-4202-PR (Santa Monica, California: RAND Corporation, August 1964).

22. cf. BLOOMFIELD and PADELFORD, *op. cit.*; BARRINGER and WHALEY, *op. cit.*; LINCOLN P. BLOOMFIELD, *Political Gaming*, United States Naval Institute Proceedings, LXXXVI (September 1960), pp. 57–64; and LINCOLN P. BLOOMFIELD and BARTON WHALEY, "The Political-Military Exercise: A Progress Report," *Orbis*, VIII (1965), 854–70.

23. R. H. DAVIS, P. B. CARPENTER, and C. W. MISSLER, *A Game for Studying the Problems of Arms Control*, SP-779 (Santa Monica, California: Systems Development Corporation, 1962).

24. PAUL SMOKER with JOHN MACRAE, "A Vietnam Simulation: A Report on the Canadian/English Joint Project," *Journal of Peace Research*, IV, No. 1 (1967), 1–25.

25. ANDREW M. SCOTT, WILLIAM LUCAS, and TRUDI LUCAS, *op. cit.*

26. JACK DANIELIAN, "Live Simulation of Affect-Laden Cultural Cognitions," *Journal of Conflict Resolution*, XI, No. 3 (1967), 312–24.

27. W. ROSS ASHBY, in Borko, *op. cit.*, p. 461.

28. From "Occasional Newsletter," *op. cit.*, No. 3, p. 4.

29. JOHN BURTON, *op. cit.*, pp. 9–10.

30. WILLIAM R. DILL, JAMES R. JACKSON, and JAMES W. SWEENEY, eds., *Proceedings of the Conference on Business Games* (New Orleans: Tulane University, April 26–28, 1961), pp. 9–11.

31. ANDREW M. SCOTT, "Simulation and National Development," prepared for Annual Meeting of the American Political Science Association, Washington, D.C., September 8–11, 1965.

32. BLOOMFIELD and WHALEY, 1965, *op. cit.*

33. ROBERT DAVIS, "The International Influence Process: How Relevant Is the Contribution of Psychologists?" *American Psychologist*, XXI, No. 3 (1966), 240–41.

34. BERNARD C. COHEN, "Political Gaming in the Classroom," *Journal of Politics*, XXIV (1962), 367–80.

35. MARTIN SHUBIK, quoted in *Proceedings on the National Symposium on Management Games* (Lawrence, Kansas: University of Kansas, Center for Research in Business, May 1959).

36. HALL T. SPRAGUE, "An Inventory of Hunches About Classroom Games and Simulations" (La Jolla, California: Western Behavioral Sciences Institute, May 1966, mimeographed).

37. CHERRYHOLMES, 1965, *op. cit.*

38. Project SIMILE, "Report to the Kettering Foundation" (La Jolla, California: Western Behavioral Sciences Institute, 1967).

39. JAMES A. ROBINSON, L. F. ANDERSON, M. G. HERMANN, and R. C. SNYDER, *op. cit.*

40. RICHARD WING, *op. cit.*, p. 33.

41. CLEO H. CHERRYHOLMES, "Some Current Research on Effectiveness of Educational Simulations: Implications for Alternative Strategies," *American Behavioral Scientist*, X, No. 2 (1966), 4–5.

42. *Ibid.*, 5–6.

43. *Ibid.*, 7.

44. cf. LAWRENCE E. METCALF, "Research on Teaching the Social Studies," in *Handbook of Research on Teaching*, ed. N. L. GAGE (Chicago: Rand McNally & Co., 1963), pp. 929–66.

45. Conversation with ALEX BAVELAS, November 11, 1967.

# 7

# VALIDITY, OR WHAT ARE GAMES REALLY GOOD FOR?

"What is Truth?"

Pontius Pilate

The question of scientific validity, even in the mature physical sciences, is so thorny and unresolved that to worry about it in the adolescent social sciences, much less in the infant field of gaming, seems premature. But worry about it we must; for if we do not constantly check our activities against the criterion of scientific soundness, we may someday find ourselves traveling down a dead-end road. Therefore, serious scholars among game and simulation builders have constantly concerned themselves with the problem of validity in respect to individual games and to the method itself.

The concept of validity is extremely complex, and I shall not attempt to deal with it completely. I shall, however, try to give the reader some feeling for the depth and scope of the problem as it applies to science in general, suggest an appropriate criterion for judging the validity of simulations and gaming, and review the thinking and research that has been directly applied to the question: "Are games and simulations valid instruments for research in the social sciences?"

## THE VARIETIES OF SCIENTIFIC VALIDITY

What is validity? According to my dictionary, "valid *implies* being supported by objective truth or generally accepted authority." (Emphasis mine.) Thus, we can speak of a "valid statement," or a "valid claim," but it is not possible to give a single, simple definition of validity, to say "validity is. . . ."

When we try to deal with validity in the context of *research*, we find ourselves in a vastly different country—in the realm of the philosophers of science, of Whitehead, Russell, Peirce, Kaplan, and the like. In the physical sciences, the connotations and denotations of the term "validity" are diverse; in the social-behavioral sciences, because they are so young, and because they deal with a quite different sort of phenomena, the matter is even more complicated. It might help to step back for a moment, as we did in Chapter 2, and talk about the question at hand in a general way.

The word "research" covers a multitude of activities and goals. For example:

(a) An investigator may want to ask, "What's going on here anyway?"—to navigate his way into an uncharted sea of phenomena. There are no data, no theory, no guideposts. To illustrate: it has been known for many years that the "shells" of diatoms—ubiquitous, single-celled marine organisms—are composed of silicon, rather than of calcium carbonate as is characteristic of other shelled creatures. Each of the thousands of species of diatoms is distinguished by the baroquely beautiful architecture of its shells. But until recently, when a handful of biologists decided to take a close look at diatoms, literally nothing was known about how living creatures can transform soluble inorganic silicon in seawater into structures of such enormous diversity in shapes and patterns. Here indeed was a *mare incognito* into which most biologists were too sensible to wade. In research of this kind, the scientist can judge the validity of his results only if they are reproducible and—but only to some extent—if they are not too wildly at variance with the pattern of known biological processes.

(b) An investigator may want to ask, "What would happen if . . .?"—if I feed cows on orange peel? . . . if I mix this chemical with that? . . . if I put a person in such-and-such a situation? Or, as a way of trying to find out "what's going on here," . . . if I deprive a diatom of silicon?

(c) Having found out "what happens if . . ." the investigator will want to ask "why" and (d) having found out *what* happens (data) and *why* (theory), it may be useful to apply the knowledge to the real world—to the solution of practical problems.

It is clear that the problem of "validity" will differ for each type of research, and that in the first two types, the investigator cannot appeal to "objective truth" or "generally accepted authority" as a criterion. He must ask two questions about both his methods and his results: Are they "reliable?" and are they "valid?" The two questions are interdependent but different; the distinction can be shown by an illustration. I want to know if X-rays *reliably* and *validly* indicate whether a subject has tuberculosis of the lungs. If I take 20 X-rays of the same subject, show them to 5 observers trained to recognize tuberculous lesions, and all 5 independently report that all the X-rays indicate a lesion, then I may say that the method is reliable. If the 5 observers agree that 10 of the X-rays show a lesion, but 10 do not, then I must conclude that the method is not reliable. Or I may show 20 different X-rays of several subjects to my 5 trained observers. If there is good agreement among them as to which X-rays show a lesion and which do not, I may equally conclude that the method is reliable.

But is a lesion a *valid* indicator of t.b.? Here I must appeal to other tests, such as the evidence of the tubercle bacillus in the subject's sputum. In fact, the chest X-ray is a highly reliable but not highly valid method for diagnosing t.b.; even though it does reveal a lesion, a lesion is often, but not always, proof of t.b. Thus, there are degrees of validity.

Endless complications aside, a valid hypothesis is one which has not been disconfirmed though strenuous efforts have been made to do so. A valid theory is one which describes processes and relationships *accurately enough* to predict new processes or additional relationships. A valid psychological test is one which interprets behavior *more* convincingly than other methods. These statements, too, imply *degrees* of validity, not an absolute.

We also must distinguish between validity of *method* and validity of *results*. A method that violates the canons of scientific procedure and therefore would certainly be termed "invalid," might nevertheless produce "valid"—that is, "true" or accurate—results. As an extreme case, let us take the spiritualist who successfully uses the "messages of the holy spirit" to diagnose disease, or the faith healer who cures by the laying on of hands. If his diagnoses are objectively correct as determined by trained medical personnel, or if the paralytic arises from his wheel chair and walks, the results are certainly valid, though the method is certainly not—since no one else can use it with similar results. But in the first case, we assume that the spiritualist is actually using "valid" but to him subliminal cues in his diagnoses, and that the paralytic is cured because his disability was of psychosomatic origin. We presuppose, as an article of faith, that the validity of the result is related to the validity of the method.

Nevertheless, scholars have been known to use impeccably valid methods only to arrive at demonstrably invalid results simply because the methods were inappropriate *in a wider context*. I will use two examples from the many possible. So-called—or probably, mis-called—intelligence tests are valid methods for measuring certain cognitive characteristics that make for academic success—memory, understanding of verbal concepts, reasoning ability, and so forth (including willingness to comply with the test-situation)—*within the context of middle-class culture*. But now we have ample evidence that standard intelligence tests do not produce valid results when the context is widened to include the poverty or black sub-culture.

Again, game theory has provided a valid method for considering the actions of a conscious opponent where there is a conflict of interests, and has been widely used in solving questions of military and business strategy. But game-theory requires that opponents *rationally* calculate their "utilities" and that they know what the pay-offs are. When the context is widened to include the element of player-*irrationality*, ignorance of the opponent's utilities—or, as Anatol Rapoport points out, ethics[1]—or ignorance of the pay-off, the quite valid rules of game theory produce "invalid" results.

The foregoing has, I hope, suggested how multi-faceted is the concept of validity; along with the concepts of "truth" or "reality," validity is the province of philosophers and epistemologists. Nevertheless, for the researcher, validity is a pragmatic question; his efforts are bootless if they do not further the increase of knowledge—and "knowledge" *implies* "validity."

The temptation is understandably great to judge the validity of a model or simulation according to how accurately and completely it represents "reality"—or, in technical shorthand, on the basis of its "isomorphism to the reference system." I shall argue that this criterion of validity is both inappropraite and *inadequate*, and that it is more consistent with modern concepts of scientific theory and more fruitful to judge the validity of a particular simulation, and indeed, that of gaming as a method, in terms of its *usefulness* in reaching particular goals. Once we couch the question in terms of usefulness, we are led to ask two further questions: "Useful for *what?*" and, "Useful *compared* to what?"

## VALIDITY AS USEFULNESS

To demonstrate the "validity" of this conception of validity, consider a model of the solar system three feet in diameter, constructed of hollow plastic balls, wires, and electric motors. Is it valid? If isomorphic replication is the criterion, such a model is absurdly invalid. Materials, distances, weights, gravitational forces, almost everything but size and distance relationships are amiss. But if we ask whether the model is *useful*, and if so for *what*, several sets of different answers emerge. The model is not useful for predicting the future of the earth, for plotting interplanetary travel routes, or for analyzing the gravitational relationship between the moon, Mercury, and the sun. But it *is* useful for helping a student understand the geometry of the solar system, and it is probably more useful for this purpose than a two-dimensional drawing, a verbal description, or a set of equations. It might conceivably be useful for answering a question of the "what happens if . . ." or "why" variety. According to the "usefulness" criterion, the model is valid.

"Usefulness" is less neat than "isomorphism" as a criterion. This is because "usefulness" does not provide an objective standard for measurement, but allows each scholar to answer the validity question for himself within the context of his own experiences and purposes. While such an individual standard raises the spectre of non-scientific, subjective evaluation, it should also be borne in mind that the "objective truth" implied in asking for isomorphism is also a phantom. Our knowledge of the "objective" world is too limited, our measures and our senses too fallible, our theories too uncertain and contradictory, and our data too ambiguous to justify any claims to real objectivity, no matter what means we might use to determine validity.

In any case, testing for isomorphic validity is difficult in the social sciences, for we are often so uncertain of the actual characteristics of the referent system that we cannot establish a standard for comparison. It takes two to tango, and when the pair consists of a referent and a replicate, it is impossible to tell whether the replicate is in step if the referent is not also clearly visible. In the social sciences, the referent is seldom more than a shadow, "seen through a glass darkly."[2]

As Crow and Noel argue:

> Establishing the "validity" of simulations or any other behavioral science method, is difficult. We believe that much more rapid progress could be made by a seemingly simple change in viewing the problem: we should shift attention from the validity of the method itself to the validity of using the information produced by the method. We suggest that validity be measured by asking: *how useful to the purpose for which it is to be gathered is the information produced by this method, as compared to some alternative method?* We believe this approach to validity brings it more closely in accord with modern concepts of scientific method, and guides research more directly to application.
>
> The most important implications of this approach are that accuracy and precision are no longer the sole considerations in evaluating a method, and that a method "valid" for some purposes may not be valid for others. It also has many implications for the procedures by which the degree of validity is established for any particular method. . . . For example, the purposes for which the information produced . . . is to be used should be detailed, available alternative methods should be specified, and . . . adequacy should be evaluated in relation to these considerations, rather than to [the simulation's] "correspondence to reality."
>
> The amount of error in the information produced by a method is an important criterion for its usefulness, but is not the sole factor, and often may not even be the most important one. A less precise method may be preferable because it produces information more quickly and/or at less cost. Moreover, the information is more likely to be used if the method by which it was obtained is familiar and acceptable to the user —an important consideration to those who must produce it. If the purpose is, for example, to generate new and unexpected contingencies as an aid to planning a hypothetical situation, then a "loose" method might be more useful (valid) than a precise one.[3]

In a sense, this view of validity has permeated the present book. When we examine the philosophy of science underlying gaming, its intellectual history, and the epistemological considerations that lead scholars to employ it, we are examining its validity—that is, its legitimacy as a scientific method. To claim that gaming is a stimulus to theory building, an incentive to gather further data, and a way of ordering previously disjoined bits of knowledge into a consistent picture, is to argue that gaming is scientifically useful, and therefore valid. And to suggest that games are arresting tools for teaching and training and that they produce worthwhile results, is again to imply that they are valid. Thus, the criterion of validity that best contributes to the increase of knowledge seems most profitable, regardless of whether it is "objective" or "subjective." This is similar to the position of such scientific philosophers as C. S. Peirce, the "pragmaticist": that the proof of the pudding is in the eating. If it is tasty and nourishing, one need not be perturbed about the ingredients, the mixing procedures, or the moral fiber of the cook. One simply enjoys and profits! But this view does not imply that accurate correspondence to reality (isomorphism) is *never* an important criterion; it merely suggests that in many instances, other criteria are more appropriate and productive.

## ISOMORPHISM AS ONLY ONE TEST OF USEFULNESS

In discussing the uses of gaming for theory construction and for teaching, for example, it was apparent that these activities may be most enhanced by use of several sorts of games—some so extremely sophisticated and complete that the theorist or student can come to understand the intricate processes involved in simulating—others crude, primitive, and perhaps even irritatingly inaccurate. The incomplete games then can be used as a basepoint from which to build a more accurate model. Gaming experience demonstrates that an interesting psychological phenomenon is at work here: the incentive to build, to construct a better model, seems to be greater when the student or theorist is presented with a crude and inaccurate game and asked to improve it than when he is expected to start from scratch. Once the game has been improved to the stage that it is, as nearly as can be determined, a faithful replicate of the referent system, a true simulation rid of annoying discrepancies, it loses some of its potency as a teaching or theory-building device. Further activities with it chiefly entail changing input parameters and exploring the model; they are assuredly valuable aids to learning, but we should not ignore the powerful impetus for learning provided by games that are intentionally primitive.

So if we judge a simulation's validity according to its usefulness for a particular purpose, then perhaps we might say that for theory-building and teaching one type of game that is "valid" is one that is simple, inaccurate, and incomplete, but that contains intriguing concepts and obvious challenges for improvement. To compare the validity of such a game with that of a highly accurate computer simulation, say of supply and demand in the steel industry, is meaningless; each game is valid in its own way, but each fulfills a different purpose—even in the context of teaching and theory-construction. And comparing the validity (i.e., "usefulness") of either type of game with that of other teaching or theory-building techniques is also difficult, since in neither case has there been objective assessment of their absolute efficacy. In this area, conclusions about the comparative validity of different methods are likely to be highly subjective for a long time.

In the specific use of gaming for research, however—for generating data, testing theory,* exploring, or the "messing around" I described earlier—the question of isomorphism is usually salient; to put it another way, isomorphism often may be a criterion of usefulness, either of a method or of its results. Theorists who have dealt with the validity of research simulations have taken different approaches. Some have concerned themselves with validity as such, whereas others have addressed the problem of isomorphism, albeit sometimes obliquely. All have been concerned with suggesting how the value of research gaming might be established and/or improved.

## FOUR CRITERIA OF VALIDITY FOR GAMES USED IN RESEARCH

The validity of social simulation games can be increased, according to Harold Guetzkow,[4] if the variables built into the game are structured to correspond to those aspects of the reference system that are being simulated. Whether this correspondence has been adequately accomplished will be revealed by the extent to which the game generates processes similar to those observed in the referent and/or outcomes similar to reference system events.

Taking a similarly inductive approach, Richard Brody considers that the "validity" of a game rests on the "validity" of the theory embodied in the game—and, in turn, confidence in the validity of the theory depends on the degree to which it enables us to predict events, processes, or relationships. Thus, says Brody, confidence in the game will be increased either if it can reproduce an actual historical event, given the actual antecedent situation, or if it reliably predicts future events. He further suggests that confidence is increased if the processes ob-

* I do not mean to imply, either here or elsewhere in this volume, that theory-testing is not related to theory-construction—the first is obviously intrinsic to the second. I am separating the two for analytic purposes, to show that gaming may play a different role in the specific task of testing hypotheses—in answering "why" questions—than it does in other aspects of the total process of generating theory—"what's going on," or "what would happen if . . ."

served in the game are those that would be predicted to occur were the game valid; or if hypotheses tested in the game are confirmed or disconfirmed in the same manner that theory predicts they would be, were they tested in the reference system. So, both Guetzkow and Brody seem to agree with Peirce that "the proof of the pudding is in the eating," and that validity is as validity does. Their conclusion is that the evidence so far indicates that games will be more useful for producing information about human interaction processes than for making predictions about specific future events.[5]

Taking a different approach, Paul Kress suggests six strategies for validating a simulation: using classical methods of inductive logic; applying sensitivity-analysis to the parameters embodied in the game; playing out similar events in the simulation and in the reference system when possible; starting with a simple game and adding components as they are validated by the above strategies; using multiple replications of a game, each focusing on a different aspect; and, finally, evaluating the amount of coherence between game elements and larger bodies of knowledge and theory.[6]

Charles F. Hermann's position is similar to mine—that it is meaningless to speak of validity except in terms of particular goals. He demonstrates that a simulation or game that is highly valid for one purpose may be entirely invalid for another. Hermann suggests that in general, validity is increased if (a) results are consistent in a number of "runs" of the game; (b) the game has "face validity," that is, it *seems* realistic; (c) it can be determined that the variables built into the game are similar to those operating in the reference system; (d) the game generates events or processes that also occur in the reference system; and (e) similar results are obtained from examining the same hypotheses both in the simulation and in the reference system.[7]

The different sets of validation criteria suggested by these theorists can, I think, be distilled into four criteria by which we can judge the usefulness of a particular game or simulation for a given *research* purpose:

1. An all-man or man-machine game used as a complex environment laboratory should provide an environment that seems realistic to the subjects (players).
2. A game is valid to the degree that its structure (the theory and assumptions on which it is built) can be shown to be isomorphic to that of the reference system.
3. It is valid to the degree that the processes observed in the game are isomorphic to those observed in the reference system.
4. It is valid to the degree that it can reproduce historical outcomes or predict the future.

It should be noted that none of these criteria can be applied to all "games" and all "simulations" in general. One can only examine a *specific* game and try to determine its validity for a *specific* purpose. Because of the considerable expense and hard work involved, this examination has been done with only a few games; we will now look at some of these efforts, since they are instructive for future validation work.

## HOW WELL DO SOME GAMES MEASURE UP?

As I indicated, all four of the criteria can be applied only to simulations that involve human participants, because the first criteria is irrelevant, and the second not feasible in judging all-computer simulations. This is so because computer simulators are not interested in using their simulations of economic or other systems as laboratories for experimentation on human behavior, so they ignore the question of environmental realism. Further, the processes that occur during the cycling of such simulations are so highly aggregated and so invisible, since they take place within the computer, that they cannot be analyzed. But economic models, at least, are structurally valid since they do incorporate variables that were validated before they were embodied in simulations, and that are subject to sensitivity analysis to determine which ones account for a lot of variance and which for little. Finally, the models have proven themselves capable of predicting—with a high degree of accuracy—gross economic trends during an ensuing six months to a year. Economists therefore feel that their simulations are valid. When these simulations are compared to other methods of economic predicting, there is little question that the simulations are superior.

Other types of social science simulations have, as a rule, differing goals, so all four criteria of validity may be applied. But it should be remembered that the creators of most of these games think of them as just that—games rather than simulations—and do not assume that the games have achieved a high degree of validity (in the sense of isomorphism) in their present state. Rather than assessing their over-all validity, the approach is to determine which aspects of the game are valid and which are not. This is certainly a legitimate research strategy. To be deplored, however, is the fact that so *few* of the scholars engaged in gaming have made serious attempts to cope with the validity question as it applies to the use of simulations for research.

The most notable effort is that of the Simulation of International Processes project at Northwestern University, under the direction of Harold Guetzkow;[8] indeed, nearly every effort to deal with research validity of social science games has either been made by members of this project, or has been catalyzed by the project. (Let me remind the reader again that we are speaking of the validity of games as research tools, not as theory-building or teaching devices—so we are in an area where isomorphism is especially relevant.) Thus, when we search for evidence related to the four criteria offered above, we must rely almost entirely on studies carried out in connection with the Northwestern project, and primarily on studies geared to an evaluation of the Inter-Nation Simulation or one of its variants. There is some evidence from other sources, which we will include, but the bulk of the material derives from the work of Guetzkow and his colleagues. Because for their purposes, the usefulness of a simulation depends to a considerable degree on its isomorphism, Guetzkow and his colleagues have used isomorphism as a criterion of validity; but they also have attended to other questions.

*Does the game provide a realistic environment in which to place subjects for research?* This question has two aspects. First, can any game be so involving that subjects forget they are conducting activities that have no future repercussions, and therefore act as do men whose decisions have important consequences for their own and others' welfare? Second, does a particular game provide the rich possibilities for involvement and action needed to stimulate a wide range of responses?

The answer to the first question has usually been a flat "no"—at least from those who have never actually taken part in a social simulation game. They maintain that it is evident that a college student, Navy recruit, or management trainee, co-opted for a few hours or days, cannot possibly operate in the same psychic environment as a company president, a legislator, or a chief of state, whose whole life and future are involved in his daily decisions. When the Central Decision-Maker (CDM) of UTRO must decide whether or not to launch a nuclear strike, they argue, his situation is not the same as that of the President of the United States confronted with a similar decision; the Utronian CDM is playing with paper, pencils, and computers, and he knows it, whereas the President of the United States is dealing with real property, human lives, perhaps the fate of the world, and *he* knows it. This is obviously true. It would be foolish to argue that game involvement is necessarily as intense as "real life" involvement; nevertheless, it is equally foolish to ignore the evidence that games are usually more involving than is frequently assumed, and that a great many "real life" situations are not particularly engaging.

Anyone who has conducted complex games can testify to the intense involvement of most players. I have witnessed fisticuffs among theological seminary students; Navy recruits who wept in the presence of their peers after losing office in a game; a participant who suffered temporary blindness and paralysis when his "country" was under attack; I know of a four star general who broke into a barracks in the middle of the night to spy out the secrets of an opponent team; and on one occasion, I had to break up a knife fight. But these examples are only the more dramatic evidences of how real the game situation may be for the players. High emotional levels, hard work for 14 to 16 hours per day, all night bull sessions, vivid dreams, and extensive independent research are "standard operating procedure" for most players.

In contrast, there is some evidence that high level governmental decision-makers tend to be insulated from the actual consequences and ramifications of their decisions. They sit in offices surrounded by papers and advisors; they move in a tight circle of their peers who pride themselves on their unemotional professionalism; and they usually develop a neutral and highly abstract terminology with which to discuss their work. (For example, the military euphemisms of "floorspace" and "population response" refer to amount of property totally destroyed and number of people killed by a nuclear blast; these are only two minor examples of language sterilization from among thousands that are verbal currency in governmental and military circles.) Furthermore, many members of such elite groups have admitted quite frankly that they enjoy their work because it gives them a sense of power and offers an intellectual challenge, not because they are motivated by altruism or feelings of responsibility for their nation. In short, the nature of their involvement and the reasons for it may be similar to those of game players.

I don't wish to push this argument too far; I merely want to point out that the assertion that game players cannot be as involved in their tasks as are their real life counterparts may be too glib a generalization; there is good evidence that the "psychic environments" are not as dissimilar as one might think. Erving Goffman has suggested that the degree of involvement in a situation is not a function of its objective "reality," but rather of the "psychological reality" of the setting. He demonstrates that a game situation designed specifically to enhance this psychological reality may frequently be *more* involving that its real life counterpart.[9] (To be sure, the extent of either a player's or a real life decision-maker's involvement also is a function of his personality or of his role.) It can be concluded that the "unreality" of gaming situations is indeed a limitation, but it is not nearly as crippling as critics often assume. The lack of a sense of reality and of personal responsibility for the consequences of one's decisions is not restricted to game participants! In any case, whatever the distortions produced by the game situation, they certainly are produced to a greater extent by other laboratory situations that are even less involving. Compared to other laboratory techniques, therefore, gaming probably has a good deal of validity. It would be possible, moreover, although it has not yet been done, to compare the behavior of subjects placed in simple and uninvolving situations—but that provide a specific range of processes and decisions—with their behavior in situations designed to be maximally involving. One could then designate "degree of involvement" as an independent variable and explore its effects on various aspects of behavior. The question, in short, is empirical.

The second question with respect to the "realistic environment" criterion is whether a particular game provides the rich possibilities for involvement and action needed to stimulate a wide range of responses. The only game that has been carefully examined from this standpoint is the Inter-Nation Simulation. The strategy of the examination has been to determine whether the players display the kinds and range of behavior we would expect if they were decision-makers in the international system. The evidence clearly shows that they do. The players develop strong "national" loyalties and ethnocentric attitudes; their behavior changes during crises in the ways one would expect were the crises real; they develop strong amities and enmities with other players, determined almost entirely by role and nation; and they respond to changes in the simulated environment much as would be expected were the environment real.[10] Further, many if not most INS-players complain that there is too much for them to do, too much information, too many possible choices, too many avenues of activity to explore, and that they feel overwhelmed with the richness of the environment. Whether these encouraging responses are elicited by games other than the INS remains to be determined. It can be said, however, that to the extent such reactions do occur in this and other complex games, the games generate a more realistic environment than do conventional laboratory experiments. As far as I know, no one working with such a laboratory has even tried to find out whether it was generating the overall effect presumed to exist in the arena to which he wants to extrapolate his findings.

I believe, then, that experience with the INS shows that games *can* provide a realistic environment to a greater extent than is often assumed, and that in any case, games are superior to other laboratory techniques in this respect. Thus, their validity is comparatively high on this dimension.

*Is the structure of the game isomorphic to that of the referent?* That is, do the assumptions on which the game is built conform to accepted theory or real-world data? We have already noted that, although the structural elements are highly aggregated in computer simulations of economic systems, they can be highly isomorphic. In simulations such as the INS or TEMPER, isomorphism is more difficult to assess. However, in a group of studies of the INS, seventy-five assumptions about basic elements or about relationships among elements were examined in the light of newly collected data on the real world (primarily derived from the Yale Data Program and the Dimensionality of Nations Project at the University of Hawaii). Questions arose as to whether many of the assumptions programmed into the model conformed to what occurs in the "real world."[11] But questioning these assumptions in the model led inevitably to an equally persistent questioning of the "real world" data upon which the criticisms were based. This intensive probling revealed that many of the measures used in deriving these data and methods used for comparing them to the INS were inadequate. When some of these problems were rectified and new measures used, the results were different and indicated a good degree of structural isomorphism on the part of the INS, insofar as data on the real world was complete enough to make comparisons possible. Guetzkow's assessment of the situation is that the then existing version of the INS showed a considerable similarity with the real world; in two-thirds of fifty-five comparisons, ranging from analyses involving personal characteristics of decision-makers through the behaviors of the international system as a whole, the simulation corresponded with "Some" or "Much" similarity. By and large, the non-correspondences were failures of the game to produce phenomena ascribed to the world systems being simulated; there were few inversions of findings, and rarely did the simulations yield nonsense results.[12]

It should be emphasized that these validity studies have been and continue to be a dynamic process. Each new version of the INS is evaluated in terms of the existing body of theory and data from international relations, and the model is constantly brought into closer conformity with those theories and data. At the same time, the existence of the model and the eagerness of its developers leads those engaged in empirical research on the international system to examine their own techniques and to ask questions of nature that they might not otherwise be stimulated to ask. It is as if the gamer says "Here are ten questions about the international system I would like to have answered. Can those of you who gather data on that system help?" Thus, the INS as an "open ended game"—as a developing simulation—is providing strong incentive to scholars to examine and revise existing verbal theory in international relations, an incentive that at least some scholars believe has long been lacking.

A different and less encouraging picture emerges when we examine a game that has been treated more as a finished product than as a continuing process. Such is the TEMPER computer-simulation, designed by Raytheon Corporation and then "delivered" as a manufactured product to the Joint Chiefs of Staff. Initial evaluations throw into serious question some basic assumptions about both structure and process in this complex model—particularly those assumptions relating to psychological and sociological dimensions. The JCS evaluation of TEMPER reports, "The TEMPER program was delivered obviously untested and error-ridden and definitely not documented. Attempts to test, verify, or even gain experience were thwarted by program errors or design weaknesses."[13] Other examinations of the model indicate that it adequately incorporated neither contemporary international relations theory[14] nor the impact of psychological and organizational variables on decision-making behavior.[15] Of course, these errors presumably can be corrected as they are recognized, but in practice, correction is difficult. The game has been defined as a completed simulation—it is in the hands of those who must justify its existence by immediate use in policy development rather than as a vehicle for its own improvement. It seems likely that TEMPER will remain in its present state and that its weaknesses will be permanent drawbacks rather than take-off points for improvement, as is the case with the INS, which remains in the hands of its builders as a dynamic research technique.

So if structural isomorphism is used as a criterion of validity, neither of the two games that have been subjected to close examination receive unqualified high marks. But the differences between the two games are crucial. The builders of INS do not claim it to be a finished product but simply a vehicles for learning, whereas the builders of the TEMPER model appear to have had an inappropriate vision of their task, and have thus aborted a malformation rather than continuing gestation. The point, I think, is clear. Any social simulation effort is not going to achieve high structural isomorphism at its early stages; the pertinent question is whether its builders are placing their highest premium on a "product" or on a process.

*Are the processes observed in the game isomorphic to those observed in the referent?* In the majority of social science games, the answer often is a qualified "yes." Most people who have observed these games in operation are struck by the extent to which the players seem to assume the behavior characteristics of real life decision-makers in language, development of attitudes, and responses to the possession of power. In a simulation such as the INS, office changes, cabinet crises, resource allocation, and other processes based on player choice rather than on pre-programming all seem to occur in appropriate manners; wars, bargaining, trading, diplomatic meetings, alliance formation and dissolution, and so forth, all happen much as they do in the particular international situation being modeled. Furthermore, the relationships among these processes appear to confirm with recognized patterns.

The small amount of research that has been done on process-coherence in simulations frequently—though not always—reinforces these observer impressions. In a comparison of the INS, TEMPER, and M.I.T.'s Political-Military Exercise, the relationship between certain processes was found to be the same in all three; that is, international conflict was closely associated with factional domestic conflict, and once begun, it tended to escalate.[16] This relationship has not firmly been established in the real world by quantitative methods but seems to merit further research on the basis of initial studies.[17] Another study, comparing the relationship between "trust" and "responsiveness" in INS participants with that in State Department officials, found the relationship to be similar in both groups.[18] In still another study, in which historical data from World War I was compared with processes that occurred in the Brody INS, the effect of alliance structure on decision-makers' expressions and perceptions of hostility was found to be similar in both.[19]

Thus, the limited evidence suggests that game processes may be more isomorphic with those in the relevant reference systems than would be expected, given the simplified structure of the games. It may be that process-validity is not highly dependent on structural isomorphism. If this is the case, then where the primary research interest is in human behavioral processes, the requirements for structural isomorphism can be lowered without compromising the validity—that is, research usefulness—of the game. Perhaps all that is required is that the structure seem realistic to the players, that it conform to *their* ideas as to what constitutes reality, not that it accurately reflect what is actually "out there." And reality, as we are beginning to see, may be different from the descriptions embodied in our standard theories. This discussion emphasizes that when we ask whether a game is more or less valid for studying human social processes as compared to other research methods, we are hard pressed for answers, since non-simulation techniques seldom generate any similar processes at all.

The reader may be led at this point to a state of utter confusion. Are the games discussed structurally and in their processes isomorphic to their references, or aren't they? The honest answer is that we don't really know. The serious attempts to find out are few, the measures weak, and the data unclear. The most that can be said is that the evidence gathered on a game such as the INS—which is being handled in the way I have argued gaming ought to be handled—is encouraging rather than discouraging, that how concerned one is about such isomorphism at a given point depends on the uses to which the game is being put—even within the research framework—and that efforts to learn more and improve our techniques for measuring structural and process isomorphism are continuing.

Finally, let us examine the fourth criterion: *can the game be used either to recapitulate historical events or to predict the future?* The record of social science games is not impressive. One of the first attempts to reconstruct history, and one of the more fascinating studies, was made by Charles and Margaret Hermann, who used an INS to see if it would reproduce the events leading up to World War I. Margaret Hermann, a psychologist, read the diaries, letters, life histories, and related documents for twenty of the key international decision-makers involved in this event. On the basis of information so gained, she filled out batteries of personality tests as she felt they would have. Identical tests were then given to high school students, and those whose scores most closely matched the personality-profiles projected for the real European decision-makers were chosen to fill the appropriate roles in one run, and students whose scores matched second best staffed a second run. A disguised scenario of the situation six weeks prior to the outbreak of the war was presented to the participants, who were otherwise free of constraints in operating the game. In neither run did war break out. Some of the game developments, however, such as the misperceptions and communication patterns, were astoundingly similar to those evident prior to the actual war, especially in the first run, where personalities were most closely matched. The Hermanns conclude that the simulation *can* be used to reconstruct some historical trends, if not the actual events, and that there is an important relation between personalities of the decision-makers and the events that occur.[20]

In the Crow and Noel study, we saw that in a disguised situation designed to be similar to that faced by Mexico prior to the Texas rebellion, about half the participants chose the course of action actually taken by the Mexican decision-makers, when probabilities indicate that the chance of such a course being chosen was only about one in ten. The authors point out that to obtain correct predictions in 45-55% of the cases in psychological testing, the validity coefficients would have to be .67-.75—extremely high for such tests, where a coefficient of .50 is considered to indicate excellent validity.[21] Now just what do these coefficients mean? Visualize a psychological test—an intelligence test, for instance. The experimenter will administer the test to a large class, then predict that those who score in the upper quartile of the test will be those who are in the upper quartile of their class in grades. To predict correctly in 45-55% of the cases, the test must have a validity coefficient of .67-.75. This percentage is considered highly valid by testers. The Crow and Noel game was able to predict correctly—or more accurately to recreate reality—in about 50% of the cases. By test standards then, it was quite valid. Further analysis of the data indicates that the actual historical response was chosen most frequently by subjects who tested low on propensity to take risks and low on nationalism, and who felt they faced extreme provocation but were somewhat sanguine about their chances of winning a war. No one has yet performed a historical analysis to determine whether this description fits the Mexican decision-makers involved in the real situation, but it would be a curious twist on validity if we found that the description does fit—and that the simulation could therefore be used to predict, or rather "post-dict," the personalities, values, and opinions of historical figures by analysis of the values, personalities, and opinions of game players who behave in almost the same way they did!

Another attempt to recreate history was made at M.I.T. "Negotiation" was a simulation of the disarmament negotiations between the United States, the Soviet Union, and the United Kingdom in the mid-1950's. The processes and outcomes of the runs were compared to those of the historical negotiations. Some were accurately reproduced and some were not; the simulation results were particularly at variance with the substance of actual concessions made in the historical negotiations. To test the postdictive ability of the "Crisiscom" simulation discussed earlier, the documents from runs of the "Negotiation" game were later used as inputs, with quite negative results.[22]

Games also have not been very successful as predictors of future events. In the single INS study of this sort (the only prediction study with any social science game that I know of), the game was set with parameters designed to reflect the contemporary situation of the real world. After several "runs" with different groups of players, the results were compared with developments in the real world during the ensuing year. In general, the outcomes of the simulation predicted neither real world trends nor discrete events. On the other hand, at the time the study was initiated, predictions were gathered from journalists and from academic and governmental personnel, and these predictions proved to be at least as far from the mark as those produced by the INS![23] If the game is poor at predicting, it is in good company.

In brief, the few games that have been checked proved to be only moderately successful at post-diction and even less so at prediction—weaknesses apparently shared by academic, governmental, and journalistic experts. But when one stops to think about what is involved in prediction, this result is hardly surprising. As Sidney Verba says:

> . . . the matching of the simulation and the real world contains many complexities. Suppose one simulates a particular situation and the results of the simulation do not match the real world. What does this mean? On the one hand, it might mean that the two systems are not isomorphic. Some significant process (significant for the problem at hand) was left out of the simulation, or some process has operated differently in the simulation than in the real world. These processes might include many that tend to contaminate experimental results involving human subjects—such as the tendency of participants to act the way they think the experimenter wants them to act. Or it might mean that though the processes have been properly identified and operate properly in the model, the variables involved were given incorrect initial values. Or—and this is the toughest problem in validating such simulations—the simulation might be a quite accurate replica, but stochastic processes are operating both in the real world and in the simulation that make outcomes probabilistic in each case, and the match between them, therefore, doubly probabilistic.[24]

Predictive power, then, is both the most desired goal and the most difficult assignment for all scientific endeavor, and gaming and simulating is no exception.

What do these assessments of game and simulation validity for research yield? I suggest that as realistic laboratories, games appear to rate very well, certainly better than the available alternatives. Their structural isomorphism with the reference system is difficult to ascertain, and where ascertainable, not very impressive, particularly when first designed; but this is an aspect that can be changed as theory and data improve. The process isomorphism of games is perhaps better, though in this respect it is difficult to compare their validity with that of other research techniques, for almost no techniques generate comparable processes. Finally, in post-dictive and predictive power, games are no worse than other methods, but whether they are better is uncertain; the experimental results are too ambiguous and contradictory. These comments all apply to the validity of games as experimental research tools, a form of validity that implies excellence as an experimental laboratory, at least some degree of structure and process isomorphism with the reference system, and some pre- and post-dictive power. As I have indicated, the validity of games as theory construction and teaching aids must be judged on different bases—i.e., do they stimulate inquiry in profitable ways. I have given my own evaluation here—and it is a highly positive one. But in the final analysis, this question can be answered only by the individual user.

There is a deeper sense in which one can ask the question of validity—a sense that is indirectly rather than directly related to the criterion of usefulness that I have emphasized. This is, does the gaming activity reflect, or is it based on, an appropriate philosophy of science? One of the main theses of this book that I want to re-emphasize here is that scientific activity is fundamentally a matter of matching patterns, or creating frameworks for inquiry, of discovering analogies, of fitting systems together, rather than of simply discovering "truth" through incremental additions of particles of fact. Gaming activity does reflect and build upon this philosophy. If the philosophy is appropriate, gaming is valid.

## A PLAYFUL MODEL FOR RESEARCH: THE DISCOVERY OF DNA

As this final chapter was being prepared, *The Atlantic Monthly* published a portion of James Watson's narrative of how he and Francis Crick discovered the structure of the DNA molecule. I have never read a more delightful and unpretentious account of "sciencing." It illuminates the basic themes just mentioned—the role of "play," and of "messing around," or, as Watson calls it, "fiddling"; the importance of pattern as a heuristic. Above all, Watson's account illuminates the highly "valid" use of modeling where isomorphism to the reference system is—hopefully—the end result, not the starting condition.[25]

Linus Pauling had established the structure of the protein molecule to be an alpha-helix—a rightward twisting spiral. But it had not been found, says Watson, "by only staring at X-ray pictures; the essential trick, instead, was to ask which atoms like to sit next to each other." In place of pencil and paper, the main working tools were a set of molecular models superficially resembling the toys of pre-school children . . . tinker-toy-like models . . . with which Pauling "played like a ten-year-old boy."

"We could see no reason," continues Watson, "why we should not solve DNA in the same way. All we had to do was to construct a set of molecular models and begin to play—with luck the structure would be a helix. Any other type of configuration would be much more complicated. Worrying about complications before ruling out the possibility that the answer was simple would have been damned foolishness."

The data on DNA obtained from X-ray crystallography were superficially compatible with a structure consisting of two, three, or four strands. Watson and Crick hoped " . . . a week of solid fiddling with the molecular models would be necessary to make us absolutely sure we had the right answer."

The two scientists decided that in building their first model, they would postulate "that the sugar-phosphate backbone was very regular, and the order of bases of necessity very irregular. . . ." But there were some difficulties to be faced: "There existed no accurate representations of the groups of atoms unique to DNA." They would have to improvise; so Watson began "adding bits of copper wire to some of our carbon-atom models, thereby changing them into the larger-sized phosphorus atoms." He had then to "fabricate representations of the inorganic ions. Unlike the other constituents, they obeyed no simple-minded rules telling us the angles at which they would form their respective chemical bonds. *Most likely we had to know the correct DNA structure before the right models could be made.*" (Emphasis added.)

"Perhaps the whole problem would fall out," continues Watson, "just by our concentrating on the prettiest way for a polynucleotide chain to fold up. So . . . I began to assemble the various atomic models into several chains . . . there was no reason to put together anything massive. As long as we could be sure it was a helix the assignment of the position for only a couple of nucleotides automatically generated the arrangement of all the other components."

They made a guess about the forces that held the chains together. "Admittedly there was no evidence . . . and so we might be sticking our necks out. On the other hand, there was absolutely no evidence against our hunch." "With luck," the addition of certain ions to the sugar-phosphate backbone "would quickly generate an elegant structure, the correctness of which would not be debatable."

But when they started "the game," as Watson calls it, the "first minutes with the models . . . were not joyous." The atoms "kept falling out of the awkward pincers set up to hold them the correct distance from one another." After ten, however, "a shape began to emerge which brought back our spirits. Three chains twisted about each other in a way . . . demanded by the X-ray crystallographic pictures. . . . Admittedly a few of the atomic contacts were still too close for comfort, but after all, the fiddling has just begun. . . . Soon, when several atoms had been pushed in or out, the three-chain model began to look quite reasonable." They might have "come up with a creature which might be the answer we were all awaiting."

And then "In the midst of further fiddling that afternoon. . . . The awkward truth became apparent that the correct DNA model must contain at least ten times more water than found in our model. This did not mean that we were necessarily wrong—with luck the extra water might be fudged into vacant regions on the periphery of our helix."

But there was "beastly uncertainty about whether $Mg^{++}$ ions were important." With this solved, "another round of model building could start, and, given luck" they might have their answer by Christmas. But "the crudely improved phosphorus atoms gave no hint they would ever neatly fit into something of value . . . we were up the creek with models based on sugar-phosphate cores. No matter how we looked at them they smelled bad . . . the impression was there that any model placing the sugar-phosphate backbone in the center of a helix forced atoms closer together than the laws of chemistry allowed. Positioning one atom the proper distance from its neighbor often caused a distant atom to become jammed impossibly close to its partner. . . . A fresh start would be necessary to get the problem rolling again."

Such are the activities of Nobel prize winners in chemistry—men who have come closer than anyone else to unlocking the ancient riddle of life. Social scientists might do well to take a lesson from them and to refuse to be apologetic about their own fiddling, tentative modeling, gaming, and hunch following. The knowledge to be gained from such insightful playing—guided by esthetics as well as by logic—may be as great as that to be gained from the most tightly structured observation of punctiform phenomena.

# CONCLUSION

In this volume, I have explored social science games and "pre-simulations." I have looked into their philosophical and epistemological bases, examined their intellectual roots and their applications in a variety of disciplines, and traced their antecedents. I have shown how they may be used as an aid in theory building, and how they have been applied to training, teaching, and experimental research. Finally, I have discussed a means of assessing how useful, or valid, they are. I have tried to do these things with enough examples, analogies, and illustrations drawn from the gaming literature to give the reader a solid "feel" for the method, a knowledge that is iconic as well as symbolic.

What of the future of gaming? It is certain that the method will come into more widespread use, and that existing games will improve, new ones be devised, and game technology further developed. Those of us who are involved in this activity believe that gaming can be a valuable tool for man to use in his quest for social progress. Like other scientific techniques, gaming can help us to bring more understanding to our view of the world, and thus more intelligent planning to the decisions we make.

But gaming also has a negative side, which should be mentioned in these concluding paragraphs. Some people, who are less optimistic about man's ability to use his knowledge wisely, are haunted by the spectre portrayed recently in one of the more exciting science fiction magazines. A future world is described in which many planets are settled and civilized, and a universal central government is in existence. One arm of this government is the Institute for Socio-Economic-Historical-Psychological-Political Studies. This Institute is nothing more than a huge computer simulation of the entire universe, with such detail and explicit predictive power that, constantly fed with new data gathered automatically from all corners of the universe, it can chart trends and predict events with complete accuracy. When it notes a depression building, a war brewing, a revolt hatching, inflation creeping, or other "counter-stabilizing" occurrences, it can isolate the exact input variable responsible for creating the problem. Thus, to "adjust" planetary conditions agents can be dispatched around the universe to drop a hundred dollar bill on the street in just the right spot, assassinate a key figure, introduce a new strain of wheat on a certain planet, or blow up a building. Any undesired trend can be altered and the future manipulated. Prosperity, peace, and stability are assured! The control of individual human beings is absolute, made possible by the ultimate refinement of just the kind of methodology we have been discussing in this volume!

There is a lot of complaint about the slow progress of the social and behavioral sciences in contrast with the physical sciences. If there is any lesson in the science fiction story just cited, it is that there are also benefits from this snail's pace progress. We are a long way from the abundant, totalitarian, computer simulation society visualized by the science fiction writer, but our methods *could* take us that direction if they became powerful enough. Fortunately, the slow pace gives us time to think, to consider what we are doing, and hopefully to avoid the blame and guilt the physicists awoke to the morning after Hiroshima. The very delays imposed by the difficulty of our task may allow us time to insure that the social sciences techniques and philosophy we develop will lead to a wider sharing of human values rather than to a destruction of those values.

Gaming—simulation—is a potent new method holding great promise as a powerful instrument of the future for the generation of knowledge. This knowledge can be used for human fulfillment or for human sorrow. The ultimate and most meaningful test of simulation validity lies in which of these choices is made.

## FOOTNOTES

1. Anatol Rapoport, *Fights, Games and Debates* (Ann Arbor: University of Michigan Press, 1960).
2. I Corinthians, XIII, 12.
3. Crow and Noel, *op. cit.*, p. 25.

4. Harold Guetzkow and Lloyd Jensen, "Research Activities on Simulated International Processes," *Background*, IX, No. 4 (1966), 261–74.

5. Richard A. Brody, "Meaning of Findings from the Inter-Nation Simulation," Memorandum to T. W. Milburn, Head, Behavioral Sciences Group, Code 014. (China Lake, California: U.S. Naval Ordnance Test Station, February 17, 1964, mimeographed.)

6. Paul F. Kress, "On Validating Simulation: With Special Attention to the Simulation of International Politics." (Evanston: Northwestern University, April 1966, mimeographed.)

7. Charles F. Hermann, "Validation Problems in Games and Simulations with Special Reference to Models of International Politics," *Behavioral Science*, XII, No. 3 (1967), 216–31.

8. Funded by contract between Northwestern University and the Advanced Research Projects Agency of the Department of Defense.

9. Erving Goffman, *op. cit.*, pp. 27–28, 69–70.

10. Harold Guetzkow, "Validation Studies in the Simulation of International Processes." (Evanston: Northwestern University, September 1966), pp. 13–26. An example of the research reported by Guetzkow is a study by Daniel Druckman, examining INS players to determine if they developed "national ethnocentrism" in the way that members of a nation in the real world do. His study showed that INS participants displayed all the behavior predicted by ethnocentrism theory. They rated members of their own nation and of allied nations as more intelligent, likeable, hard-working, and so on, than members of non-allied or enemy nations; they rated former enemies who had become allies more favorably than long-term allies; they rated former allies who had become enemies less favorably than long-term enemies, they respected strong enemies but did not like them, whereas they liked weak enemies more but did not respect them; and the more favorable the "in-group" ratings (the greater the "patriotism"), the less favorable the "out-group" ratings. Members of a nation who had more personal contact with members of other nations displayed less of these ethnocentric behaviors. ("Ethnocentrism in the Inter-Nation Simulation," *Journal of Conflict Resolution*, Vol. XII, Number 1, March, 1968, pp. 45–68.)

11. cf. Terry Nardin, "An Inquiry into the Validity of a Simulation of International Relations." (Evanston: Northwestern University, Simulated International Processes Project, August 1965, mimeographed.) Charles D. Elder and Robert E. Pendley, "An Analysis of Consumption Standards and Validator Satisfaction in the Inter-Nation Simulation in Terms of Contemporary Economic Theory and Data." (Evanston: Northwestern University, December 1966, mimeographed.) Robert E. Pendley and Charles D. Elder, "An Analysis of Officeholding in the Inter-Nation Simulation in Terms of Contemporary Political Theory and Data on the Stability of Regimes and Governments" (Evanston: Northwestern University, December 1966, mimeographed). Richard W. Chadwick, "Developments in a Partial Theory of International Behavior: A Test and Extension of Inter-Nation Simulation Theory," Ph.D. dissertation, Northwestern University, 1966. Richard W. Chadwick, "Relating Inter-Nation Simulation Theory with Verbal Theory in International Relations at Three Levels of Analysis." (Chicago: Illinois Institute of Technology, July 1966, mimeographed.)

William D. Coplin, "Inter-Nation Simulation and Contemporary Theories of International Relations," *American Political Science Review*, LX, No. 3 (1966), 562–78.

12. Harold Guetzkow, "Some Correspondences Between Simulations and 'Realities' in International Relations," abstract of a paper to appear in *New Approaches to International Relations*, ed. Morton A. Kaplan. (New York: St. Martin's Press, 1967.)

13. *Technological, Economic, Military and Political Evaluation Routine (TEMPER): An Evaluation*, *op. cit.*, p. 8.

14. Gordon Morton, "International Relations Theory in the TEMPER Simulation." (Philadelphia: University of Pennsylvania, March 15, 1967, mimeographed.)

15. Crow and Noel, *op. cit.*

16. Hayward R. Alker, Jr. and Ronald D. Brunner, "Simulating International Conflict: A Comparison of Three Approaches." (New Haven: Yale University, April 1966, mimeographed.)

17. Michael Haas, "Social Change and National Aggressiveness, 1900–1960," in *Quantitative International Politics: Insights and Evidence*, ed. J. David Singer. (New York: The Free Press, 1968), pp. 215–46. Rudolph J. Rummel, "The Relationship Between Attributes and Foreign Conflict," in Singer, ed., *op. cit.*, pp. 187–214.

18. Dean G. Pruitt, "Two Factors in International Agreement." (Evanston: Northwestern University, August 1961, mimeographed.)

19. Dina A. Zinnes, "A Comparison of Hostile State Behavior in Simulate and Historical Data," *World Politics*, XVIII, No. 3 (1966), 474–502.

20. Charles F. Hermann and Margaret G. Hermann, "An Attempt to Simulate the Outbreak of World War I," *American Political Science Review*, LXI, No. 2 (1967), 400–416.

21. Crow and Noel, *op. cit.*, pp. 20–21.

22. Matthew G. Bonham, "Aspects of the Validity of Two Simulations of Phenomena in International Relations." (Cambridge, Massachusetts: Massachusetts Institute of Technology, August 31, 1966, mimeographed.)

23. Harry R. Targ and Terry Nardin, "The Inter-Nation Simulation as Predictor of Contemporary Events." (Evanston: Northwestern University, Simulated International Processes Project, August 1965, mimeographed.) Also conversations with Dr. Dorothy Meier, co-director of this project.

24. Sidney Verba, op. cit., p. 513.

25. James D. Watson, "The Double Helix," *The Atlantic Monthly*, January 1968, 77–99. The following quotations are from pp. 87–99.

# BIBLIOGRAPHY

## INTRODUCTION

BERNE, ERIC, *Games People Play*. New York: Grove Press, Inc., 1964.

BOGUSLAW, ROBERT, *The New Utopians: A Study of System Design and Social Change*. Englewood Cliffs, N.J.: Prentice-Hall, 1965.

GUETZKOW, HAROLD, CHADWICK ALGER, RICHARD BRODY, ROBERT NOEL, and RICHARD SNYDER, *Simulation in International Relations: Developments for Research and Teaching*, pp. 211–12. Englewood Cliffs, N.J.: Prentice-Hall, 1963.

HUIZINGA, JOHAN, *Homo Ludens*. Boston: Beacon Press, 1950.

MCMILLAN, CLAUDE, and R. F. GONZALES, *Systems Analysis: A Computer Approach to Decision Models*. Homewood, Ill.: Richard D. Irwin, Inc., 1965.

ORCUTT, GUY H., MARTIN GREENBERGER, JOHN KORBEL, and ALICE RIVLIN, *Microanalysis of Socioeconomic Systems: A Simulation Study*. New York: Harper & Row, 1961.

SCOTT, ANDREW M., WILLIAM A. LUCAS and TRUDI LUCAS, *Simulation and National Development*. New York: John Wiley & Sons, Inc., 1966.

## CHAPTER I

BOGUSLAW, ROBERT, *The New Utopians: A Study of System Design and Social Change*. Englewood Cliffs, N.J.: Prentice-Hall, 1965.

CROW, WAYMAN J., "The Role of Simulation-Model Construction in Social Research on Post-Nuclear Attack Events," pp. 11–12. La Jolla, Calif.: Western Behavioral Sciences Institute, 1967.

DAWSON, RICHARD E., "Simulation in the Social Sciences," in *Simulations in Social Science: Readings*, ed. HAROLD GUETZKOW, p. 3. Englewood Cliffs, N.J.: Prentice-Hall, 1962.

DEUTSCH, KARL W., "On Theories, Taxonomies, and Models as Communication Codes for Organizing Information," *Behavioral Science*, XI, No. 1 (1966), 3.

Kaplan, Abraham, *The Conduct of Inquiry: Methodology for Behavioral Science*, pp. 264–5. San Francisco: Chandler Publishing Co., 1964.

Miller, James G., "Living Systems: Basic Concepts," *Behavioral Science*, X, No. 3 (1965), 209.

Verba, Sidney, "Simulation, Reality, and Theory in International Relations," *World Politics*, XVI, No. 3 (1964), 491.

## CHAPTER II

Barber, James, "Government Committees in the Small Group Laboratory," prepared for delivery at the 1963 Annual Meeting of the American Political Science Association, New York, September 4–7, mimeographed, Yale University.

Berelson, Bernard, and Gary Steiner, *Human Behavior: An Inventory of Scientific Findings*. New York: Harcourt, Brace and World, Inc., 1964.

Campbell, Donald T., "Pattern Matching as an Essential in Distal Knowing," in *The Psychology of Egon Brunswick*, ed. K. R. Hammond, p. 81, 83, pp. 99–102. New York: Holt, Rinehart, and Winston, 1966.

Crow, Wayman J., "Simulation: The Construction and Use of Functioning Models in International Relations," in *The Psychology of Egon Brunswick*, ed. K. R. Hammond, pp. 341–58. New York: Holt, Rinehart, and Winston, 1966.

Crow, Wayman J., and Robert Noel, "The Valid Use of Simulation Results." La Jolla, Calif.: Western Behavioral Sciences Institute, June 1965.

Dawson, Richard E., "Simulation in the Social Sciences," in *Simulations in Social Science*, ed. Harold Guetzkow. Englewood Cliffs, N.J.: Prentice-Hall, 1962.

Deutsch, Morton, and Robert M. Krauss, "Studies of Interpersonal Bargaining," *Journal of Conflict Resolution*, VI, No. 1 (1962), 52–76.

Farson, Richard E., James Johannson, and Lawrence Solomon, "Studies in Group Leadership." La Jolla, Calif.: Western Behavioral Sciences Institute, 1965.

Goffman, Erving, *Encounters: Two Studies in the Sociology of Interaction*. Indianapolis: Bobbs-Merrill, 1961.

Green, Philip, *Deadly Logic: The Theory of Nuclear Deterrence*. Columbus: Ohio State University Press, 1966.

Hovland, Carl I., Irving L. Janis, and Harold H. Kelley, *Communication and Persuasion: Psychological Studies of Opinion Change*. New Haven: Yale University Press, 1953.

MADGE, JOHN, *The Tools of Social Science*. London: Longmans, Green & Co., 1953.

ORCUTT, GUY H., MARTIN GREENBERGER, JOHN KORBEL, and ALICE M. RIVLIN, *Microanalysis of Socioeconomic Systems: A Simulation Study*. New York: Harper & Row, 1961.

POPPER, KARL, "Unity of Method in the Natural and Social Sciences," in *Philosophical Problems of the Social Sciences*, ed. D. BRAYBROOKE, pp. 33–41. New York: The Macmillan Company, 1965.

RAPOPORT, ANATOL, and CAROL ORWANT, "Experimental Games: A Review," *Behavioral Science*, VII, No. 1 (1962), 1–37.

"Science and the Citizen," *Scientific American*, December 1967, p. 48.

SKINNER, B. F., "Is a Science of Human Behavior Possible?" in *Philosophical Problems of the Social Sciences*, ed. D. BRAYBROOKE, p. 24. New York; The Macmillan Company, 1965.

## CHAPTER III

ABELSON, ROBERT P., and ALEX BERNSTEIN, "A Computer Simulation Model of Community Referendum Controversies," *Public Opinion Quarterly*, XXVII, No. 1 (1963), 93–122.

BARRINGER, RICHARD E., with BARTON WHALEY, "The M.I.T. Political-Military Gaming Experience," *Orbis*, IX, No. 2 (1965), 437–58.

BENSON, OLIVER, "A Simple Diplomatic Game," in *International Politics and Foreign Policy: A Reader in Research and Theory*, ed. JAMES N. ROSENAU. Glencoe, Ill.: The Free Press of Glencoe, 1961.

BOGUSLAW, ROBERT, ROBERT H. DAVIS, and EDWARD B. GLICK, "A Simulation Vehicle for Studying National Policy Formation in a Less Armed World," *Behavioral Science*, XI, No. 1 (1966), 48–61.

BORKO, HAROLD, *Computer Applications in the Behavioral Sciences*. Englewood Cliffs, N.J.: Prentice-Hall, 1962.

BRODY, RICHARD A., "Some Systemic Effects of Nuclear Weapons Technology: A Study Through Simulation of a Multi-Nuclear Future," *Journal of Conflict Resolution*, VII, No. 4 (1963), 663–753.

BUCHLER, IRA RICHARD, ed., *Applications of the Theory of Games in the Behavioral Sciences*, Final Technical Report, ONR Grant Nonr (G)-00042-66, University of Texas, December 1966.

BURDICK, EUGENE, *The 480*. New York: McGraw-Hill, 1964.

CARTWRIGHT, DORWIN, and A. F. ZANDER, *Group Dynamics Research and Theory*. Evanston, Ill.: Row, Peterson and Co., 1953.

COHEN, KALMAN J., and ERIC RHENMAN, "The Role of Management Games in Education and Research," *Management Science*, VII, No. 2 (1961), 131–66.

COLEMAN, JAMES S., "Mathematical Models and Computer Simulation," in *Handbook of Modern Sociology*, ed. ROBERT E. FARIS. Chicago: Rand McNally, 1964.

DEUTSCH, MORTON, and ROBERT M. KRAUSS, "Studies of Interpersonal Bargaining," *Journal of Conflict Resolution*, VI, No. 1 (1962), 52–76.

FREDERIKSEN, NORMAN, "In-Basket Tests and Factors in Administrative Performance," Invitational Conference on Testing Problems, Proceedings, October 1960.

FROMM, G., and L. R. KLEIN, "The Brookings—S. S. R. C. Quarterly Econometric Model of the United States: Model Properties," Reprint 100, Washington, D.C.: The Brookings Institution, 1965.

GAMSON, WILLIAM A., *SIMSOC: A Manual for Participants*. Ann Arbor, Michigan: Campus Publishers, 1966.

GOLDHAMER, HERBERT, and HANS SPEIER, "Some Observations on Political Gaming," *World Politics*, XII, No. 1 (1959), 71–73.

GUETZKOW, HAROLD, "Isolation and Collaboration: A Partial Theory of Internation Relations," *Journal of Conflict Resolution*, I, No. 1 (1957), 48–68.

GUETZKOW, HAROLD, "Simulations and Gaming of International Military Political Behaviors: Survey of Activities." Evanston: Northwestern University, Simulated International Processes Project, May 1966.

GULLAHORN, JOHN T., and JEANNE E. GULLAHORN, "A Computer Model of Elementary Social Behavior," *Behavioral Science*, VIII, No. 4 (1963), 354–62.

HARE, A. PAUL, E. F. BORGATTA, and R. F. BALES, eds., *Small Groups: Studies in Social Interaction*. New York: Alfred A. Knopf, 1966.

ISARD, WALTER, and STANISLAW CZAMANSKI, "A Model for the Projection of Regional Industrial Structure, Land Use Patterns and Conversion Potentialities," *Peace Research Society (International) Papers*, V (1966), 1–13.

KAPLAN, ABRAHAM, *The Conduct of Inquiry: Methodology for Behavioral Science*, p. 4. San Francisco: Chandler Publishing Co., 1964.

KELMAN, HERBERT, *International Behavior: A Social Psychological Analysis*. New York: Holt, Rinehart, and Winston, 1965.

MARCH, JAMES G., and HERBERT A. SIMON, with HAROLD GUETZKOW, *Organizations*. New York:John Wiley & Sons, Inc., 1958.

"Occasional Newsletter About Uses of Simulations and Games for Education and Training," La Jolla, Calif.: Western Behavioral Sciences Institute, Project SIMILE, No. 1, September 1965.

ORCUTT, GUY H., MARTIN GREENBERGER, JOHN KORBEL, and ALICE M. RIVLIN, *Microanalysis of Socioeconomic Systems: A Simulation Study*. New York: Harper & Row, 1961.

POOL, ITHIEL DE SOLA, and ROBERT ABELSON, "The Simulmatics Project," *Public Opinion Quarterly*, XXV, No. 2 (1961), 167–83.

POOL, ITHIEL DE SOLA, and ALLAN KESSLER, "The Kaiser, the Tsar, and the Computer," *American Behavioral Science*, VIII, No. 1 (1965), 31–38.

RAPOPORT, ANATOL, and CAROL ORWANT, "Experimental Games: A Review," *Behavioral Science*, VII, No. 1 (1962), 1–37.

RAPOPORT, ANATOL, "Games Which Simulate Deterrence and Disarmament," *Peace Research Reviews*, I, No. 4 (1967). Clarkson, Ontario: Canadian Peace Research Institute.

RAPOPORT, ANATOL, *Strategy and Conscience*. New York: Harper & Row, 1964.

RASER, JOHN R., and WAYMAN J. CROW, *Winsafe II: An Inter-Nation Simulation Study of Deterrence Postures Embodying Capacity to Delay Response*. La Jolla, Calif.: Western Behavioral Sciences Institute, July 1964.

ROBINSON, JAMES A., and RICHARD C. SNYDER, "Decision-Making in International Politics," in *International Behavioral: A Social-Psychological Analysis*, ed. HERBERT C. KELMAN. New York: Holt, Rinehart and Winston, 1965.

ROBINSON, JAMES A., LEE F. ANDERSON, MARGARET G. HERMANN, and RICHARD C. SNYDER, "Teaching with Inter-Nation Simulation and Case Studies," *American Political Science Review*, LX, No. 1 (1966), 53–65.

SAYRE, FARRAND, *Map Maneuvers and Tactical Rides*. Springfield, Massachusetts: Press of Springfield Printing and Binding Company, 1908.

SCOTT, ANDREW M., WILLIAM A. LUCAS, and TRUDI LUCAS, *Simulation and National Development*. New York: John Wiley & Sons, Inc., 1966.

SHERIF, MUZAFER, *et al.*, *Intergroup Conflict and Cooperation: The Robbers' Cave Experiment*. Norman: University of Oklahoma, 1961.

SHUBIK, MARTIN, "Bibliography on Simulation, Gaming, Artificial Intelligence, and Allied Topics," *Journal of the American Statistical Association*, LV, No. 292 (1960), 736–51.

SIMON, HERBERT A., D. W. SMITHBURG, and V. A. THOMPSON, *Public Administration*. New York: Alfred A. Knopf, 1950.

SNYDER, RICHARD C., H. W. BUCK, and BURTON SAPIN, eds., Foreign Policy *Decision-Making: An Approach to the Study of International Politics*. Glencoe, Ill.: The Free Press of Glencoe, 1962.

SPECHT, ROBERT D., "War Games," P-1041, pp. 7–19. Santa Monica, California: The RAND Corporation, March 1957.

*Survey of the State of the Art: Social, Political, and Economic Models and Simulations*. Cambridge, Mass.: Abt. Associates, Inc., November 1965.

*Technological, Economic, Military, and Political Evaluation Routine (TEMPER): An Evaluation*, National Military Command System Support Center Technical Memorandum, Number TM–11–66, July 27, 1966.

THOMAS, CLAYTON J., "The Genesis and Practice of Operational Gaming," Proceedings of the First International Conference on Operations Research. Baltimore: Operations Research Society of America, 1957.

TUSTIN, A., *The Mechanism of Economic Systems*. Cambridge, Mass.: Harvard University Press, 1953.

WEINER, M. G., "An Introduction to War Games," P-1773. Santa Monica, Calif.: The RAND Corporation, August 17, 1959.

# CHAPTER IV

ASHBY, W. R., "Simulation of a Brain," in *Computer Applications in the Behavioral Sciences*, ed. HAROLD BORKO, p. 456. Englewood Cliffs, N.J.: Prentice-Hall, 1962.

COPLIN, WILLIAM D., "Inter-Nation Simulation and Contemporary Theories of International Relations," *American Political Science Review*, LX, No. 3 (1966), 577–8.

CROW, WAYMAN J., "The Role of Simulation-Model Construction in Social Research on Post-Nuclear Attack Events," pp. 12–14. La Jolla, Calif.: Western Behavioral Sciences Institute, March 1967.

GEERTZ, C., "The Impact of the Concept of Culture on the Concept of Man," *Bulletin of the Atomic Scientists* (1966), 3.

HOMANS, GEORGE, *Social Behavior: Its Elementary Forms*, pp. 10–11. New York: Harcourt, Brace and World, 1961.

JENSEN, LLOYD, "United States Elites and Their Perceptions of the Determinants of Foreign Policy Behavior." Evanston, Ill.: Northwestern University, paper delivered to the Midwest Conference of Political Scientists, April 29, 1966.

KAPLAN, ABRAHAM, *The Conduct of Inquiry: Methodology for Behavioral Science*, pp. 268–9. San Francisco: Chandler Publishing Co., 1964.

POLANYI, MICHAEL, *Personal Knowledge: Towards a Post-Critical Philosophy*. Chicago: University of Chicago Press, 1958.

RASER, JOHN R., and WAYMAN J. CROW, *Winsafe II: An Inter-Nation Simulation Study of Deterrence Postures Embodying Capacity to Delay Response*. La Jolla, Calif.: Western Behavioral Sciences Institute, July 1964.

ROBINSON, JAMES A., "Simulating Crisis Decision-Making," pp. 13–14. Paper prepared for panel on Foreign Policy and Affairs at Joint Meeting of the Institute of Management Sciences and the Operations Research Society of America, Minneapolis, October 7, 1964.

SCHELLING, THOMAS C., "Experimental Games and Bargaining Theory," *World Politics*, XIV, No. 1 (1961), 57.

SIMON, HERBERT A., "New Developments in the Theory of the Firm," *American Economic Review*, LII, No. 1 (1962), 13.

SINGER, J. DAVID, "Data-Making in International Relations," *Behavioral Science*, X, No. 1 (1965), 68–80.

VERBA, SIDNEY, "Simulation, Reality, and Theory in International Relations," *World Politics*, XVI, No. 3 (1964), 499.

# CHAPTER V

BALDWIN, JOHN, "The Economics of Peace and War: A Simulation," *Journal of Conflict Resolution*, XI, No. 4 (1967), 383–97.

BOGUSLAW, ROBERT, R. DAVIS, and E. GLICK, "A Simulation Vehicle for Studying National Policy Formation in a Less Armed World," *Behavioral Science*, XI, No. 1 (1966), 48–61.

BRODY, RICHARD, ALEXANDRA BENHAM, and JEFFREY MILSTEIN, "Hostile International Communication, Arms Production, and Perception of Threat: A Simulation Study." Stanford: Institute of Political Studies, Stanford University, July 1966.

BRODY, RICHARD A., "Some Systemic Effects of Nuclear Weapons Technology: A Study Through Simulation of a Multi-Nuclear Future," *Journal of Conflict Resolution*, VII, No. 4 (1963), 633–753.

BURGESS, PHILIP, "Memorandum re Simulation Project—OSU/INS/03 of J. Robinson, P. Burgess, and E. Fedder," Columbus: Ohio State University, March 1966, mimeographed.

CHAPMAN, ROBERT L., J. L. KENNEDY, ALLEN NEWELL, and WILLIAM C. BIEL, "The Systems Research Laboratory's Air-Defense Experiments," in *Simulations in Social Science: Readings*, ed. HAROLD GUETZKOW, pp. 172–88. Englewood Cliffs, N.J.: Prentice-Hall, 1962.

CHERRYHOLMES, CLEO H., "The House of Representatives and Foreign Affairs: A Computer Simulation of Roll Call Voting." Ph.D. dissertation, Northwestern University, 1966.

CROW, WAYMAN J., and JOHN R. RASER, "A Cross-Cultural Simulation Study." La Jolla, Calif.: Western Behavioral Sciences Institute, November 1964.

CROW, WAYMAN J., and LAWRENCE SOLOMON, "A Simulation Study of Strategic Doctrines." La Jolla, Calif.: Western Behavioral Sciences Institute, 1962.

CROW, WAYMAN J., and ROBERT NOEL, "The Valid Use of Simulation Results." La Jolla, Calif.: Western Behavioral Sciences Institute, June 1965.

DAWSON, RICHARD E., "Simulation in the Social Sciences," in *Simulations in Social Science: Readings*, ed. HAROLD GUETZKOW, pp. 12–13. Englewood Cliffs, N.J.: Prentice-Hall, 1962.

DEUTSCH, MORTON, YAKOV EPSTEIN, DONNAH CANAVAN, and PETER GUMPERT, "Strategies of Inducing Cooperation: An Experimental Study," *Journal of Conflict Resolution*, XI, No. 3 (1967), 345–60.

Driver, Michael, "The Perception of Simulated Nations: A Multidimensional Analysis of Social Perception as Affected by Situational Stress and Characteristic Levels of Cognitive Complexity in Perceivers." Ph.D. dissertation, Princeton University, 1962.

Driver, Michael, "A Structural Analysis of Aggression, Stress, and Personality in an Inter-Nation Simulation." Lafayette, Indiana: Purdue University, June 1966.

Geisler, Murray A., "The Simulation of a Large-Scale Military Activity," *Management Science*, V, No. 4 (1959), 359–69.

Gullahorn, John T., and Jeanne E. Gullahorn, "A Computer Model of Elementary Social Behavior," *Behavioral Science*, VIII, No. 4 (1963), 354–62.

Hermann, Charles, "Crises in Foreign Policy Decision-Making: A Simulation of International Politics." Princeton: Princeton University, April 1965.

Hermann, Margaret G., *Stress, Self-Esteem, and Defensiveness in an Inter-Nation Simulation*. China Lake, Calif.: Project Michelson, U.S. Naval Ordnance Test Station, April 1965.

Jennings, Norman, and Justin Dickens, "Computer Simulation of Peak Hour Operations in a Bus Terminal," in *Simulations in Social Science: Readings*, ed. Harold Guetzkow, pp. 153–4. Englewood Cliffs, N.J.: Prentice-Hall, 1962.

Kaplan, Morton A., A. L. Burns, and Richard E. Quandt, "Theoretical Analysis of Balance of Power," *Behavioral Science*, V, No. 3 (1960), 240–52.

Orcutt, Guy H., Martin Greenberger, John Korbel, and Alice M. Rivlin, *Microanalysis of Socioeconomic Systems: A Simulation Study*. New York: Harper & Row, 1961.

Orcutt, Guy H., "Simulation of Economic Systems," in *Simulations in Social Science*, ed. Harold Guetzkow, p. 95. Englewood Cliffs, N.J.: Prentice-Hall, 1962.

Osgood, Charles, *An Alternative to War or Surrender*. Urbana, Ill.: Illinois Books, 1962.

Phillips, Bernard S., *Social Research: Strategy and Tactics*, p. 152. New York: The Macmillan Company, 1966.

Pool, Ithiel de Sola, "Simulating Social Systems," *International Science and Technology*, XXVII, (1964), 62–71.

Rapoport, Anatol, and Carol Orwant, "Experimental Games: A Review," *Behavioral Science*, VII, No. 1 (1962), 1–38.

Rapoport, Anatol, and Melvin Guyer, "A Taxonomy of 2 x 2 Games," *Peace Research Society (International) Papers*, VI (1967), 11–26.

Raser, John R., and Wayman J. Crow, *Winsafe II: An Inter-Nation Simulation Study of Deterrence Postures Embodying Capacity to Delay Response*. La Jolla, Calif.: Western Behavioral Sciences Institute, July 1964.

RASER, JOHN R., "Cross Cultural Simulation Research," *Journal Internationale de Psychologie*, II, No. 1 (1967), 59–68.

RIDENOUR, LOUIS, "Pilot Lights of the Apocalypse: A Playlet in One Act," *Fortune*, XXXIII (1946), 116.

ROBINSON, JAMES A., and A. WYNER, "Information Storage and Search in an Inter-Nation Simulation." Columbus: Ohio State University, May 1965.

ROBINSON, JAMES A., "Simulating Crisis Decision-Making," paper prepared for panel on Foreign Policy and Affairs at Joint Meeting of the Institute of Management Sciences and the Operations Research Society of America, Minneapolis, October 7, 1964.

ROME, BEATRICE, and SIDNEY ROME, "Communication and Large Organization," SP 1690/000/000. Santa Monica, Calif.: Systems Development Corporation, September 1964.

SHAPIRO, MICHAEL, "Cognitive Rigidity and Perceptual Orientation in an Inter-Nation Simulation." Evanston: Northwestern University, April 1966.

SHAPIRO, MICHAEL, "The House and the Federal Roll: A Computer Simulation of Roll Call Voting." Ph.D. dissertation, Northwestern University, 1966.

SINAIKO, H. WALLACE, and GLEN P. CARTWRIGHT, *Careful: A Pilot Study of the Effects of Heavy Target Load on Human and Automatic Decision-Making*, p. 35. Coordinated Science Lab Report, No. R-115, 1959.

SINGER, J. DAVID, and HIROHIDE HINOMOTO, "Inspecting for Weapons Production: A Modest Computer Simulation," *Journal of Peace Research*, II, No. 1 (1965), 18–38.

SISSON, ROGER L., and RUSSELL L. ACKOFF, "Toward a Theory of the Dynamics of Conflict." Philadelphia: University of Pennsylvania, Management Center, n.d., mimeographed.

SNYDER, RICHARD C., "Some Perspectives on the Use of Experimental Techniques in the Study of International Relations," in *Simulation in International Relations*, GUETZKOW, *et al.*, pp. 9–10. Chicago: Rand McNally, 1963.

STREUFERT, SIEGFRIED, PETER SUEDFELD, and MICHAEL J. DRIVER, "Conceptual Structure, Information Search, and Information Utilization," *Journal of Personality and Social Psychology*, II, No. 5 (1965), 736–40.

TERHUNE, KENNETH, and JOSEPH M. FIRESTONE, *Psychological Studies in Social Interaction and Motives (SIAM) Phase 2: Group Motives in an International Relations Game*, CAL Report No. VX-20 18-G-2. Buffalo: Cornell Aeronautical Laboratory, Inc., March 1967.

VERBA, SIDNEY, "Simulation, Reality, and Theory in International Relations," *World Politics*, XVI, No. 3 (1964), 499–501.

ZELDITCH, MORRIS, and WILLIAM EVAN, "Simulated Bureaucracies: A Methodological Analysis," pp. 48–60. In GUETZKOW, ed., 1962, *op. cit.*

## CHAPTER VI

ALGER, CHADWICK, "Use of the Inter-Nation Simulation in Undergraduate Teaching," pp. 152–4. In GUETZKOW, *et al.*, 1963, *op. cit.*

AVERCH, H., and M. M. LAVIN, *Simulation of Decision-Making in Crisis: Three Manual Gaming Experiments*, RM-4202-PR. Santa Monica, Calif.: RAND Corporation, August 1964.

BARRINGER, RICHARD E., with BARTON WHALEY, "The M.I.T. Political-Military Gaming Experience," *Orbis*, IX, No. 2 (1965), 437–58.

BLOOMFIELD, LINCOLN P., Political Gaming, U.S. Naval Institute Proceedings, LXXXVI (September 1960), pp. 57–64.

BLOOMFIELD, LINCOLN P., and BARTON WHALEY, "The Political-Military Exercise: A Progress Report," *Orbis*, VIII (1965), 854–70.

BLOOMFIELD, LINCOLN P., and NORMAN J. PADELFORD, "Three Experiments in Political Gaming," *American Political Science Review*, LIII, No. 4 (1959), 1105–1115.

BURTON, JOHN, "International Relations Simulation on the Cheap." Evanston: Northwestern University, 1966, multilith.

CHERRYHOLMES, CLEO H., "Developments in Simulation of International Relations in High School Teaching," *Phi Delta Kappan*, January 1965, 227–31.

CHERRYHOLMES, CLEO H., "Some Current Research on Effectiveness of Educational Simulations: Implications for Alternative Strategies," *American Behavioral Scientist*, X, No. 2 (1966), 4–5.

COLEMAN, JAMES A., "In Defense of Games," *American Behavioral Scientist*, X, No. 2 (1966), 3–4.

DAVIS, R. H., P. B. CARPENTER, and C. W. MISSLER, *A Game for Studying the Problems of Arms Control*, SP-779. Santa Monica, Calif.: Systems Development Corporation, 1962.

GIFFEN, SIDNEY F., *The Crisis Game: Simulating Internation Conflict*. Garden City, New York: Doubleday and Company, 1965.

GOFFMAN, ERVING, *Encounters: Two Studies in the Sociology of Interaction*. Indianapolis: Bobbs-Merrill, 1961.

GOLDHAMER, HERBERT, and HANS SPEIER, "Some Observations on Political Gaming," *World Politics*, XII, No. 1 (1959), 71–73.

HELMER, OLAF, *Strategic Gaming*, P-1902. Santa Monica, Calif.: The RAND Corporation, February 10, 1960.

HELMER, OLAF, and R. E. BICKNER, *How to Play SAFE—Book of Rules of the Strategy and Force Evaluation Game*, RM-2865-PR. Santa Monica, Calif.: RAND Corporation, November 1961.

METCALF, LAWRENCE E., "Research on Teaching the Social Studies," in *Handbook of Research on Teaching*, ed. N. L. GAGE, pp. 929–66. Chicago: Rand McNally & Co., 1963.

"Occasional Newsletter About Uses of Simulations and Games for Education and Training," La Jolla, California: Western Behavioral Sciences Institute, Project SIMILE, No. 1, p. 4, and No. 2, p. 2.

PAXON, E. W., *War Gaming*, RM-3489-PR. Santa Monica, Calif.: RAND Corporation, February 1963.

PRICE, T., "Applying Wargaming to the Cold War," *PROD*, III (1959), 3–6.

Project SIMILE, "Report to the Kettering Foundation." La Jolla, Calif.: Western Behavioral Sciences Institute, 1967.

ROBINSON, JAMES A., LEE F. ANDERSON, M. G. HERMANN, and R. C. SNYDER, "Teaching with Inter-Nation Simulation and Case Studies," *American Political Science Review*, LX, No. 1 (1966), 53–65.

SCHELLING, THOMAS C., "Experimental Games and Bargaining Theory," *World Politics*, XIV, No. 1 (1961), 47.

SNYDER, RICHARD C., "Some Perspectives on the Use of Experimental Techniques in the Study of International Relations," in *Simulations in International Relations: Developments for Research and Teaching*, HAROLD GUETZKOW, CHADWICK ALGER, RICHARD BRODY, ROBERT NOEL and RICHARD SNYDER, p. 12. Chicago: Rand McNally & Co., 1963.

SPRAGUE, HALL T., "Changing Education in America." La Jolla, Calif.: Western Behavioral Sciences Institute, September 1966, mimeographed.

WEINER, M. G., *War Gaming Methodology*, RM-2413. Santa Monica, Calif.: RAND Corporation, July 10, 1959.

WHALEY, BARTON, PETER C. ORDESHOOK, and ROBERT H. SCOTT, *INDEX III*, C/64–33. Cambridge, Mass.: Center for International Studies, Massachusetts Institute of Technology, October 1964.

WING, RICHARD L., "Two Computer-Based Economics Games for Sixth Graders," *American Behavioral Scientist*, X, No. 3 (1966), 31.

## CHAPTER VII

ALKER, HAYWARD R. JR., and RONALD D. BRUNNER, "Simulating International Conflict: A Comparison of Three Approaches." New Haven: Yale University, April 1966, mimeographed.

BONHAM, MATTHEW G., "Aspects of the Validity of Two Simulations of Phenomena in International Relations." Cambridge: Massachusetts Institute of Technology, August 31, 1966, mimeographed.

Brody, Richard A., "Meaning of Findings from the Inter-Nation Simulation," memorandum to T. W. Milburn, Head, Behavioral Sciences Group, Code 014. China Lake, Calif.: U.S. Naval Ordnance Test Station, February 17, 1964.

Chadwick, Richard, "Developments in a Partial Theory of International Behavior: A Test and Extension of Inter-Nation Simulation Theory." Ph.D. dissertation, Northwestern University, 1966.

Chadwick, Richard, "Relating Inter-Nation Simulation Theory with Verbal Theory in International Relations at Three Levels of Analysis." Chicago: Illinois Institute of Technology, July 1966.

Coplin, William D., "Inter-Nation Simulation and Contemporary Theories of International Relations," *American Political Science Review*, LX, No. 3 (1966), 562–78.

*Corinthians I*, XIII, 12.

Crow, Wayman J., and Robert Noel, "The Valid Use of Simulation Results." La Jolla, Calif.: Western Behavioral Sciences Institute, June 1965.

Druckman, Daniel, "Ethnocentrism in the Inter-Nation Simulation," *Journal of Conflict Resolution*, XII, No. 1 (1968), 45–68.

Elder, Charles D., and Robert E. Pendley, "An Analysis of Consumption Standards and Validator Satisfaction in the Inter-Nation Simulation in Terms of Contemporary Economic Theory and Data." Evanston: Northwestern University, December 1966.

Goffman, Erving, *Encounters: Two Studies in the Sociology of Interaction*. Indianapolis: Bobbs-Merrill, 1961.

Guetzkow, Harold, and Lloyd Jensen, "Research Activities on Simulated International Processes," *Background*, IX, No. 4 (1966), 261–74.

Guetzkow, Harold, "Some Correspondences Between Simulations and 'Realities' in International Relations," abstract of a paper to appear in *New Approaches to International Relations*, ed. Morton A. Kaplan. New York: St. Martin's Press, 1967.

Guetzkow, Harold, "Validation Studies in the Simulation of International Processes." Evanston: Northwestern University, September 1966.

Haas, Michael, "Social Change and National Aggressiveness, 1900–1960," in *Quantitative International Politics: Insights and Evidence*, ed. J. David Singer, pp. 215–46. New York: The Free Press, 1968.

Hermann, Charles F., and Margaret G. Hermann, "An Attempt to Simulate the Outbreak of World War I," *American Political Science Review*, LXI, No. 2 (1967), 400–416.

Hermann, Charles F., "Validation Problems in Games and Simulations with Special Reference to Models of International Politics," *Behavioral Science*, XII, No. 3 (1967), 216–31.

Kress, Paul F., "On Validating Simulation: With Special Attention to the Simulation of International Politics." Evanston: Northwestern University, April 1966, mimeographed.

MORTON, GORDON, "International Relations Theory in the TEMPER Simulation." Philadelphia: University of Pennsylvania, March 1967.

NARDIN, TERRY, "An Inquiry into the Validity of a Simulation of International Relations." Evanston: Northwestern University, Simulated International Processes Project, August 1965.

PENDLEY, ROBERT E., and CHARLES D. ELDER, "An Analysis of Office-holding in the Inter-Nation Simulation in Terms of Contemporary Political Theory and Data on the Stability of Regimes and Governments." Evanston: Northwestern University, December 1966.

PRUITT, DEAN G., "Two Factors in International Agreement." Evanston: Northwestern University, August 1961.

RAPOPORT, ANATNOL, *Fights, Games, and Debates*. Ann Arbor: University of Michigan Press, 1960.

RUMMEL, RUDOLPH J., "The Relationship Between National Attributes and Foreign Conflict," in *Quantitative International Politics: Insights and Evidence*, ed. J. DAVID SINGER, pp. 187–214. New York: The Free Press, 1968.

TARG, HARRY R., and TERRY NARDIN, "The Inter-Nation Simulation as a Predictor of Contemporary Events." Evanston: Northwestern University, Simulated International Processes Project, August 1965.

*Technological, Economic, Military and Political Evaluation Routine (TEMPER): An Evaluation*, National Military Command System Support Center Technical Memorandum, Number TM-11-66, July 27, 1966.

VERBA, SIDNEY, "Simulation, Reality, and Theory in International Relations," *World Politics*, XVI, No. 3 (1964), 513.

WATSON, JAMES D., "The Double Helix," *The Atlantic Monthly*, January 1968, 77–99.

ZINNES, DINA A., "A Comparison of Hostile State Behavior in Simulate and Historical Data," *World Politics*, XVIII, No. 3 (1966), 474–502.

# INDEX